Postcommunist Belarus

Postcommunist Belarus

EDITED BY STEPHEN WHITE, ELENA KOROSTELEVA,
AND JOHN LÖWENHARDT

ROWMAN & LITTLEFIELD PUBLISHERS, INC.
Lanham • Boulder • New York • Toronto • Oxford

ROWMAN & LITTLEFIELD PUBLISHERS, INC.

Published in the United States of America
by Rowman & Littlefield Publishers, Inc.
A wholly owned subsidiary of The Rowman & Littlefield Publishing Group, Inc.
4501 Forbes Boulevard, Suite 200, Lanham, MD 20706
www.rowmanlittlefield.com

P.O. Box 317, Oxford OX2 9RU, UK

Copyright © 2005 by Rowman & Littlefield Publishers, Inc.

All rights reserved. No part of this publication may be reproduced, stored in a retrieval system, or transmitted in any form or by any means, electronic, mechanical, photocopying, recording, or otherwise, without the prior permission of the publisher.

British Library Cataloguing in Publication Information Available

Library of Congress Cataloging-in-Publication Data

Postcommunist Belarus / edited by Stephen White, Elena Korosteleva, and John Löwenhardt.
    p. cm.
Includes bibliographical references and index.
ISBN 0-7425-3555-X (cloth : alk. paper)
    1. Political culture—Belarus. 2. Post-communism—Belarus. 3. Belarus—Social conditions—1991- 4. Belarus—Politics and government—1991- I. White, Stephen, 1945- II. Korosteleva, Elena A. III. Löwenhardt, John.
    JN6649.A15P67   2005
    306.2'09478—dc22
                                                                              2004021899

Printed in the United States of America

∞™ The paper used in this publication meets the minimum requirements of American National Standard for Information Sciences—Permanence of Paper for Printed Library Materials, ANSI/NISO Z39.48-1992.

Contents

	List of Tables	vii
	List of Figures	ix
	Preface	xi
	Maps	xiii
1	Post-Soviet Belarus: In Search of Direction *Ronald J. Hill*	1
2	Patterns of Political Culture *Stephen White and Ian McAllister*	17
3	The Emergence of a Party System *Elena Korosteleva*	35
4	Lukashenko and the Postcommunist Presidency *Stephen White and Elena Korosteleva*	59
5	The Dynamics of the 2001 Presidential Election *Uladzimir Padhol and David R. Marples*	79
6	The Belarus Economy: Suspended Animation between State and Markets *D. Mario Nuti*	97
7	Belarus and the East *Clelia Rontoyanni*	123
8	Belarus and the West *John Löwenhardt*	143
9	Belarus and Postcommunist Democratization *Christian W. Haerpfer*	161
	Appendix: Selected Socioeconomic Data	181
	Index	185
	About the Contributors	191

Tables

2.1	The "Best" and "Worst" Features of Communist Rule in Belarus, 2000 and 2004 (percentages)	19
2.2	A Scoreboard of Freedoms, 2000 (percentages)	20
2.3	Age and Perceptions of Political and Economic Systems (correlation coefficients)	23
2.4	Trust in Institutions, 2004	25
2.5	Attitudes toward the Electoral Mechanism (percentages)	26
2.6	Corruption and Government, 2004	27
2.7	Past, Present, and Future by Political Type	29
2.8	Policy Choices by Political Type	31
3.1	The Spectrum of Belarusian Parties, 2003	38
3.2	Election Results to the Supreme Soviet of 1995	47
3.3	Results of the Parliamentary Elections in 2000	50
4.1	The Dynamics of Lukashenko's Electoral Support, 1997–2003 (percentages)	66
5.1	Voters' Attitudes to the Two Leading Candidates during the Presidential Electoral Campaign, July–September 2001 (percentages)	88
5.2	Voters' Attitudes to the 2001 Presidential Election (percentages)	89
5.3	Results of the Belarusian Presidential Election, September 9, 2001	92
6.1	Belarus: EBRD Transition Progress Scores, 1995–2003	100
6.2	Belarus: Transition Assessments, 1995–2003	104
6.3	Belarus: Economic Performance, 1992–2003	110
7.1	Belarusian Trade with Russia (millions of US dollars)	130

7.2	Voting in a Hypothetical Referendum on the Adoption of the Constitution of a Union State of Belarus and Russia	134
7.3	Preferred Form of Integration of Belarus and Russia (percentages)	135
8.1	"In what language do you usually converse at home?" (percentages)	146
8.2	"How proud are you to be a citizen of your country?" (percentages)	147
8.3	"How important is it in your opinion for Belarus to have good relations with the following countries?" (percentage answering "very important")	148
8.4	"Are your impressions of the aims and activities of the European Union generally . . . "	150
8.5	"Do you think [country] could be a substantial threat to security and order in the world?"	151
8.6	"Please indicate for each of these points what in your view would be the most likely results of our country becoming a member of the EU" (row percentages)	152
9.1	Nostalgia for Communist Rule	162
9.2	Support for Communist Restoration	164
9.3	Support for Current Government	165
9.4	The Future of National Parliaments	167
9.5	Popular Support for National Parliaments	170
9.6	Support for a Strong Authoritarian Leader	171
9.7	Alternatives to Democracy: Support for a Military Regime	173
9.8	Alternatives to Democracy: Support for a Monarchy	175
9.9	Support for Democracy as a Political Regime (the "Churchill Hypothesis")	176

Figures

2.1	Assessing Political Systems: Past, Present, and Future	22
2.2	A Typology of Political Orientations	29
4.1	The Dynamics of Electoral Preference for President Lukashenko, 1997–2003	66
4.2	Trust in Civic and Political Institutions, 1997–2003 (percentages)	67
4.3	The Lukashenko Electorate, 2003	68
5.1	Voters' Readiness to Support Candidates of Their Choice, July–September 2001	88

Preface

Belarus is one of Europe's larger countries, located—as Belarusians themselves calculate it—at the very center of the continent. It is also one of the larger of the countries that are "in transition" from communist rule to a variety of still uncertain destinations. For many, Belarus is scarcely in transition at all: it is "Europe's last dictatorship," a regime so intolerant of political diversity that Freedom House has placed it in the same category as Equatorial Guinea and North Korea. But for the Belarusian authorities themselves, it represents a very different model: one in which there is substantial or even majority support for its powerful president, and one that shows the virtues of a more cautious approach to economic reform that emphasizes full employment and the maintenance of the living standards of ordinary people.

For political scientists, yet another view is possible: that Belarus provides a rich array of instructive examples for their repertoire. President Lukashenko, for instance, is arguably a "charismatic" leader, of the kind that was defined many years ago by Max Weber. The powers of the Belarusian presidency help us to understand the variety of ways in which "institutions matter." The weakness of the Belarusian party system reflects a common pattern across the former Soviet republics, but we can identify the distinctive influence of history (as parties that date from the late nineteenth century are revived) as well as social and economic circumstances. Belarusians are less likely to identify their government as corrupt than their counterparts in Russia and Ukraine; we suggest this may have systemic consequences. And they are more likely to think they have at least a limited influence on the actions of government, in spite of the harassment of the independent press. Arguably, this shows the extent to which "Soviet" forms of participation offer a form of leverage of a kind that liberal-democratic forms have not yet provided.

Nor are these the only lessons that Belarus provides for comparativists. How viable, for instance, is the "Belarusian model" of economic management, and to what extent does it represent a realistic alternative to "shock therapy"? How satisfactorily can we classify its political system in terms of the "quality of democracy"? How does Belarus fit into larger frameworks of "democratization"?

And internationally, what does the Belarusian experience tell us about alliance formation among postcommunist states, bound together more by natural resources than by a proletarian ideology?

To discuss these and other themes we have brought together a variety of authors from inside and outside the region, and from both sides of the Atlantic. Two of the three editors (White and Löwenhardt) came together through their participation in a project that became known as "The Outsiders," exploring the implications for Russia, Ukraine, and Belarus of EU and NATO enlargement. Elena Korosteleva, who had already convened a conference on contemporary Belarus at Bath University, joined the team at Glasgow University as a British Academy research fellow. Clelia Rontoyanni, who completed her doctorate at Glasgow, has been closely associated with our work since the outset. Ronald Hill was a member of the project team, and is himself a country specialist; so too are David Marples and Uladzimir Padhol. Ian McAllister had previously collaborated with Stephen White in the analysis of postcommunist politics, drawing upon his statistical as well as comparative skills, and Christian Haerpfer had previously worked on Belarus within a broadly comparative framework and sometimes from a Glasgow location. Formally coedited, this is nonetheless a volume in which there is a very high degree of shared authorship.

Bringing this collection to a conclusion, it is time to remember the institutions that helped us to carry out the research on which we have drawn in successive chapters. The Economic and Social Research Council in the United Kingdom assisted us materially through grant L213252007 to Stephen White, Margot Light, and John Löwenhardt, and through grant RES230146 to Stephen White, Margot Light, and Roy Allison. The support of INTAS (99-245) and especially of the British Academy (SG-31102, SG-35130, and PDF/2001/174) is gratefully acknowledged by Elena Korosteleva. We are also glad to acknowledge the assistance and commentary offered by Professor Oleg Manaev of the Independent Institute of Socio-Economic and Political Research in Belarus, and Professor David Rotman of the Centre for Social and Political Research at the Belarusian State University. Lorton House, a charity that supports the study of communism and related movements, made a small grant toward the costs of production.

Finally, a few points of style. We have followed "Russian" usage in this volume, rather than Belarusian, on the grounds that it will be familiar to more readers: so we have Lukashenko rather than Lukashenka, and Grodno rather than Hrodna. We have followed the *Europe–Asia Studies* style in our citations, other than for names and places that have become familiar in English. A brief appendix contains a selection of official data that may be found useful for reference and comparative purposes. The final version was prepared by Ronald Hill, and reflects his close attention to detail as well as technical skill; he has our grateful thanks.

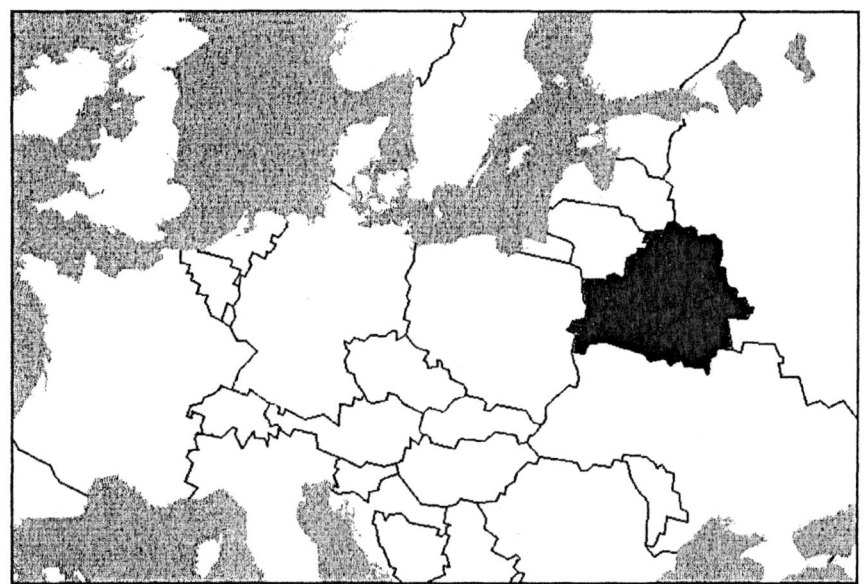

Map 1: Belarus in Europe

Map 2: Belarus: Main Administrative Centers

1 Post-Soviet Belarus: In Search of Direction

Ronald J. Hill

Belarus is, along with Moldova, perhaps the least-studied European state to emerge from the collapse of the Soviet Union in 1991. Even in the Soviet era, when it was one of the most successful of the constituent republics, very few Western specialists paid much attention to its affairs. In much of the post-Soviet era, as a result of the broadly anti-Western policies and undemocratic practices of the incumbent president, Alexander Lukashenko, the country has been largely isolated diplomatically, and scholarly interest has been restrained.

Nevertheless, patriotic Belarusians are pleased to note that the country is geographically at the very center of "Europe" (assuming that the east–west axis stretches from the Atlantic to the Urals), and it constitutes a sensitive border region between Russia and the western part of the continent. Some of its neighbors have recently become members of the European Union, and its immediate western neighbor, Poland, with which it shares a long common history, is already a member of the NATO military alliance. Sandwiched between Russia and western Europe, and on a direct line of march between Germany (or Prussia) and Russia, Belarus has been directly affected by every turn in the fraught relations between these dominant powers in northern Europe. In the modern era its sense of identity has been strongly influenced by its destruction in the Second World War, as it bore the brunt of the Nazi onslaught in the front line of the Soviet defenses, its population brutally treated during the occupation and about a third of them left for dead. That experience has strongly affected national sentiment as the country under Lukashenko attempts to forge an identity of separateness combined with a close association with Russia.

The brief history of Belarus in the period leading up to and following independence in 1991 can be summarized in precisely such a search for identity. To the outside observer it may appear that the country has been grappling with challenges that it is ill-equipped to deal with, and those challenges are conceptual or psychological as much as political, economic, and social. National independence, it appears, was thrust upon a nation that was unsure how to handle it.

Western commentators use various phrases to encapsulate the process. For David R. Marples, Belarus is "a denationalized nation";[1] George Sanford sees postindependence Belarus as "[combining] weak or divided national consciousness with an insignificant experience of independent statehood";[2] Ed Jocelyn stresses a similar theme, arguing that in Belarus "national consciousness is a highly problematic concept," adding that "Belarusian national identity is fragmented, and its roots lead in different directions";[3] Richard and Ben Crampton note that Belarus "has little sense of nationhood and little experience in practical politics," pointing out that "there was no church with which Belorussians could associate" in their establishment of a distinct identity;[4] and Kathleen J. Mihalisko stresses the "retreat to authoritarianism" under President Alexander Lukashenko and relates this, in part, to his "deft exploitation of every defect in the national, political, and social psyche."[5] Grigory Ioffe says that "there is no single Belarusian identity," suggesting that to the extent that there is an identity it is "Janus-faced."[6] A similar emphasis on the psychological dimension—essentially the question of national consciousness—in modern Belarus is to be found in works by other writers, East and West.[7]

The course of events leading up to independence, and in the dozen or so years since then, illustrates this. However, the question of identity is rooted in the long history of involvement with the nations and states surrounding the geographical center of Europe, and those somewhat further afield. Statehood, in its modern conception, essentially came to the Belarusian nation late: indeed, it can be argued that it is rooted in the experience of quasi-statehood in the form of the Belorussian Soviet Socialist Republic, during the twentieth century.[8] During that period the modern apparatus of statehood was established, which, even though part of the strongly centralized Soviet political system in which power was focused in Moscow, was significantly more independent than during the previous century as part of the Russian Empire.[9] Also during the Soviet period, one of the most formative experiences was the tragedy of the Second World War, when Belarus took the main force of the Nazi attack and forged a sense of national unity *in defense of the Soviet Union* that has been a source of pride and satisfaction in subsequent decades: this, indeed, is seen as a "pivotal experience" in the history of modern Belarus.[10] The Soviet period also, through its policy of rapid and extensive industrialization, effected a social restructuring that brought urbanization and heavy industrial production to what had been essentially a traditional society of landowners and peasants—in short, a process of modernization, from which society benefited through education, health care, widened lifestyle opportunities, and rising prosperity. In addition, as Michael Urban has demonstrated, in the post–Second World War period the republic's political leadership, first under a group of Second World War veterans led by Kirill T. Mazurov

(Mazurau) and later under his protégé Piotr Masherov (Masherau), acquired a level of independence from Moscow that permitted Masherov, in particular, to win a measure of genuine popularity.[11] It has even been suggested that "Within the framework of the Soviet order . . . the BSSR had been since the mid-sixties, if not earlier, a self-governing republic."[12] In recent years, Masherov has become something of a cult historical figure, used by the regime to win legitimacy in what one commentator has referred to as the "retro-utopian" worldview of President Alexander Lukashenko.[13]

The evident economic success of the republic in the Soviet period[14] undoubtedly helped to secure a degree of loyalty both to the republic and to the larger Soviet system within which it flourished. Such loyalties were enhanced by Soviet propaganda, which—as in the case of all nations—presented the union with Russia (in the late eighteenth century, as a consequence of the partitions of Poland) in highly positive, "progressive" terms. The Soviet era was presented to an even greater extent as an identity-forming period in the life of the nation. By the same token, the historical associations with Lithuania and with Poland were played down, even though those relationships over many centuries had contributed to the formation of an identity distinct from that of Russia.

Yet, the experience of the past century seems to have been dominant in those generations that gained independence with the collapse of the Soviet Union in 1991. It is symptomatic that, unlike the position in the Baltic States, for example, or Ukraine, there was no strong demand for independent statehood that threatened the integrity of the Soviet system; similarly, there was no significant dissident movement or *samizdat* activity, unlike Russia, Ukraine, the Baltic republics, and elsewhere.[15]

Background to Independence

Although a loyal member of the Soviet system, and headed by one of the more "conservative" communist leaderships among the Soviet republics during the late 1980s, Belarus could not remain unaffected by the fissiparous tendencies that beset many national units in the period of *perestroika* and *glasnost'*, particularly given the leading role of Lithuania in challenging the authority of the center. This was the *Zeitgeist* or "spirit of the time" across the USSR. In the case of Belarus, a number of specific elements prompted an awakening of national consciousness, a social, cultural, and political development referred to as *Adradzhenne*, or Renaissance. Particularly significant was the nuclear catastrophe at Chernobyl', in Ukraine, not far from southeast Belarus, on April 26, 1986. Given the prevailing wind at the time, 70 percent of the radioactive fallout emitted in the explosion fell on the territory of Belarus, rendering thousands of hectares unusable for hundreds, perhaps thousands, of years, and visiting a lethal poison on the population of that region. Similar environmental concerns stimulated nationalist sentiment in other parts of the Soviet Union, notably the Baltic States, and the presence of nuclear weapons on the territory of the Belorussian Soviet Socialist Republic reinforced a sense of national vulnerability that had been part of the price paid for the benefits of membership of the Union.

A second significant stimulant arose as a result of the greater freedom of expression under *glasnost'*, including freedom to undertake new historical research. This was the discovery, by the archaeologist Zenon Poznyak in a wooded site at Kuropaty, near Minsk, of some 500 mass graves of victims of Stalin's Great Terror of 1937–1941. Up to 300,000 victims lay buried for half a century, and their discovery led to widespread public outrage and demonstrations in 1988, and the establishment by various intellectuals' organizations of a new association, "Martyrology of Belarus," which aimed to use the discovery to rekindle a sense of national historical memory. This association in turn established the Belarusian Popular Front, with Poznyak as its president, analogous to similar new movements formed in other republics.

This cultural and political development was also a response to a third factor that fed into the growing national self-awareness: action by a group of twenty-eight intellectuals in December 1986 to draw attention to the decline in the use of the Belarusian language and, more broadly, the erosion of national culture. During the Soviet era, statistics in national censuses showed a steady downward trend in the use of Belarusian and a concomitant rise in the use of Russian in the republic. Whether or not this was an indicator of a deliberate policy of Russification—a charge naturally denied by the authorities in Moscow—there can be no doubt that Russian was gaining, particularly in the cities, and Belarusian came to be associated with the rural, peasant way of life that was steadily passing into history. In this, Belarus was not unique; this was a common feature elsewhere in the Soviet Union. Moreover, the language issue appears not to have been something that fired the passions of the masses: it is above all intellectuals who are usually concerned about the erosion of such forms of identity.[16]

A key purpose in *Adradzhenne* was to demonstrate that the Belarusian nation had a history and identity apart from Russia; in the Golden Age of the thirteenth to the sixteenth centuries, the language had been used officially in the Grand Duchy of Lithuania, and that culture flourished at a time when Russia was still under the Tatar yoke. Even so, no strong sense of nationhood had developed—and probably still has not. In the period of the Empire, Belarus and Ukraine were both seen as "little Russias"—parts of the Russian nation that were on their way to becoming full-fledged members; such a perception was maintained during the Soviet period, and has been carried forward into the present.[17] This ambivalence in, or uncertainty about, national identity helps to explain the course of politics in the first few years of independence. The *Adradzhenne* movement, however, given added resonance by the effects of Chernobyl' and the grisly discoveries at Kuropaty, encouraged the Belarusian Popular Front in its quest for independence from the Soviet Union.

The period immediately preceding, and the two or three years following, the collapse of the Soviet Union was the time when the nation came closest to recovering and asserting the non-Russian side of its identity. The Belarusian Popular Front led the way in pushing for independence from Russia and a reassertion of traditional identities, and events in 1991 allowed it expression.

In the 1990 elections to the republic's legislature, although the communist authorities retained control, their support waned. While the previous incumbent, Nikolai Dementei (Mikalai Dzemiantsei), was elected chairman of the Supreme Soviet, a leading reformer, Stanislav Shushkevich, vice-rector of the Belorussian State University, was elected first deputy chairman; Vyacheslav Kebich, a conservative communist, remained prime minister, but a number of his former deputies and several ministers lost their positions. In these changed circumstances, as Jan Zaprudnik and Michael E. Urban expressed it, "Dzemiantsei and Shushkevich forged a tactical alliance on the seminal question of Belarus' political future."[18] On July 27, the government adopted a Declaration on State Sovereignty, declaring the country's military neutrality, stating it to be a nuclear-free zone, and asserting the right to raise an army and security forces and to create a national bank and issue separate currency. Events moved swiftly forward during 1991. Following the August *putsch* against the Soviet president, Mikhail Gorbachev, which was supported by Dementei, the Belarusian Supreme Soviet chairman was forced to resign, and Shushkevich replaced him; the communist prime minister, Kebich, resigned from the Communist Party and retained his position. On August 25, the independence of Belarus was declared.

As the year declined, the Soviet Union steadily unraveled in the political battle between the Russian president, Boris Yeltsin, and the Soviet president, Mikhail Gorbachev, progressively deprived of the means to implement his decrees and the laws of the central Soviet government. The final deathblow for the old system was struck in Belarus in early December, when President Boris Yeltsin of Russia, Leonid Kravchuk of Ukraine, and Shushkevich on behalf of Belarus met at the Belavezha hunting lodge in western Belarus and reached agreement on establishing a Commonwealth of Independent States, headquartered in Minsk, as the successor to the Soviet Union.

The Post-Soviet Period

With Shushkevich at the helm, the soon-independent Republic of Belarus moved swiftly to establish a separate identity. In September 1991, it abandoned the Soviet symbols in favor of a white–red–white flag (the colors, if not the precise design, reflecting the old association with Poland) and a coat-of-arms depicting a knight on horseback (almost identical to the state emblem of Lithuania);[19] it declared Belarusian to be the state language, and introduced other practical and policy measures that indicated a turning away from exclusive association with

Russia and a reassertion of historical ties. New political parties emerged (without the hyperpartism of neighboring countries, although thirty-five were said to be in existence in 1997[20]), the Belarusian Popular Front turned itself into a political party, and independent press organs appeared. The country accepted the START-1 and Nuclear Non-Proliferation treaties, and Shushkevich delayed signing the CIS collective security pact. In a further indication of a more western orientation, in September 1992 the country was granted special guest status at the Council of Europe.

Nevertheless, the communists and their allies retained a dominant position, and this had a retarding effect on reform. Opposition democratic parties and movements campaigned for the dissolution of the Supreme Soviet and the calling of fresh elections, a move that was resisted, despite a strong popular signature-gathering campaign. The prime minister, Kebich, and Shushkevich became bitter political rivals, with the parliamentary leader and the prime minister adopting competing policies, with the support of different constituencies—industrial and business leaders backing Kebich, nationalists (notably among the intelligentsia) supporting Shushkevich. While Shushkevich nudged the country in a western direction, Kebich signed preliminary agreements on monetary union and free trade with Russia, and engaged in political machinations to undermine the position of the chairman of parliament. This led to the ultimate sacking of Shushkevich in January 1994, amid corruption charges aimed at the government. This represented a severe blow to the movement for a Belarus independent of Russia. Over the next two or three years, the western orientation of the BNF and Shushkevich was effectively defeated by the pro-Russian tendency, which has dominated until the present.

The key event in post-Soviet politics was the election in July 1994 of Alexander Lukashenko as president of the republic, which was as decisive as it was unexpected. Following the removal of Shushkevich, a new constitution was drawn up in February, giving substantial powers to the office of president, on the assumption that the first incumbent would be Kebich. Six candidates ran for election to the office on June 23, including Shushkevich, Kebich, Poznyak (leader of the BNF), and Lukashenko. The last-named candidate was not among the most prominent of the country's politicians, having served as director of a state farm in the Mogilev (Mahileu) district and been elected to the BSSR Supreme Soviet in that capacity. He is said to have been the lone Supreme Soviet deputy to vote against the dissolution of the Soviet Union—an indication, perhaps, of his real political values. In the immediately previous period he had served as chairman of a parliamentary committee investigating corruption in public life, a position that allowed him to make assertions to discredit his rivals; they could later not be substantiated, but the damage was done. Lukashenko received some 45.1 percent of the votes, against 17.1 percent gained by Kebich; 12.9 percent went to Poznyak, and the three remaining candidates each polled less than 10 percent. In the runoff between Lukashenko and Kebich on July 10,

Lukashenko gained an overwhelming 80.1 percent of the vote. It was an impressive use of democratic procedures—the last occasion on which such propriety can be said to have been observed.

Lukashenko as President

Lukashenko did not move immediately to undermine the processes that had been set in train in the previous four or five years.[21] Economic reform continued, and some of his appointments appeared to betoken continuity rather than a reversal of orientation;[22] and in January 1995 the country joined NATO's Partnership for Peace program. Nevertheless, at the end of his first three months in office it was becoming clear that he would tolerate no opposition to his policies, and within six months of his electoral victory evidence of censorship was apparent in the publication of newspapers with blank spaces; parliament censured the president for this. As the year 1995 advanced, the president proposed that the Supreme Soviet should dissolve itself, and piled on the pressure with a referendum—against which some Supreme Soviet deputies protested by a hunger strike, which was ended when they were evicted from the parliament by special armed forces.

Lukashenko "won" the referendum of May 14, 1995, overwhelmingly; on a turnout of about 65 percent, 83 percent voted to recognize Russian as a second state language (rendering it unnecessary for Russian speakers to learn Belarusian), 82 percent supported the idea of economic integration with Russia, three-quarters voted to abandon the newly restored traditional symbols of state in favor of slightly modified versions of the Soviet-era flag and coat-of-arms, and 78 percent upheld the idea of a strong presidency. Fresh parliamentary elections took place in several rounds during 1995, and, while not all 260 parliamentary seats were filled, the nationalist and democratic opposition to Lukashenko was devastated. A further referendum on November 24, 1996, conducted with less-than-scrupulous observance of democratic conventions, offered the electorate a choice of "chaos and anarchy" or "discipline, order, and change for the better."[23] It enhanced the powers of the president, divided the Supreme Soviet into two houses, and approved constitutional amendments so major as to amount to a new constitution that enshrined a strong presidential system—even though it was illegal to alter the fundamental law by referendum. Lukashenko declared that the constitution now gave him a new five-year term of office—thereby claiming two years beyond the term for which he had been elected in 1994. In addition, finding the Supreme Soviet elected in 1995 unwilling to submit to his authority, he nominated some of its members to a new House of Representatives and ignored the remaining members and the institution. A presidential republic was now in place, two and a half years after Lukashenko's election as president.[24] In 1999, when Lukashenko's term of office nominally ended, improvised voting for a replacement was organized on May 16, and there were serious demonstrations around July 20, the date of the formal completion of his term; Western governments declared him to have lost legitimacy. Yet he carried on regardless.

Meanwhile, strong-arm tactics against all challengers to the president's rule became the norm. Unsanctioned demonstrations were declared illegal, even those that were permitted were heavily policed, and demonstrators were frequently beaten up by the militia and interior ministry forces. The state press and broadcasting became a massive propaganda empire of the president, while the private media were subjected to interference of many varieties: closure of newspapers and sacking of editors; direct censorship; refusal to print (leading some newspapers to move to the Lithuanian capital Vilnius and smuggle copies into Belarus); seizure of copies containing articles deemed critical of the regime and its policies; harassment of journalists; frequent searches of editorial offices and inspections by the state financial inspectorate; and other measures intended to intimidate and to prevent the circulation of alternative ideas. This all reflected a reversion to the Soviet practice of equating "thinking differently" (*inakomyslie*) with "dissent," "dissidence," and "opposition," and as such something to be rooted out.

The resort to authoritarian methods was accompanied by a *rapprochement* with Russia, including an agreement on military installations, under Russian control, in Belarus, the establishment of a customs union and proposals for a joint customs service and border control, a treaty of friendship, and various other agreements. In April 1996, the two countries announced the formation of a Community of Sovereign Republics, a declaration that proved stillborn but was replaced a year later by an Act of Union, ratified by the parliaments of both countries in June 1997. Progress in creating a single union-state has been slow, however, principally for lack of enthusiasm on the part of Russia, given the precarious nature of the Belarusian economy and, no doubt, the reactionary tendencies of the current president of Belarus. Moreover, there have been occasional frictions, such as when journalists from the Russian television station ORT were detained by the authorities in Belarus, and Russian journalists were arrested.[25] Nevertheless, it is widely assumed that a Russian-oriented Belarus is seen by the Russian elite to be in Russia's interests, so the long-term prospects for independence and neutrality seem slim, unless there is a fresh awakening of national consciousness—also unlikely under the rule of "the quintessential Little Russian, Alyaksandr Lukashenka."[26] Even so, Lukashenko's indignation at President Putin's "offer" to incorporate Belarus's six provinces into the Russian Federation[27] indicates that relations between the two countries and their leaders are complicated, and therefore also unpredictable.

Relations with the West, including western Europe, Belarus's central European neighbors, the United States, and international agencies such as the Soros Foundation, deteriorated sharply meanwhile.[28] Given the values that Western agencies aim to promote—human rights; personal freedoms, particularly freedom of speech and the press; the democratic values of popular sovereignty and limited government—the authoritarian tendencies manifest since 1994 have led to the country's virtual isolation. Special status at the Council of Europe was suspended in January 1997; the Soros Foundation was effectively forced to withdraw, by the expedient of demanding high taxation on its donations; Western governments and the European Union severely curtailed their activities in the republic in the last years of the 1990s, and expressed their growing concerns at the lack of progress toward democratic norms. However, in one sense this played into the hands of the regime: by severing assistance to government-sponsored projects, Western agencies *ipso facto* ended up giving financial and other support to bodies deemed part of the opposition—independent trade unions, independent mass media, human rights groups. This gave the regime a perfect opportunity to discredit such bodies for accepting support from foreign opponents of the regime.

Lukashenkism

There is little doubt that by the mid-1990s, Alexander Lukashenko dominated political life in Belarus, and both citizens and commentators were speaking of "Lukashenkism."[29] This phenomenon in post-Soviet Belarusian politics has been identified as comprising four features: (1) "an authoritarian style of leadership, with a growing reliance on the police and special forces, censorship and tight control of the media"; (2) "a discernible contempt and disregard for democratic institutions and procedures"; (3) "an aversion to and avoidance of vital economic reform with an expressed preference for the state-led policies of the Soviet era"; and (4) "an active policy of reuniting Belarus with Russia."[30] Associated with these are suspicion, contempt, and fear in dealings with the West.

However, the incumbent president's negative relationship with Western leaders and his domestic intelligentsia does not necessarily extend to the whole population. Indeed, it seems clear from the manifest support that he enjoys in the population at large—far from universal, but certainly widespread—that Lukashenko reflects popular values and aspirations: his regime has been accurately depicted as populist.[31] Even among those who oppose him, the goals of the BNF—a completely separate existence, revival of the Belarusian language as the vernacular in everyday use, and so forth—are not accepted. It is difficult to re-establish a separate identity after two centuries of close integration with Russia, particularly when living memory includes the formative experience of the Second World War, modernization under the Soviet system (which has transformed the existence of millions and given education and life opportunities that their grandparents could not have dreamt of), and a relatively high standard of living, which the post-Soviet experience of their neighbors in Ukraine and Russia has still to match. Economic reform, such as it is, was slow to bring the expected benefits, although it did bring hyperinflation, which saw a five-million-ruble banknote in circulation in early 2000. If Lukashenko insists on retaining the familiar, Soviet-style form of economic management, which permits the country to avoid the high levels of unemployment experienced by all the country's neighbors, while also avoiding the extremes of poverty seen in neighboring states, that wins plaudits.

Anti-Western rhetoric also strikes a chord with those brought up in the Cold War era. It also avoids another difficulty familiar across various borders: the lack of experience in management of a market system, and the lack of local capital that has ultimately led to the transfer of ownership to nonnative entrepreneurs, which is easy to depict as a surrender of control to foreigners. Moreover, despite the lack of economic modernization—and the economy still produces heavy industrial goods that cannot compete in the international market—change has been taking place. Intercity roads have been maintained; the Minsk underground rail system continues to expand; new housing developments and shopping centers continue to be built; popular literature—including Western—is made available (unlike works for the intelligentsia), and selected Western firms are permitted to trade, giving an impression of change. For much of the population, unaccustomed to other measures of a successful society, these factors outweigh the antidemocratic features of Lukashenko's rule.

However, popular acquiescence—even acceptance—cannot mitigate the damage to democracy and to the country's international image and reputation caused by the crude infringements of democratic norms. Opposition to the president is not tolerated. Members of the administration are treated as creatures of the president, to be sacked at whim, and in some cases thrown in prison, with or without trial. It is noteworthy that the former leader of the BNF, Poznyak, fled to the United States and was granted political asylum in August 1996. Others, including leading politicians, journalists, a diplomat, and political activists, have sought asylum in other countries; the distinguished writer, Vasil Bykov (Vasil Bykau), left for Finland in June 1998 at the age of 74;[32] others have simply disappeared. Western ambassadors have been vilified and their functioning was interfered with. Foreigners are treated with suspicion—while official "friendship" flourishes through the Soviet-style "Society for Friendship with Foreign Peoples." Even charitable donations and funding through development programs are required to pass through the state channels and are subject to taxation.

Challenges Facing Belarus in the New Century

In many ways, the presence of Alexander Lukashenko, and his likely tenure of office into the future (perhaps circumventing constitutional limitations on his office[33]) constitutes a major challenge for the state and the nation of post-Soviet Belarus. It is, after all, his policies and behavior that have effectively isolated the country from contact with the rest of Europe and much of the world, even if he has done so with the acquiescence of his compatriots. By the same token, the modernization that has influenced the country's neighbors, particularly those to the north and west, in part associated with their intended adherence to the European Union, is not allowed to take effect. The regime's virulent anti-Westernism turns the country into a bastion of continuity with the Soviet past in a world that has changed significantly in the past decade and a half. The evident rigidity leads many critics to resort to the all-too-easy word "crisis" to depict the state of the economy, society, and polity.

In fact, the problems that the new nation-state inherited from the collapse of the Soviet Union cannot be addressed without major changes in attitudes, if not in orientation. These include the economic legacy of heavy engineering applied to building products for which there is no clear market,[34] a difficulty exacerbated by the collapse of the integrated market and supply system of the former Soviet Union. The economy is still wholly dependent on Russia for the supply of energy and other raw materials, which places it in a potentially vulnerable position if it wishes to retain any semblance of independence; the reports of high subsidies on gas prices emphasize the dependence. The country has to find its own way in the world, and that means paying for imports by exporting goods and services, few of which encounter significant demand. While it is true that Belarus was a leader in the early Soviet computer industry, worldwide advances in that field have left Belarus far behind, and a thoroughgoing modernization of the economy is desperately needed. The issues of product design and quality, reliability, and servicing have not been addressed; the agricultural sector remains particularly backward, still based on state and collective farms; rural life is relatively primitive; urban life remains bland and lacking in vibrancy, despite the symbolic presence of a few Western firms.[35]

Moreover, modernization is a very broad concept, embracing more than the economy. A switch to capital-intensive rather than labor-intensive production is only a part of what is understood by a process that embraces the whole of society. This, in the twenty-first century, implies the use of computers throughout society, with broad ramifications, including increased contact with the outside world plus the opening up of the society to greater freedom of information and opinion, with knock-on implications for personal expression, leading to loss of political control by the regime—an issue that was grasped by Gorbachev in the Soviet Union, but that Lukashenko regards with mistrust.[36]

Without such changes, including greater openness, contact with the outside world, and external investment to generate efficient economic production, to update the infrastructure, and to clean up the environment, the country seems condemned to isolation and a steady deterioration, if not in absolute terms then at least in comparison with those neighbors to the west that began their independent existence in approximately the same position economically, socially, and politically. Awareness of this among the population can hardly be avoided in an era of satellites and other forms of rapid communication.

The fact is that the country is not as isolated as it was as part of the Soviet Union. Direct flights between Minsk and a number of European countries exist, although they are neither frequent nor plentiful; visas for Western visitors are more readily available than in the Soviet era, and it is easier for Belarusian citizens to travel to the West—subject also to the suspicions of Western governments. It is also clear that many of the educated generation of young adults have a keen interest in the outside world, despite the introspection of the regime and of the older generation.

Under Lukashenko, the country is run in an authoritarian fashion, and many inside the country share the term "dictatorship," regarded as appropriate in the West, although some would add the term "mild."[37] Still aged barely fifty and firmly in office, Lukashenko has much opportunity to shape the further development of his nation. He has contrived to isolate the country from the problems of transition that neither he nor, it seems, the population has been prepared to face. But it seems inconceivable that the country can hold out permanently against the wider pressures of democratization and economic reform that is transforming its neighbors, including his large neighbor to the East. Western governments, which have pursued a policy of isolation of the regime while supporting Western-oriented nationalist movements and groups that would form a civil society, have manifestly failed to have the kind of influence on the country's post-Soviet development that they would like. Western governments clearly need to reassess their approach to dealing with a regime that many find perplexing—not to say frustratingly annoying, particularly as Lukashenko heads a country that lies immediately beyond the European Union's eastern border. It may well prove that the greatest influence over the coming years is a Russia that is embracing more of the Western way of life than many expected a decade ago, or than Lukashenko and many of his countrymen feel comfortable with.[38]

Be that as it may, the omens are not propitious. As Vladimir Putin's Russia appears to be turning toward a more authoritarian style, particularly in response to the challenge posed by Chechen separatists, Lukashenko seems safe from eastern pressure to liberalize. In September 2004, in a bid to extend his rule he announced his intention to hold a referendum, accompanying parliamentary elections scheduled for October 17. This would allow him to run for a third term of office and authorize a constitutional amendment to remove the two-term restriction on a president. If granted, and if subsequent developments conform to his obvious scenario, the outside world will have to deal with this irritant until at least the end of the present decade—conceivably much longer. Western countries may find new approaches through the country's neighbors Poland and Lithuania, perhaps taking advantage of the personal contacts of politicians from the communist era, more effective than the policy of isolation pursued in the past.[39] Ukraine, too, may serve as a future conduit for influence. Either way, the challenge posed by this maverick regime in eastern Europe seems likely to grow rather than diminish in the coming years.

Notes

1. David R. Marples, *Belarus: A Denationalized Nation* (Amsterdam: Harwood, 1999). Such a view is echoed by Volodymyr Zviglyanich, who attributes the rise of "Lukashenkism" (see below) to "the virtual denationalization of the Belarusan [*sic*] political elite, the annihilation of its more active members during the second world war and Stalin's purges"; see Volodymyr Zviglyanich, "The Lost World: Belarus as a Model of Political Necromancy," *Prism* (The Jamestown Foundation), Vol. 5, Issue 10 (21 May 1999), www.jamestown.org/pubs/view/pri_005_010_004.htm.
2. George Sanford, "Nation, State and Independence in Belarus," *Contemporary Politics* 3, no. 3 (1997): 225–45 (227).
3. Ed Jocelyn, "Nationalism, Identity and the Belarusian State," in *National Identities and Ethnic Minorities in Eastern Europe*, ed. Ray Taras (Basingstoke, England: Macmillan, 1998), 73–83 (73 and 81).
4. Richard and Ben Crampton, *Atlas of Eastern Europe in the Twentieth Century* (London: Routledge, 1996), 223.
5. Kathleen J. Mihalisko, "Belarus: Retreat to Authoritarianism," in *Democratic Changes and Authoritarian Reactions in Russia, Ukraine, Belarus, and Moldova*, ed. Karen Dawisha and Bruce Parrott (Cambridge: Cambridge University Press, 1997), 223–81 (275).
6. Grigory Ioffe, "Understanding Belarus: Belarusian Identity," *Europe–Asia Studies* 55, no. 8 (2003): 1241–72 (1263).
7. For example, Steven M. Eke and Taras Kuzio, "Sultanism in Eastern Europe: The Socio-Political Roots of Authoritarian Populism in Belarus," *Europe–Asia Studies* 52, no. 3 (2000): 523–47; Dmitrii Furman and Oleg Bukhovets, "Belorussian Self-Awareness and Belorussian Politics," *Russian Law and Politics* 34, no. 6 (1996): 5–29 (translation of "Belorusskoe samosoznanie i belorusskaya politika," *Svobodnaya mysl'*, no. 1 [1996]: 57–75).
8. That is the argument of Jocelyn, "Nationalism, Identity and the Belarusian State."
9. For a similar argument in relation to Ukraine, see Taras Kuzio, "Ukraine: Coming to Terms with the Soviet Legacy," *Journal of Communist Studies and Transition Politics* 14, no. 4 (1998): 1–27.
10. Jan Zaprudnik and Michael Urban, "Belarus: From Statehood to Empire?," in *New States, New Politics: Building the Post-Soviet Nations*, ed. Ian Bremmer and Ray Taras (Cambridge: Cambridge University Press, 1997), 276–315 (283).
11. See Michael E. Urban, *An Algebra of Soviet Power: Elite Circulation in the Belorussian Republic, 1966–1986* (Cambridge: Cambridge University Press, 1989). On Masherov's popularity as the nation's "first president" and "a man who united the nation" see Slavomir Antonovich, *Pëtr Masherov: Zhizn', Sud'ba, Pamyat'. Dokumental'naya povest'* (Minsk: Yunatstva, 1998); his death in a car crash in October 1980, possibly at the hands of the KGB in a politically inspired assassination, remains a matter of controversy; on this, see Amy W. Knight, "Pyotr Masherov and the Kremlin Leadership: A Study in Kremlinology," *Survey* 26, no. 1 (1982): 151–68. A recent history textbook distinguishes both Mazurov and Masherov among the "authoritative and competent" leaders during the Soviet period; Masherov's leadership is particularly praised for fostering rapid

economic and cultural development: see *Hystorya Belarusy, Chastka II: Lyuty 1917 g.–2000 g.*, 2nd edn. (Minsk: Universitetskae, 2000), 323.

12. Zaprudnik and Urban, "Belarus: From Statehood to Empire?," 285.

13. Zviglyanich, "The Lost World."

14. Grigory Ioffe, "Understanding Belarus: Economic and Political Landscape," *Europe–Asia Studies* 56, no. 1 (January 2004): 85–118; for Ioffe Belarus was "a major Soviet success story" (85–9).

15. Zviglyanich, "The Lost World."

16. For a challenging interpretation of these trends see Grigory Ioffe, "Understanding Belarus: Questions of Language," *Europe–Asia Studies* 55, no. 7 (November 2003): 1009–47. This was the first in a three-part series of articles, the second and third of which appeared in subsequent issues of the journal and are cited above.

17. See Kuzio, "Ukraine: Coming to Terms."

18. Zaprudnik and Urban, "Belarus: From Statehood to Empire?," 290.

19. As Ioffe reminds us, these were also symbols used by the collaborators with the Nazi regime during the Second World War; see "Understanding Belarus: Belarusian Identity": 1255–6.

20. Some of these "parties" had fewer than 1,000 members, and some were the product of splits within existing parties; see www.belarusian.com/belarus/ratings.html #042499.

21. For a more detailed account and assessment of Lukashenko as president of Belarus, see chapter 4.

22. Marples, *Belarus*, 71–2.

23. Sanford, "Nation, State and Independence in Belarus," 242; see also Marples, *Belarus*, 96–9.

24. Marples, *Belarus*, 99.

25. Marples, *Belarus*, 118–19.

26. Kuzio, "Ukraine: Coming to Terms," 15. For a fuller discussion of issues concerning Russia–Belarus integration, see below, chapter 7, by Clelia Rontoyanni; also, for a recent collection of essays by Belarusian scholars, *Belarus–Russia Integration: Analytical Articles*, ed. Valer Bulhakaw (Warsaw and Minsk: Minsk Analytical Group, 2003).

27. On this see, for example, Natalia Yefimova, "Putin Slams Belarussian Union Plan," *The St. Petersburg Times*, 18 June 2002, at www.stptimes.ru/archive/times/778/t_6703.htm; Andrei Ryabov, "The Common Cause of Putin and Yeltsin," reported in Johnson's Russia List, 2 July 2002, at www.cdi.org/russia/johnson/6334_6.cfm. Lukashenko was later reported to have called Putin "worse than Stalin"; see Alexander Kornilov, "Putin Is Worse Than Stalin," *Gazeta*, 22 August 2002, http://gazeta.ru/2002/08/22/Putinisworse.shtml.

28. Relations with the West are discussed in detail later by John Löwenhardt (see chapter 8).

29. See Margery MacMahon, "Aleksandr Lukashenko, President, Republic of Belarus," *The Journal of Communist Studies and Transition Politics* 13, no. 4 (December 1997): 129–36.

30. MacMahon, "Aleksandr Lukashenko," 129. Another writer sees Lukashenkism as "a symbiosis of communism, chauvinism and populism, in the Latin American style"; see Zviglyanich, "The Lost World."

31. Kamitaka Matsuzato, "A Populist Island in an Ocean of Clan Politics: The

Lukashenka Regime as an Exception among CIS Countries," *Europe–Asia Studies* 56, no. 2 (March 2004): 235–61. Lukashenko's popularity is not at a constant level, however.

32. For details see www.belarusian.com/chronology/asylum.html>; Bykov subsequently moved to Germany and the Czech Republic, where he was operated on for stomach cancer; he died in Minsk in June 2003; his funeral was all but ignored by the regime.

33. In June 2001 there was a call to extend his first term by at least seven years to avoid "wasting time and money" on an election campaign: see *RFE/RL Newsline*, 5, no. 108, Part II (7 June 2001); the call was made by deputy Viktor Anan'ev in the Chamber of Deputies' debate to set the date for the 2001 presidential election. Numerous web sites by émigré and opposition groups refer to Lukashenko as "President-for-Life," linking his supposed intentions with the actuality of Saparmurat Niyazov in the post-Soviet state of Turkmenistan.

34. This is at least the perception of some of the country's own articulate citizens, as reported by John Löwenhardt (chapter 8).

35. For a detailed analysis of the economy, see chapter 6, by D. Mario Nuti; a relatively upbeat and positive assessment of the country's economic performance is provided in Ioffe, "Understanding Belarus: Economic and Political Landscape," especially 89–95; in Ioffe's view, much Russian and Western commentary overstates the "doom and gloom" and there are significant countervailing social trends, including a high volume of exports, albeit principally to Russia (90–93).

36. For an exposition of this issue in relation to the Soviet Union in the 1980s, see Marshall I. Goldman, *Gorbachev's Challenge: Economic Reform in the Age of High Technology* (New York: Norton, 1987).

37. At the time of the 2001 presidential election, one English-language newspaper published in Minsk referred to Lukashenko as "Europe's last dictator," *Belarus Today*, 28 August 2001, 1. Such a depiction of the president is common in conversations in the country.

38. A similar argument has been made by Marples; see *Belarus*, 122–23.

39. The Lithuanian prime minister and former president Aldirgas Brazauskas made such a suggestion in a private conversation with the present author in Dublin on November 7, 2003. Similar ideas are also put forward by some Polish thinkers; for example, Ignacy Rutkiewicz, "Do Not Close the Door," *Lithuania* (Warsaw), 2004, no. 1(45): 168–71.

2 Patterns of Political Culture

Stephen White and Ian McAllister

Belarus, as we have seen, has a complex of legacies. It is a Christian nation, but a part of the Orthodox community that stems from the Eastern rather than the Western Church. Overwhelmingly Orthodox, it also has substantial Catholic and Jewish minorities. In medieval times its present territory was part of the Kievan state, and then of the kingdom of Poland and Lithuania; but at the end of the eighteenth century it passed into the Russian Empire, and after that into the USSR. In Huntington's terms, the "cultural border of Europe" runs through the middle of the republic, with its western regions in the Western Christian world and its eastern regions a part of an Orthodox and Islamic civilization, although in more recent times it could be seen as "part of Russia in all but name."[1] Within the USSR it was certainly one of the most "loyal" republics: the one that voted by the largest margin in favor of the retention of a union in the March 1991 referendum, and one in which there was no sign of the kind of independence movement that had swept the Baltic and the Caucasus in the final years of Soviet rule.

As an independent state, postcommunist Belarus faced a new range of choices, but choices that were informed by its previous experience. Internationally, what kind of orientation should it adopt: a "European choice" that would bring it closer to the European Union and NATO, or a "Slavic choice," that would bring it even closer to its powerful Slavic neighbor and perhaps into a confederal union?[2] Economically, how could it combine the advantages of central planning—including stable prices and the avoidance of large-scale unemployment—with the sensitivity to consumer choices that was a characteristic of the market? Socially, what could take the place of the comprehensive and state-funded welfare systems that had been maintained over the years of Soviet rule? And politically, what was the optimal balance between a strong executive—particularly a powerful presidency, which had been introduced in almost all the post-Soviet states—and a representative parliament with real authority?

In part, all of these were matters of institutional design. There was nothing inevitable about a powerful presidency; it was introduced with the constitution that was adopted by parliamentary vote in 1994, and taken further in 1996 by a referendum that (for many observers) should not have taken place at all. But the politics of independent Belarus also reflect a larger cultural and historical context—of religious and linguistic affinities, of the impact of war, of the kind of social structure that was the product of seventy years of Soviet rule, and arguably of a much longer period of time (it was particularly important, to writers such as Huntington, that there had been no prosperous landowning class that might have limited the powers of the monarchy[3]). Later chapters of this book focus on the institutions and policy choices of the postcommunist years; in this chapter we identify some of the assumptions that have helped to define these choices, and the decisions that followed them. We rely, for the most part, upon the evidence of national surveys conducted in 2000 and 2004; and we consider not only the distribution of opinion within Belarus itself, but also the corresponding patterns in Russia, Ukraine, and a wider range of European countries.

Looking Backward, Looking Forward

Successor regimes, and their citizens, have immediately to define themselves: what do they retain from their inheritance, and what do they repudiate? These choices are more acute when the transition is a "triple transformation"[4] from an economic and social system based upon public ownership and central management, and a political system based upon the hegemony of a single party. As other inquiries have made clear, postcommunist citizens will typically take a disaggregated approach to the system within which most of them have grown up. A couple of years after the demise of the USSR, it was "job security" that was most generally recognized as a valuable feature of Soviet rule; but there was also praise for the way in which "peace between nationalities" and "economic stability" had been maintained. On the other hand, communist rule was thought to have "too much bureaucracy," some thought it "suppressed human rights," and others thought it had allowed too much corruption.[5] What did Belarusians, at the start of a new century, think was positive, and what did they think was negative, in the system from which they had emerged less than ten years earlier?

It was a mixed, and not entirely unfavorable, verdict (see table 2.1). The former system certainly had features that were still widely respected after almost a decade of postcommunist rule. Most of all, it provided full employment—even if incomes were low, and not everyone was doing something useful. Its other most welcome features were also connected with the comprehensive social assurances that communist rule had at least nominally provided. Prices, for instance, were low and regulated; and there was little friction among the hundred or more nationalities that made up the Soviet state—at least until the Nagorno-

Karabakh dispute broke out in the late 1980s. There was also firm public order, compared with the high levels of criminality and antisocial behavior that were characteristic of the postcommunist years. Very few (just 1 percent) thought the communist system had no positive features of this or any other kind.

On the debit side, it was inefficiency rather than oppression that mattered the most. Above all, it was "too much bureaucracy" that our respondents identified as a failing of the former system, followed by "economic stagnation," a judgment that reflected the steady fall in the rate of economic growth that had been experienced since the 1960s. "Corruption" was also a failing of the communist system, and so was the "suppression of human rights"—although it was striking that objections of this kind, based on a concern for individual liberties, were not more prominent. Atmospheric pollution was another shortcoming of communist rule, and one with which the successor regimes had increasingly to reckon, but there were slightly more who thought communist systems had no shortcomings at all. Across the region, Belarusians (together with Ukrainians) were in fact the most positive about their former system of government: more than two-thirds (68 percent) thought it "a good way of running things," or at least "tolerable"; this compared with 48 percent across the postcommunist countries as a whole, and much less than this in Poland (36 percent) and the Czech Republic (37 percent).[6]

Table 2.1. The "Best" and "Worst" Features of Communist Rule in Belarus, 2000 and 2004 (percentages)

"Best" features	2000	2004	"Worst" features	2000	2004
Job security	24	28	Bureaucracy	26	26
Economic stability	22	19	Economic stagnation	20	22
Interethnic peace	22	22	Corruption	13	7
Law and order	11	7	Human rights	12	10
Equality	9	14	None	8	10
None	4	1	Pollution	7	9

Question wording: Respondents, from a list provided, were asked to identify "one best" and "one worst feature of the communist system."

Source: National representative surveys conducted for the authors and associates by Novak in April 2000 and by Russian Research in January 2004; further details of this and our other surveys are provided in the appendix.

We explored these perceptions in a different way by asking what more particular changes our respondents believed had taken place since the end of communist rule. By a very large majority, there was agreement that individual liberties had been enhanced (see table 2.2). The most conspicuous change, so far

Table 2.2. A Scoreboard of Freedoms, 2000 (percentages)

	Belarus		Russia		Ukraine		New Democracies	
	more	*less*	*more*	*less*	*more*	*less*	*more*	*less*
Religion	80	2	80	2	88	1	84	2
Organization	69	6	76	3	76	5	82	3
Participation	65	4	69	3	73	3	72	3
Speech	50	10	77	6	85	3	78	6
Arrest	30	20	24	19	36	19	57	11
Government	20	22	15	28	16	33	33	20
Fairness	17	31	12	51	8	53	32	27

Question wordings: "Compared with the Soviet period, would you say that today (1) Everyone has freedom of choice in religious matters, (2) You can join any organization you wish, (3) Everyone can decide individually whether or not to take part [in the New Democracies: "an interest"] in politics, (4) Everyone is free to say what he thinks, (5) People need not worry about illegal arrest, (6) People like you can influence the government, (7) Government treats everyone equally and fairly?"

Source: As table 2.1. Figures for eleven "new democracies," including Belarus and Ukraine, are drawn from Richard Rose and Christian Haerpfer, *New Democracies Barometer V: A 12-Nation Survey* (Glasgow: Centre for the Study of Public Policy, University of Strathclyde, SPP 306, 1998), 55–8.

as respondents were concerned, was in the freedom to practice—or not to practice—a religion. But there had also been substantial changes in the freedom to join any organization they might wish, and to decide whether or not to take part in politics (under the previous system, as some had put it, everything that wasn't banned had been compulsory). The freedom to travel was similarly thought to have improved since the end of communist rule—although there were financial, if no longer political barriers to availing of these new opportunities. And freedom of speech was widely agreed to have improved since Soviet times.

There was rather less agreement that the relationship between regime and citizen had changed in fundamental ways. No more than three out of every ten respondents thought they were less likely to suffer arbitrary or illegal arrest—in spite of a formal commitment to the independence of the courts, and a presumption of innocence. Two out of every ten thought they were actually *more* likely to be arrested improperly, and half saw no improvement. About half of all respondents, similarly, thought their postcommunist government was no more likely to treat individual citizens fairly and equally, and twice as many thought they were *less* likely to be fairly treated as took the view that there had been an improvement. In terms of their influence over government, more generally, half of our respondents thought there had been no improvement, and again, more thought they had *less* influence over government than in the communist period, in spite of the introduction of the formal procedures of liberal democracy.

These results were characteristic of the postcommunist region as a whole, although they applied more obviously to the post-Soviet republics than to other "new democracies." There was overwhelming agreement, across the region, that individual liberties had been strengthened, such as the freedom to practice a religion, to join an organization, or to choose whether or not to take part in political life. There was less consistency in terms of freedom of speech: Russians and Ukrainians recorded large perceived improvements, Belarusians were more cautious. But in every case there was little belief that citizens had fundamentally improved their position in relation to government. Many, certainly, thought they were less likely to suffer illegal arrest, but still larger numbers saw no change. And there were more across the three countries who thought their influence over government had *diminished* than who thought it had increased, although once again the largest numbers saw no change. Most remarkably of all, a majority of our Russian and Ukrainian respondents—even larger numbers than in Belarus—thought governments treated citizens less fairly and impartially than they had done in the communist period.

Belarusians, as these figures suggest, were less likely than their Slavic neighbors to believe their individual freedoms had been enhanced—by a small margin in the case of the right to join any organization they might wish, but a substantial margin in terms of their right to say what they thought. These were results that accorded with the conclusions of international monitoring bodies, which agreed that the Belarusian media were heavily censored and subject to arbitrary action by the authorities.[7] But comparisons in terms of the relationship between citizen and the state were almost exactly the reverse: Belarusians were *less* likely than their Slavic neighbors to think they had suffered a loss of influence over government, and *less* likely to believe government treated them more unfairly. This was, arguably, an accurate reflection of the more limited nature of the changes that had taken place in Belarus since the communist period. Individual freedoms had been enhanced, but less so than in Russia and Ukraine; on the other hand, there was still some opportunity to use the channels of political influence (however unsatisfactory) that had existed within the framework of communist rule, while Russians and Ukrainians had lost these opportunities but had not yet found a satisfactory postcommunist alternative.

Finally, in what is sometimes called a "heaven and hell" exercise, we asked each group of respondents to rate their political and economic systems at three points in time: the communist period, the present, and five years into the future. A version of this question has regularly been asked as part of the World Values Survey, although there are no questions about the economic system, and the prospective assessment is set ten years into the future—risking the danger, in countries that have experienced very rapid and fundamental change, that predictions of this kind become almost entirely speculative, with large numbers who feel able to offer no response at all. Responses, in our own inquiries, could vary between +100 (for the most enthusiastic) and –100 (for the most hostile). We

Figure 2.1. Assessing Political Systems: Past, Present, and Future

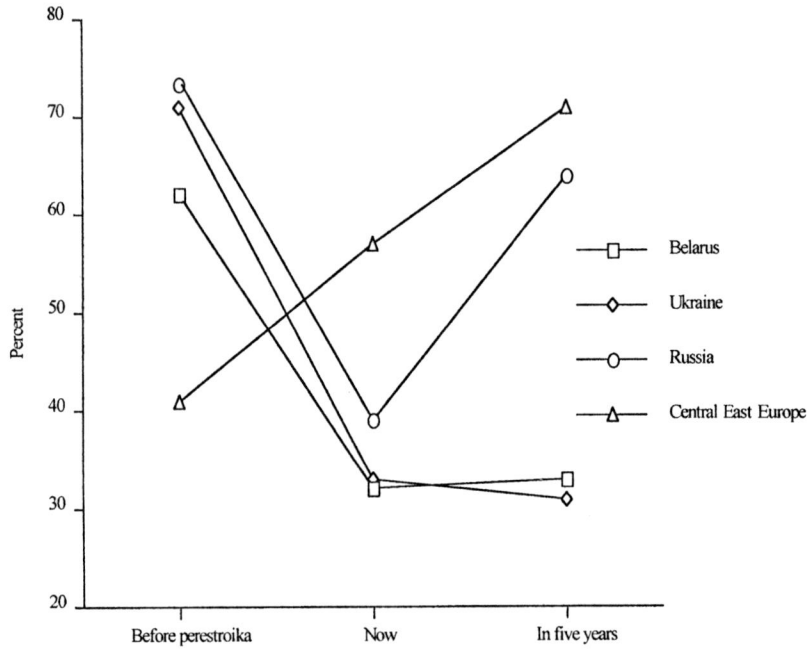

Question wordings: "Now I am going to show you a scale for the assessment of the political system, on which the highest figure, plus 100, represents the most positive evaluation, and the lowest, minus 100, represents the most negative. Where on this scale would you place: (i) the political system we had before perestroika? (ii) Our present political system? (iii) The political system we will have in five years?'

Source: As table 2.1; Rose and Haerpfer, *Trends in Democracies and Markets*, 53.

have included results, not only for Belarus, but also for Russia and Ukraine (see figure 2.1). Several conclusions emerge.

First of all, the communist period merits the most positive assessment in each of the three countries, in political and still more so (data not shown) economic terms. The future was also likely to be assessed more positively than the present, although this was not universally the case, and there were substantial levels of uncertainty that are not readily apparent in these figures, which show only the positive responses. Belarusians, compared with Russians and Ukrainians, were slightly less positive about the past, but very similar to Ukrainians in their assessment of the present and future. Russians stood out in their positive assessment of the future: a reflection, perhaps, of the euphoria of the early months of the Putin premiership and acting presidency, as well as the economic recovery that had followed the devaluation of the ruble in August 1998 and high world oil prices.

Attitudes toward the previous economic and political system were positive across the entire postcommunist region, and tending to become more positive with the passage of time.[8] However, there were significant differences between attitudes toward the past, present, and future in Belarus and the other post-Soviet republics, and attitudes in central Europe. Belarusians, and most of their counterparts in the former Soviet republics, thought better of the past than of the present, and thought their economic and political situation five years into the future would be little improvement upon the present. Central Europeans, by contrast, rated the present more highly than the past, and the future more highly again than the postcommunist present. Even in war-torn former Yugoslavia in the late 1990s, there was more optimism about the future than in post-Soviet Ukraine; elsewhere in the region, large majorities were "consistently hopeful."[9]

Attitudes toward the past, present, and future have typically varied widely by age-group. The older generation, especially pensioners, have positive memories of the comprehensive welfare system that prevailed under communist rule; younger age groups have more often been willing to take their chances in a market environment, and in any case have little personal experience of the previous regime. Older respondents, in our own inquiries, were certainly more likely to approve of the economic and political system of the communist past. In Belarus, unusually, they were also more likely to approve of the present and the future—a reflection, perhaps, of the extent to which Soviet-period welfare policies have been continued under Lukashenko, to the advantage of those who might

Table 2.3. Age and Perceptions of Political and Economic Systems (correlation coefficients)

	Belarus	Ukraine	Russia
Political system			
Before perestroika	.21**	.08**	.18**
Current	.09**	−.08**	−.05*
Five years	.09*	−.07*	−.03
Economic system			
Before perestroika	.19**	.13**	.19**
Current	.04	−.15**	−.13**
Five years	.09*	−.19**	−.07**

** Significant at $p < .01$, * $p < .05$, both two-tailed.

Sources: As table 2.1.

otherwise find it more difficult to sustain their living standards (see table 2.3). Differences of this kind were nonetheless a minor variation within a larger picture in which all sections of the society took a positive view of the political and economic system under which they have previously been living, and a negative view of the political and economic system they were currently experiencing or thought they were likely to experience in the near future.

Citizen and State

Whether they preferred it or not, Belarusians obviously lived in the postcommunist present; and the political system to which they most immediately related was the one that had been established under the Lukashenko presidency after 1994. Did ordinary Belarusians trust the government that spoke in their name within this postcommunist system, or the institutions that claimed to represent their interests, or any of the other institutions of civil society? The evidence of earlier research was that the predominant attitude, across the region, was skepticism (53 percent evaluated all institutions in this way) followed by distrust (31 percent), with trust (16 percent) well behind them. Institutions across the region, it appeared, had "yet to overcome the widespread antagonism generated in the Communist era"; and ordinary citizens were not simply antigovernment, but also antisocial, in that they distrusted a wide range of social institutions as well as the structures of government.[10] Belarusians and Ukrainians, in these earlier inquiries, were in turn more distrustful of government, and of civic institutions in general, than citizens of the other "new democracies."[11]

Belarusians, at the start of a new century, were still distrustful (table 2.4). They were actually less distrustful of their civic and social institutions than their counterparts in Russia and Ukraine, on our evidence, with an average level of support for all institutions of 37 percent compared with 31 percent in Ukraine and 30 percent in Russia; levels of confidence were higher in all cases than in Russia and Ukraine. But considered within a broader context, it is the general lack of confidence that stands out most clearly. Belarusians were rather more supportive of their religious institutions than, for instance, their counterparts in the EU member states; but in almost every other respect they were more skeptical, with the largest discrepancies in relation to the armed forces, the courts, parliament, and (by an enormous margin) the police. The central institution of representative politics, the political party, enjoyed the least support of all, although this was also true in the member countries of the European Union.

A low level of confidence in civic institutions, particularly the institutions of representative democracy, was reflected in a more general disillusion with the quality of the political system as a whole. How satisfied, for instance, were our Belarusian respondents with the "level of democracy" in their country? No more than a fifth (22 percent) expressed approval, with three times as many dissatis-

Table 2.4. Trust in Institutions, 2004

	Belarus	Russia	Ukraine	EU 15
Church	68	48	48	44
Army	58	49	49	70
President	38	22	30	48
Private enterprise	38	16	20	33
Courts	37	18	20	51
Trade unions	30	21	19	39
Police	28	18	16	67
Parliament	25	12	10	51
Parties	13	9	7	18

Question wording: "To what extent do you trust each of the organizations I am going to name to defend your interests?" Responses were coded from 1 (complete absence of trust) to 7 (complete trust), with don't know and no answer options; "trust" is defined as the percentage of respondents that chose points 5–7 inclusive.

Source: As table 2.1. Figures for the EU's fifteen member countries are derived from the *Standard Eurobarometer 56* (2002), fieldwork October–November 2001, 10–11, accessed at www.europa.eu.int/comm./public_opinion/archives/eb/eb56/eb56_en.htm. Figures for "president" relate to the "national government," and for "private enterprise" to "big companies."

fied (65 percent)—higher levels of support than in Ukraine but much lower than those that prevailed among the member countries of the European Union, where there was more satisfaction than dissatisfaction.[12] In terms of human rights, similarly, 28 percent of our Belarusian respondents thought they were respected to some degree, but 67 percent took the opposite view. These responses were once again more positive than those of our Ukrainian and Russian respondents, but well below the kinds of levels that were characteristic of the postcommunist region as a whole—let alone those of the established European democracies.[13]

What, then, about the nature of the interaction that took place between regime and citizen? To what extent, for instance, did our respondents believe they were treated "equally and fairly" by the state officials with whom they came in contact? As we have seen, this was the respect in which our respondents across the region as a whole were most likely to believe there had been a deterioration, not an improvement, since the communist period; and absolute levels of satisfaction were very low indeed. Among our Belarusian respondents, just 12 percent thought government officials treated them "equally and fairly"; levels in Ukraine were even lower, with just 4 percent believing government officials treated them fairly and an overwhelming 93 percent taking the opposite view. Responses were very similar when we asked a related question: whether it was "difficult for ordinary people to secure their legal rights." In Belarus, 77 percent agreed and a mere 18 percent took a different view; in Ukraine and Russia the level of agreement was even greater (88 percent).

Belarusians, like their counterparts in Ukraine and Russia, had little doubt that it was desirable to have competitive elections with a choice of candidates and parties, and little doubt that it was appropriate for them to take part in such exercises (see table 2.5). They also believed, by rather smaller majorities, that voting could "give people like yourself some say in how the government runs things," and that elections could make some difference to the country's "future direction." Belarusians were more convinced of the effectiveness of the electoral mechanism than either their Ukrainian or Russian counterparts, perhaps because theirs was one of the few postcommunist countries that had changed its leadership and political orientation through the ballot box (in 1994, when Lukashenko defeated the outgoing prime minister Vyacheslav Kebich for the newly established presidency). A majority of our Belarusian respondents thought elections gave them some influence over government, but only a minority did so in Russia and Ukraine. Similarly, a majority of our Belarusian respondents thought elections could change their country's future direction; Ukrainians and Russians were much more doubtful.

We asked another question, which was the one that most directly related to levels of political efficacy—the belief, whether or not it is realistic, that ordinary citizens can exercise some influence over the government that rules in their name. It is a characteristic of Western liberal democracies that levels of political efficacy are high (although falling), and it was a characteristic of Soviet-type

Table 2.5. *Attitudes toward the Electoral Mechanism (percentages)*

	Belarus		Russia		Ukraine	
	yes	no	yes	no	yes	no
Favor competitive elections	61	28	77	22	74	20
Approve of voting	74	20	66	33	76	21
Believe voting gives some influence	51	40	29	62	40	54
Believe voting can change country's future direction	64	29	42	49	53	41

Question wordings: "What do you think of parliamentary and presidential elections in which there is a wide choice of candidates and parties?"; "How do you think people like you should behave when there are national elections?"; "Do you think taking part in national elections gives people like you an opportunity to influence the government [*upravlenie*] of the country or not?"; "Some people say that elections can change the future course of events in our country. Others say that whether you vote or not, the state of things won't change. What do you think?"

Source: As table 2.1.

systems, at least in the view of Western scholars, that political efficacy was low, reflecting the position of ordinary people in relation to a regime in which they were "subjects" rather than "citizens," allowed to do no more than "demonstrate to the authorities that they support[ed] official policy enthusiastically and [were] exerting their full efforts to assist in its implementation."[14] Levels of political efficacy in Belarus are certainly low in comparative terms—fewer than a quarter of our respondents thought they had "a lot" (3 percent) or "some" (23 percent) influence over government, about half the level that obtains in the established democracies.[15] But once again, these were somewhat higher levels than in Ukraine (where just 4 percent thought they had "a lot" and 12 percent "some" influence over government) and Russia (where just 1 percent thought they had "a lot" and 11 percent thought they had "some" influence, but a massive 84 percent thought they had none or very little).

There was at least one obvious reason for ordinary people to believe they had lost influence upon government—or failed to gain it in the first place: increasing levels of corruption, which advantaged those who were able to give bribes or, in some cases, to occupy executive office themselves. In none of the three countries we considered was there majority support for the idea that government had come close to the idea of a "law-governed state," which had been one of the objectives of Gorbachev's *perestroika* and which found reflection in the constitutional commitment throughout the region to the "supremacy of law" (see table 2.6). Belarus, however, approximated to this more closely than either of its Slavic neighbors. The incidence of bribery and corruption was significantly less in Belarus than in either Ukraine or Russia—not just as our respondents perceived it, but also on the evidence of Transparency International.[16] And Belarusians were much less likely to take the view that bribery and corruption had increased since the Soviet period, when overt criminality of all kinds had

Table 2.6. Corruption and Government, 2004

	Belarus	Russia	Ukraine
A law-governed state?	39	30	36
How widespread bribery and corruption?	59	77	77
More than in Soviet times?	55	89	78

Question wordings: "How close is the [country] government to the idea of a law-based state?"; "In your opinion, how widespread are bribery and corruption in the central government in [capital]?"; and "Compared with the Soviet period, would you say that the level of bribery and corruption in [country] has increased significantly/somewhat/remained the same/fallen somewhat/significantly?" Figures show percentage agreement.

Source: As table 2.1.

been limited by the repressive legislation that was a consequence of authoritarian government.

How citizens view government has important implications for their political behavior. Other things being equal, those who believe they have influence over government, and that government will respond to the wishes of voters, are more likely to vote, to make an effort to influence governmental actors and, as a consequence of these activities, to express greater satisfaction with the system of government itself.[17] The type of electoral system, the perceived fairness of voting arrangements, and the responsiveness of the judicial system to the redress of grievances have all been seen as of particular importance in shaping such popular support.[18] Equally, the comparative evidence suggests that "[t]he higher the level of corruption in a new democracy, the less likely individuals are to support the new regime."[19] Viewed from this perspective, there were several features of the Belarusian system that appeared to matter more than others in generating higher levels of generalized approval than in Ukraine or Russia: most of all, lower levels of perceived corruption and a greater degree of confidence in the courts, the electoral system, and government itself.

A Typology of Political Orientations

In the final part of this chapter we relate some of the dimensions already discussed in order to develop a typology of attitudes toward the Belarusian political system and its future destiny. We distinguish, in the first place, between higher and lower levels of electoral efficacy—whether ordinary Belarusians support a choice of parties and candidates, believe they should vote, believe they can exercise political influence through the ballot box, and that elections can "change the future course of events"—and, on the other, between higher and lower levels of trust in civic institutions. We identify four distinct types on this basis. "Civics," as we define them, have a high level of trust in the system under which they live and at the same time a high sense of electoral efficacy; they account for about 23 percent of the electorate, and are slightly more likely to be male and to have a higher self-perceived level of income. Our second group, "Deferentials," shares a high level of trust in institutions, but has a low sense of electoral efficacy; they account for about 26 percent of the electorate, and are somewhat older, more female, and less well educated.

Our other two groups are less supportive of the regime, though in different ways. The "Disaffected," as we define them, have low levels of trust in civic institutions, but high levels of confidence in their ability to effect change through the ballot box. On our evidence, they make up about 17 percent of the electorate; they are slightly younger than the sample as a whole, more likely to be male, and more likely to have a higher education, and they represent the most obvious constituency for a more pluralist politics. Our fourth group, "Mar-

Figure 2.2. A Typology of Political Orientations

		Efficacy of Electoral Institutions	
		High	Low
Trust in Institutions	High	*Civics* (23%)	*Deferentials* (26%)
	Low	*Disaffected* (17%)	*Marginals* (33%)

ginals," is by far the largest, accounting for 33 percent of the entire electorate. Like the Disaffected, they are distrustful of existing institutions, but at the same time they are very skeptical of their ability to exercise any influence through the electoral mechanism. "Marginals," on our evidence, are disproportionately female, less well educated, and less prosperous (in their own view) than the sample as a whole; they also represent a constituency for more pluralist politics, but of a more latent kind. We set out these four groups schematically in figure 2.2.

We would expect these different groups to take different views of the past, present and future; and indeed they do (see table 2.7). "Civics," with higher levels of trust in existing institutions and greater confidence in their ability to exercise electoral influence, are in nearly every case the most optimistic. They are certainly the most positive about the present economic system, and the most positive about the economic system as they expect it to be in five years' time—though it still falls short, in their view, of the economic system of the communist past. Civics are the only group to take a positive view of the current political system, and they are the only group to place the future political system—by a

Table 2.7. Past, Present, and Future by Political Type

	Civics	Deferentials	Disaffected	Marginals
Economic system				
Past	55	57	38	47
Current	−12	−24	−35	−36
Future	39	28	−1	4
Political system				
Past	43	44	21	32
Current	10	−7	−21	−21
Future	45	31	16	4
(N)	(224)	(254)	(169)	(323)

Question wordings: As in figure 2.1.

Source: As table 2.1.

very small margin—above the political system of the communist period. Overall, they give high marks to the Soviet past; but they also identify with the current administration and the policies it is promoting, in many cases (presumably) with their active participation. Deferentials take a very similar view of the Soviet past, as their social characteristics would lead us to expect; but they are somewhat more reserved about the present and immediate future, reflecting lower levels of efficacy.

Our other two groups are less positive about the Soviet past, but also less positive about the present and the immediate future. The "Disaffected" reflect the outlook of younger professionals, confident of their ability to exercise influence but alienated from the political and economic systems in the form in which they exist at present. They are positive about the Soviet past, but less so than all other groups, and (with Marginals) they are the most dissatisfied with the present and the immediate future—except for the immediate political future, where their belief in their capacity to exercise a direct influence offers some grounds for optimism. Marginals are more positive about the Soviet past, but they are just as dissatisfied as the Disaffected about the present, and they are the least optimistic of all the groups about the immediate political future.

As these patterns suggest, there were relatively few who took a positive view of their current situation, but up to half of the electorate were optimistic about the near future (counting Deferentials as well as Civics). Conversely, even the "Disaffected," reserved about the Soviet past and critical of the present, held out some hope for the future, and Marginals were evenly divided. The same impression, of an electorate in which many had still to define their position, emerged from other questions that we asked more directly. Well over half (58 percent), for instance, felt unable to place themselves on the left, right, or center of the political spectrum; and just under 50 percent felt unable to identify with a "party family"—communist, pro-market, nationalist, or whatever. This meant, in turn, that there was little association between either of these measures and our political types: in every case, more than half were unable to define themselves in terms of left or right, and more than two-thirds had no commitment to a party family.

There were similar differences on current policies, and these were again distributed in the manner we would have expected (table 2.8). Few favored an economic system that was entirely in private hands; but as between the remaining options, Civics and Deferentials were more likely to favor state control, while the Disaffected and Marginals were more likely to favor an economic system that combined public and private management. Similarly, the most generally favored party system was the one that currently existed, or one in which there were fewer parties; but the Disaffected were less likely than any of the other groups to favor the single-party system of the communist past, or a system in which there were no parties at all. When we asked about a range of political systems, once again, Civics and Deferentials were the most likely to favor the resto-

Table 2.8. Policy Choices by Political Type

	Civics	Deferentials	Disaffected	Marginals
Preferred economic system				
State management	38	43	24	34
Equal state/private	43	38	50	50
Private management	19	19	16	16
Preferred party system				
One party	22	23	9	17
Multiparty as now	31	19	44	22
Multiparty, few parties	31	39	44	48
No parties	15	19	1	12
Preferred political system				
Restore communism	34	41	11	26
Army rule	6	10	5	13
Strong leader	23	28	15	33
Return to monarchy	12	13	13	13

Question wordings asked respondents to choose "which economic system is necessary for Belarus" from a set of options ranging from "state management of the economy without any private enterprise" to "freedom of private enterprise without any state interference"; to choose "which system would be best for Belarus today" from "a single-party system," "a multiparty system as at present," "a multiparty system with fewer parties than at present" or "no parties at all"; and to agree or otherwise that "it would be better to restore the communist system," that "the country should be run by the army," that "it would be better to do without parliament and elections and have a strong leader who could quickly resolve all problems," and that "it would be better to return to the Russian state monarchy." Figures show percentage agreement in each case.

Source: As table 2.1.

ration of communist rule, while the Disaffected were the most strongly opposed (a strongly autocratic regime found some support across all four groups, particularly Marginals, but not military rule or a return to monarchy).

The immediate future of Belarusian politics will certainly be defined by its dominant presidency. But in the longer run public preferences, mediated through the electoral system and in other ways, are likely to exert a gravitational pull. On our evidence those preferences are still amorphous, with high levels of uncertainty and relatively little confidence in the ability of ordinary people to influence affairs of state. Belarusians, admittedly, are less alienated from their political system than Russians or Ukrainians: less inclined to distrust their institutions, more likely to believe they will be treated fairly by state officials, more inclined to have faith in the electoral mechanism, and more likely—rightly or wrongly—to believe they can exercise some influence over the government that rules in their name. They are less despairing of corruption, and less likely to believe it has become worse since the communist period. But no more than 9 percent think of themselves as "close to a party" (considerably fewer than in Russia or Ukraine), and not much more than a third (37 percent) find it possible even to define themselves as a supporter or opponent of the present administration.

This remains, accordingly, a largely "Soviet" political culture. The mechanisms of authoritarian rule are still in place, particularly in the mass media; but so too are the ways in which the Soviet system allowed for consultation with its citizens, through trade unions, or residents' committees, or letters to the newspapers. And so is the "social contract" upon which the Soviet system was based, including virtually full employment and subsidies for basic necessities. Belarusians, accordingly, have had little opportunity to discuss their future destinies, and they have certainly had little opportunity to advance organized alternatives within a competitive political environment. But at the same time authoritarian politics has limited the scope for state officials to pursue their own economic interests and for public assets to be taken over by a privatizing *nomenklatura*. Ironically, the more the Belarusian system allows for political competition, the more its political system may become one in which ordinary people are removed still further from effective control of their own affairs, with few means at their disposal to hold to account a political class that—across the region—has become increasingly synonymous with oligarchic wealth and organized crime.

Appendix

Our primary source is a national representative survey conducted by Russian Research of London and Moscow in association with the project on "Inclusion without Membership? Bringing Russia, Ukraine and Belarus closer to 'Europe'," which is funded by the UK Economic and Social Research Council under grant RES-00-23-0146. Fieldwork took place between December 21, 2003, and January 16, 2004. The number of respondents was 2000, selected according to the agency's normal sampling procedures; it was representative of the Russian population aged eighteen and over, using a multistage proportional representation method with a random route method of selecting households. Interviews were conducted face to face in respondents' homes. The response rate was 57 percent. The sample was then weighted in accordance with sex, age, and education in each region. There were ninety-seven sampling points, and 150 interviewers were employed.

We draw also upon a national representative survey conducted by Novak under the direction of Andrei Vardomatsky. Fieldwork took place between April 13 and 27, 2000. There were sixty-two sampling points, and 90 interviewers conducted face-to-face interviews in respondents' homes. The total number of interviews was 1,090, using the agency's normal three-stage stratified sampling model to secure adequate representation of the resident population aged 18 and over. All seven of the country's regions were included. A full set of results may be consulted in Stephen White and Richard Rose, *Nationality and Public Opinion in Belarus and Ukraine* (Glasgow: Centre for the Study of Public Policy, University of Strathclyde, SPP 346, 2001).

We acknowledge the support of the UK Economic and Social Research Council under grant L213252007 to Stephen White, Margot Light, and John Löwenhardt, and under grant RES-000-23-0146 to Stephen White, Margot Light, and Roy Allison.

Notes

1. Samuel P. Huntington, *The Clash of Civilizations and the Remaking of World Order* (London: Touchstone, 1998), 158–59, 164.

2. For a recent discussion of these issues see Stephen White, Ian McAllister, Margot Light, and John Löwenhardt, "A European or a Slavic Choice? Foreign Policy and Public Attitudes in Post-Soviet Europe," *Europe–Asia Studies* 54, no. 2 (March 2002): 181–202.

3. Huntington, *Clash of Civilizations*, 71 (which contrasts the strength of the feudal aristocracy in western Europe and its weakness in Russia, among other places).

4. Claus Offe, "Capitalism by Democratic Design? Democratic Theory Facing the Triple Transition in East Central Europe," *Social Research* 58, no. 4 (Winter 1991): 865–92.

5. William L. Miller, Stephen White, and Paul Heywood, *Values and Political Change in Postcommunist Europe* (London: Macmillan and New York: St Martin's, 1998), 86–88.

6. These data are drawn from the New Democracies Barometer as reported in Christian W. Haerpfer, *Democracy and Enlargement in Post-Communist Europe* (London: Routledge, 2002), 16.

7. See, for instance, the annual Press Freedom Survey maintained by Freedom House (www.freedomhouse.org) or the periodic reports of Article 19.

8. Haerpfer, *Democracy and Enlargement*, chapter 2.

9. Richard Rose and Christian Haerpfer, *Trends in Democracies and Markets: New Democracies Barometer 1991–98* (Glasgow: University of Strathclyde, Centre for the Study of Public Policy, SPP 308, 1998), 30.

10. Richard Rose, William Mishler, and Christian Haerpfer, *Democracy and Its Alternatives: Understanding Post-Communist Societies* (Cambridge, England: Polity, 1998), 155.

11. For instance, just 15 percent trusted government in Belarus and Ukraine compared with 28 percent across ten postcommunist countries taken together: Richard Rose and Christian Haerpfer, *New Democracies Barometer IV: A 10-Nation Survey* (Glasgow: Centre for the Study of Public Policy, University of Strathclyde, SPP 262, 1996), 78–83. Similar evidence is presented in Fritz Plasser, Peter A. Ulram, and Harald Waldrauch, *Democratic Consolidation in East–Central Europe* (Basingstoke,

England: Macmillan, 1998), 110–15.

12. On Eurobarometer data, 44 percent were satisfied compared with 38 who were dissatisfied with the "way democracy [was] developing in their country"; *Standard Eurobarometer* 56 (2002), 17, accessed at www.europa.eu.int/comm./public_opinion/archives/eb/eb56/eb56_en.htm.

13. See for instance Plasser et al., Democratic Consolidation in East–Central Europe, 84.

14. Frederick C. Barghoorn, "Soviet Russia: Orthodoxy and Adaptiveness," in *Political Culture and Political Development*, ed. Lucian W. Pye and Sidney Verba (Princeton, NJ: Princeton University Press, 1965), 452.

15. Plasser et al., Democratic Consolidation in East–Central Europe, 137.

16. In Transparency International's 2003 survey, for instance, Belarus ranked 53 out of 133, between Greece and the Czech Republic; Russia ranked 86 and Ukraine a dismal 106: see www.transparency.org/cpi/2003/cpi2003.en.html (18 October 2003).

17. See Max Kaase and Kenneth Newton, eds., *Beliefs in Government* (New York: Oxford University Press, 1995); and Hans-Dieter Klingemann and Dieter Fuchs, eds., *Citizens and the State* (New York: Oxford University Press, 1995).

18. See Ian McAllister, "The Economic Performance of Governments," in *Critical Citizens: Global Support for Democratic Governance*, ed. Pippa Norris (Oxford: Oxford University Press, 1999), 188–203.

19. Rose, Mishler, and Haerpfer, *Democracy and Its Alternatives*, 188. A more comprehensive study is available in William L. Miller, Ase B. Grodeland, and Tatyana Y. Koshechkina, *A Culture of Corruption? Coping with Government in Post-Communist Europe* (Budapest: Central European University Press, 2001).

3 The Emergence of a Party System

Elena Korosteleva

Transitions to democracy in the former Soviet Union have been more problematic than those of the former socialist states of central and eastern Europe. This has been particularly true of Belarus, and especially of the development of the classic institutions of representative democracy, including elections and political parties. After twelve years of anticipated democratization the party system in Belarus remains nascent, with dissipated and ineffective parties that appear to be the least trusted institution in the country.[1] Furthermore, there have been rising tensions between the principles of representative government and an increasingly authoritarian leadership. The ensuing legal and institutional framework has left little room for parties to acquire authority in the decision-making process, which raises serious questions about their future role in a system of strong presidential rule and nonpartisan politics.

The first two sections of this chapter focus on the initial period of party system formation, in the immediate aftermath of the collapse of the USSR. The third section discusses the parliamentary elections of 1995 and 2000, and a concluding section considers some of the issues that emerge from this experience.

The Emergence of a Belarusian Party System

The period 1990–1991 was formative in the history of the new Belarusian state. On March 3, 1990, parliamentary elections to the Belarusian Supreme Soviet took place. Traditionally the Communist Party had dominated parliament, but shortly afterward it lost its monopoly of power. Three months later, a totally new political force consisting of thirty-seven members of the Belarusian Popular Front (BNF) and communist MPs formalized as the "Democratic Club" and began to press for radical change in Belarusian politics. As a result, on July 27, 1990, the Belorussian Supreme Soviet adopted a Declaration of State Sovereignty of the Belorussian Soviet Socialist Republic; and in September that year it approved a "National Program for the Development of the Belarusian Language" as the official language of a new state. Developments of this kind were not welcomed by the old-guard elite, and the first secretary of the Communist Party Efrem Sokolov raised concerns about the upsurge of "chauvinism, nationalism, and separatism" in the republic, calling for an all-union referendum to preserve the existence of the Soviet Union (which took place in March 1991).[2] These conservative undercurrents, however, did not prevent the reformist faction in parliament from formulating a concept of national independence and sovereignty, which finally took shape in the Declaration of Independence of August 25, 1991, the day after a similar declaration had been approved in neighboring Ukraine. The Communist Party of Belarus had already seceded from the CPSU; however, it soon found itself suspended after the attempted coup of August 19–21, 1991. The national parliament subsequently elected a democratically minded speaker, university professor Stanislav Shushkevich, and in December 1991 the Belavezh Treaty was signed by Russia, Belarus, and Ukraine to establish the Commonwealth of Independent States, marking a break with the Soviet Union and its monopolistic party politics.

In Belarus, as in many other postcommunist states, the end of the 1980s was associated with the rise of nationalist and pro-market movements, drawing on the slogans of independence, sovereignty, and democratic change. This initially took the shape of informal youth organizations and clubs, such as Talaka, Spadchyna, Krynichka, Svitanak, Suchasnik, and Minskaya Alternativa,[3] which were primarily concerned with the issues of national revival, ecology,[4] and Belarus's historical past. A collective petition of the Belarusian intelligentsia to Mikhail Gorbachev facilitated their crystallization into registered political organizations in 1987, pleading for the prevention of the "spiritual extinction" of the Belarusian nation. This was subsequently followed by a large protest movement in Minsk to commemorate the genocide in the Kuropaty Forest committed by the Soviet regime on Stalin's orders. Increasing public awareness and nationalist sentiment led in turn to the registration in 1989 of the Belarusian Popular Front, which defined itself as a "mass socio-political movement" whose goal was "to create a society and to renew the identity of the Belarusian nation . . . [and guarantee] the irreversibility of reforms in the BSSR."[5] The BNF became the first and the biggest mass organization in postcommunist Belarus, and its formation helped to encourage the emergence of social-democratic, liberal, and nationalist parties.

The human and intellectual capacity of the BNF movement and democratic aspirations in society established a basis for the formation of political organizations across a broad spectrum. Thus, in November 1990, the core of the Suchasnik Club and some members of a reformist wing of the Belarus Communist Party (KPB) in parliament formed the United Democratic Party of Belarus (ODP)—the first officially registered political party in the republic. Alexander Dobrovol'sky, later a prominent opposition politician, became its leader.[6] In

1995, in conjunction with the Civic Party (1994) led by Stanislav Bogdankevich, it formed the United Civic Party (OGP) of the Russian-speaking liberal (right-wing) elite, which remains influential even today. That year a splinter of the Civic Party relaunched itself as a public union under the name of "Yabloko," nominally a sister organization of the Russian party "Yabloko" although it drew more upon its name than upon its ideological orientation or beliefs.[7]

In February 1991 another right-wing liberal organization, the Belarusian Peasant Party, emerged, representing the first functional network of partisan forces in the regions. Its major strongholds were in the Minsk and Vitebsk regions, and it drew upon the support of the rural and agricultural intelligentsia. In June the same year the radical Nationalist Democratic Party of Belarus was registered; and in July the Belarusian Christian-Democratic Union held its first congress as a historical successor to the liberal nationalist party that had existed in western Belarus in the 1920 and 1930s, during the Polish partition. Later the same year, members of the BNF who were in disagreement with its radical economic program and had an incremental approach to reform established the Belarusian Social-Democratic Gromada (BSDG)—a center-right organization, which by its name rather than program represented the historical successor of the Belarusian Socialist Gromada that had originally been founded in 1903. They were led by Mikhail Tkachev and, after his death in 1992, by Oleg Trusov. The same year the Communist Party of Belarus (PKB) called its first congress, although its formal registration did not take place until May 1992. Thus, the 1990–1991 period witnessed a sharp increase in party activity; however, only six national parties (four right-wing, one center-right, and one communist) had formally registered their presence with the authorities.

Fewer parties were formed in 1992. On the left, two new organizations emerged—the United Agrarian-Democratic Party led by Semion Sharetsky (in 1994 it was renamed the Agrarian Party of Socialist Orientation), and the Party of Popular Consent (PNS) headed by Gennadii Karpenko, a former mayor of Molodechno and Deputy Speaker of the 1995 parliament (who died in 1999). On the center left were "The Greens," the first ecological party in Belarus, headed by Nikolai Kartash; and on the center-right the Slavic Assembly "White Russia," which favored a closer association with Russia and Ukraine. The PNS, however, soon found itself in ideological disarray between its dominant left- and right-wing factions, and split, subsequently to rejoin BSDG on the center-right and ODP at the right end of the spectrum. The Slavic Assembly, for its part, moved increasingly toward the presidential camp from 1995 onward.

A new upsurge of parties occurred during 1993–1995, and the spectrum expanded to thirty-four officially registered organizations by the 1995 parliamentary elections. Many newly emerged parties were of centrist orientation, with the exception of the BNF, which registered as a party in response to the mistreatment of its petition for a referendum that had been received in parliament a year earlier. Thus, on the left of the center the Belarusian Party of Labor (BPT) had

Table 3.1. The Spectrum of Belarusian Parties, 2003

Party Name	Date of registration	Membership on registration (1999)	Reported membership (2002)	Structure	Ideology
Belarusian Green Party	December 30, 1992	620 (1992)	Merged with BEZ	Cells in Gomel and Minsk	Center, ecological
Belarusian Ecological Party (BEZ)	October 9, 1999	Above 1,000	1,500	Regional Centers	Center, ecological
Belarusian Social-Democratic Party "Narodnaya Gromada" (BSDP NG)	March 3, 1991 as BSDG; reregistered on January 29, 1997, and September 9, 1999	Above 2,000	4,076	112 regional cells	Center-left
Liberal-Democratic Party of Belarus (LDPB)	May 2, 1994; reregistered June 15, 1999	35,855	17,637	District and regional cells	Center-right
Slavic Union "White Russia"	March 23, 1995; did not reregister	1,500 (1995)	Ceased	Regional cells in Gomel and Vitebsk	Center-right
Belarusian Women's Party "Nadzeya"	April 28, 1994; reregistered June 21, 1999; split 2002	Above 260	—	Regional and city centers	Center-left
Belarusian Social-Democratic Gromada (BSDG)	September 9, 1999	1,071	Above 2,000	Minsk and regional centers	Center-right, social-democratic
Agrarian Party (AP)	June 13, 1992; reregistered September 22, 1999	250	Above 1,000	Local branches	Left-wing, socialist
Party of Communists of Belarus (PKB)	January 30, 1995; reregistered July 5, 1999	15,000	7,878	143 local, 6 regional and Minsk branches	Left-wing, communist
Belarusian Party of Labor (BPT)	April 18, 1995; reregistered September 10, 1999	1,000	1,077	Party clubs, and local cells	Left-wing, socialist

Party	Registration	Membership (claimed)	Membership (official)	Regional branches	Orientation
Belarusian Patriotic Party (BPP)	October 8, 1994, did not register in 1999	12,000 (1994)	Ceased	Not known	Pro-Lukashenko
Belarusian Social Sports Party (SSP)	February 22, 1995; reregistered September 13, 1999	7,000	7,000	Not known	Pro-Lukashenko
Social Democratic Party of Popular Consent (SD PNS)	September 10, 1999	Above 1,000	—	Regional centers	Pro-Lukashenko
Communist Party of Belarus (KPB)	November 2, 1996; reregistered September 9, 1999	7,000	7,000	90 District, regional, and city branches	Pro-Lukashenko, communist
Republican Party of Labour and Justice (RPTS)	March 31, 1995; reregistered June 10, 1999	1,300	1,629	Not known	Pro-Lukashenko, socialist
Republican Party (RP)	March 27, 1995; reregistered in 1999	Above 1,000	—	Not known	Center-left
Conservative-Christian Party of BNF	February 28, 2000	1,267	1,267	Regional centers	Right (far), nationalist
Belarusian Popular Front (BNF)	December 26, 1994; reregistered September 30, 1999; ceased to exist on February 24, 2000	5,000 Reported 18,000	Ceased	Branches in all regions of Belarus	Right, nationalist
Belarusian Peasant Party (BKP)	February 23, 1991, did not reregister in 1999	12,000	Ceased	Local organizations in many regions	Right-wing, liberal
Party of BNF	February 24, 2000	Above 1,000	2,500	Branches in all regions	Right-wing, nationalist
United Civil Party (OGP)	October 1, 1995; reregistered July 30, 1999	3,500	3,125	Minsk, 6 regional; 28 city, and 66 district branches	Right-wing, liberal, conservative

Source: Adapted from *Belaruskii rynok*, issue 9, 10 March 2002, pp. 4–5, and the Official Bulletin of the Ministry of Justice, 2003 (electronic version).

Note: For more detailed information see *Politicheskie partii Belarusi*, ed. Vladimir Bobkov et al. (Minsk: BGEU, 1997); Mikhail Chudakov et al., *Politicheskie partii: Belarus i sovremennyi mir* (Minsk: Tesei, 2002); and Igor' Kotlyarov, *Politicheskie partii Belarusi: mezhdu proshlym i budushchim* (Minsk: MIU, 2003).

formalized itself by 1993, and so had the Republican Party of Labor and Justice (BRPTS). Two more ecological parties became legally established—the Belarusian Ecological Party (BEP), and "The Green World." In October 1998 they united in one ecological force known as "The Greens" (BEZ), headed by Nikolai Kartash and Mikhail Fridlyand, with a joint membership of 1,500 and regional cells throughout the country. Many smaller and often short-lived center-oriented organizations also came into existence. These included the Party of All-Belarus Unity and Consent (PVES), the Belarusian People's Party (BNP), the Belarusian Humanitarian Party (BGP), the Socialist Party, and the Party of Common Sense, all of which either vanished or became subservient to the president after 1996.

In 1994, on the right of the political spectrum the Beerlovers' Party (PLP), the Women's Party "Nadzeya," the Christian-Democratic Union, the Liberal-Democratic Party (LDPB), and the Republican Party crystallized as individual parties. Other organizations that formed for the first time after 1995 were generally not ideologically but politically oriented, responding to the opportunities that had emerged with the election of Lukashenko as president in 1994.

The beginning of 1998 witnessed the culmination of party growth, when the total reached 41—the record number of parties in the modern history of Belarus. Under the legislation on political parties introduced in 1999, the total fell sharply to eighteen.[8] Before 1998, however, the existing parties covered the full range of the political spectrum—from the communists on the left to the nationalists and liberal conservatives on the right.[9] Table 3.1 provides summary details of the party spectrum as it stood in the early years of the new century.[10]

Despite these changes in the direction of a pluralist society, the government *nomenklatura* had effectively remained in place, and had been working hard to secure the mechanisms of power. After parliament rejection of the BNF's call for a referendum in 1992, the hard-line *nomenklatura* began to advance. Within a few months an independent television station (TV-6) was closed, and the course of reform was suspended. In February 1993 the Supreme Soviet repealed the Parliamentary Decree "On the Temporary Ban of the Activities of the Communist Party of Belarus–Communist Party of the Soviet Union on the Territory of the Republic of Belarus," allowing the Party of Communists in Belarus to reestablish itself and facilitating the organization of an orthodox-communist parliamentary caucus "For the New Belarus," led by Vyacheslav Kebich. This slowly became a political force of a kind that had counterparts in all the former Soviet republics—a "party of power," composed of Kebich's allies and the old-guard *nomenklatura*. Thus the struggle for the survival of democratic parties began.

A Survey of the Contemporary Party System

The party system that seemed to have crystallized in Belarus by the mid-1990s had a simple tripartite shape, with the communist, socialist, and other satellite organizations on the left, through the moderate center to the liberal and nationalist right. Apart from the obvious left-right divide, a clear geographical cleavage could also be observed. At the national level it included a "center–periphery" divide in relations between Moscow and Belarus, and at the regional level a clear "urban–rural" divide between Minsk and rural centers. The parties on the left, by and large, had established themselves as "mass organizations" with a relatively large membership, a network of branches, and fairly strong ideological backgrounds (PKB, AP, and LDPB). The BNF represented the only exception to the rule, being a mass nationalist right-wing organization. All the other new parties (including OGP, BSDP Gromada, BPT, and Nadzeya) were elite organizations—"top-down" in structure, urban-centered, and often parliament-based. Let us look more closely at some of them by membership type to identify their structure, leadership, and programs.

Mass Membership Parties

The Party of Communists of Belarus (PKB) was launched in December 1991, and officially registered in May 1992. However, only a few regarded the new party as a true successor to the Belarusian Communist Party of the Soviet Union. The relegalization of the original Communist Party took place in February 1993; however, this did little to help clarify its true allegiance. In May 1993 the two parties—PKB and KPB—united at a joint congress and were named after the officially registered PKB, having inherited much of KPB's organizational structure, partisan loyalty, and material resources, embracing over 18,000 members. However, in circumstances of considerable social and economic change, the original PKB underwent an internal evolution, resulting in its ideological fragmentation and eventually an informal split in 1996 between hard-liners (led by Viktor Chikin) and "pink" or democratic communists, led by Sergei Kalyakin. As a result the party adopted a more flexible policy, which sought to retain a state-led moderate reform program and to continue the public ownership of land. The party has been the primary sponsor of economic and political alliance with Russia, which involved support of the agreement to establish the CIS in 1991 and of a collective security pact and monetary union in 1993. Over time its membership declined and its leadership became increasingly elderly. Eventually, as a result of internal frictions following the dissolution of the Supreme Soviet in 1996, the party formally split, and a conservative-communist splinter organization (the KPB) emerged. Led by Chikin, twenty-four members of the KPB joined the 1997 House of Representatives. The original PKB lost some 4,000 members, and many regional and local organizations ceased their activities at the beginning of 1998. On registration in 1999 it reported a total membership of 7,878, with 19 urban, 119 regional, and 534 local organizations in operation.[11]

Having assumed leadership of the rump KPB, Chikin in September 1998 became executive secretary of the pro-Lukashenko Belarusian Patriotic Union, reportedly gathering the support of thirty smaller parties loyal to the president and supporting the Belarus–Russia Union. The alliance did not last, however, and Chikin soon was replaced by Valerii Zakharchenko. Under its new leadership the KPB obtained six seats in the October 2000 parliamentary elections.

Another mass type of organization, the *Agrarian Party* (AP), registered in 1992 and soon grew into a party of left orientation representing the Belarusian peasantry. Its membership increased from 250 to reportedly over 12,000 supporters in 1995. The AP's chairman, Semion Sharetsky, was elected Speaker of the 1995 Parliament, and later became an active signatory of Charter-97, an oppositional nongovernmental organization.[12] With the 1996 crisis the party split and ceased to exist, defeated by the growing power of the president. About half of its members, nevertheless, managed to resurface as members of the House of Representatives on Lukashenko's initiative, organized into the new Agrarian Party under the leadership of Mikhail Shimansky. The latter was chief editor of the pro-government newspaper *Narodnaya gazeta*, whose only programmatic pledge was to "constructively co-operate with the incumbent government." In his opinion, the party should defend the interests of peasants by entering all branches of government and taking an active part in the parliamentary elections in 2000.

On the political right, the mass-type *Belarusian Popular Front*[13] followed the course of nationalist movements in the Baltic States, and like many of them was led by a group of national intellectuals, including the renowned writer Vasil Bykov (who died in 2003) and the archaeologist Zenon Poznyak, the Front's elected chairman. The BNF had originally organized itself as an inclusive political movement, extending its appeal beyond the core nationalist constituency, and positioning itself as an umbrella movement for all democratic forces; however, failing to achieve that, the BNF refused to dissolve into any form of "alliance" with other political forces, and this subsequently became a stumbling block in its further development.

The BNF was formally established on May 30, 1993, at the third congress of the movement, and registered in December of the following year. Officially the party and the movement were separate organizations, although in practice their organizational structures (leadership and core membership) largely coincided. This eventually was a cause of conflict over the leadership and strategy, which led the organization to a formal split in 1999.

The BNF is governed by a biennial congress and between congresses is managed by a Soim (council), which is appointed by congress. The Soim in turn appoints an executive body to implement party strategy on a day-to-day basis. Before 1999, leadership was shared between the chairman[14] and his six deputies: Liavon Borschevsky (who was acting chairman until 1999), Stanislav Gusak, Yuri Khodyko, Anatol' Krivorot, Vintsuk Vecherka, and Sergei Popkov. The party was highly disciplined and organized as a hierarchy with a central collective decision-making body. However, with Poznyak's subsequent deportation abroad, party governance acquired a more directive style and was often based on Poznyak's unilateral decisions transmitted through the limited channels of communication that were available. This was understandably a source of conflict and disagreement, especially on party strategies and tactics. After 1995 the party divided into two factions. The dominant radical wing was headed by Poznyak, and pursued extreme nationalist policies offering no compromise toward any political forces that favored a closer association with Russia. This made it difficult to establish any dialogue between the nationalist parties, which were attempting to unite in opposition to the growing power of the president. In late 1999 the radical wing separated off, having formed a splinter right party —the Conservative-Christian Party of BNF (CCP)[15] headed by Poznyak. The liberal center-right party, headed by Vecherka, re-registered as the Party of BNF and followed a policy of compromise and cooperation with other political forces.

The BNF was one of the most complex and pervasive political organizations in the country; it also retained a distinct ideological position. It had satellite youth and women's movements, and before the split in 1999 it had an extensive regional network with cells in every region of Belarus, especially in the west. Official party membership exceeded 5,200 supporters. Thanks to a new policy of flexible membership, which extended to anyone who could consistently contribute to the party's objectives, the number of party "supporters" allegedly reached over a million and incorporated 18 percent of the country's voting population. When the party split, the original BNF led by Vecherka had a core membership of 2,500, and Poznyak's group claimed to have about 1,400 members.

On the OSCE Advisory and Monitoring Group's initiative, a coordinating council (KRDS) of opposition groups was formed in 1999 to unite the BNF and other parties. This action nevertheless failed to carry through an alternative presidential election in 1999, and instead led to a boycott of the October 2000 legislative elections.

On the center-left of the political spectrum is the *Liberal-Democratic Party of Belarus* (LDPB), another mass-type organization, whose ideology and structure were similar to those of the LDPR in Russia. However, with the latter's decline in Russia, the LDPB began to distance itself from its parent organization in a more liberal nationalist direction. It was established at a regional level in 1991 but was not registered until 1994, and has a personalized style of politics based upon its leader Sergei Gaidukevich. The LDPB has been working on developing its regional network in Belarus, and claims to have established a membership of about 18,000 registered supporters. Gaidukevich himself jokes that it could have been more, if more drink had been provided. The party offers no clear program or ideology, and used financial incentives to motivate electors to vote for its leader in the 2001 presidential election. These efforts, nevertheless, failed spectacularly (see chapter 5), and the party itself became an increasingly marginal presence within the Belarusian political spectrum.

Elite Parties

Among the "elite parties" on the center-left is the *Party of Labor* (BPT), founded in 1993 and registered in 1995, which aims to represent the interests of the official trade unions in parliament. The Party of Labor pursues the traditions and principles of the international social-democratic and labor movements, and has been led by the party chairman, Alexander Bukchvostov, since 1996. The party is based on a modest network of regional political clubs, which are governed by the Regional Association of the BPT. The party was relatively effective in its negotiations with the authorities until 1999, when a presidential decree brought an end to the existing system of trade unions based on the payment of dues and allocation of bonuses. The party consequently suffered a considerable decline in membership. At present it remains Minsk-based and moderately anti-Lukashenko, and takes part together with Narodnaya Gromada in the activities of the Coordinating Council of Democratic Forces (KRDS).

Its partner, the *Belarusian Social-Democratic Gromada* (BSDG),[16] was founded in 1991 and expanded in 1995, merging with the Party of Popular Consent (PNS). Although it was originally formed as a merger of former KPB and BNF members, the party distanced itself from both, and even supported its own candidate, Stanislav Shushkevich, in the 1994 presidential election, in opposition to Poznyak. This action led to internal frictions and a change of leadership within the party in 1995. Nikolai Statkevich, an engineer and leader of a Belarusian Assembly of Armed Forces that had been banned in 1993, became party chairman, and its policies began to drift to the left, aiming to create a wide social-democratic coalition. In 1995 it was joined by part of the PNS and the Party of All-Belarus Unity and Consent (PVES), having formed a Social-Democratic Alliance (SDS) for the election campaign. It subsequently won two seats and later formed an eighteen-member parliamentary group entitled "Union of Labor." However, in January 1997 the former PNS left the SDS to form its own Belarusian Social-Democratic Party of Popular Consent (BSDP NS), under the leadership of Leonid Sechka. In September 1997 the remaining SDS formally split into two parties: the BSDP NG, with a center-left orientation, led by Statkevich, and the Belarusian Social-Democratic Gromada, with a center-right orientation (BSDG), led by Shushkevich. After 1998 the Statkevich party continued its independent strategy, and unlike other oppositional parties it did not boycott the 2000 parliamentary election. According to the Ministry of Justice, the BSDP NG has a membership of 4,076 activists, and Shushkevich's party claims to have a much smaller number of about 2,000 supporters.[17]

The *Belarusian Women's Party "Nadzeya"* [Hope] is another new party of the center-left, first registered in 1994. The party leader, Valentina Polevikova, had maintained very close links with the official trade unions led by Vladimir Goncharik, and was his campaign manager during the 2001 presidential election. The party has no ideological mission statement, and focuses on helping families, women, and children. Perhaps surprisingly, the party has survived and prospered, and its original membership of 200 had swelled to 5,000 by 1999. In August 2002 at a special convention of the party Valentina Polevikova was replaced by Valentina Matusevich. According to Matusevich, the convention was intended to reanimate Hope and prevent it from disappearing from the political map of Belarus following its announced merger with the two social democratic parties, splinter BSDP NG and BSDG. The merger, nevertheless, took place on August 24, 2002, on the initiative of the BSDP NG splinter organization led by Aleksei Karol' and Stanislav Shushkevich, and a new United Democratic Party was launched.

On the right is the *United Civic Party* (OGP),[18] the leading liberal conservative party of Belarus. It was established in October 1995 as a result of the merger of two like-minded parties—the United Democratic Party (formed in 1990) and the Civic Party (formed in 1994). It stands for an independent, sovereign Belarus based upon human rights, democratic forms of government, private property, free enterprise, and a market economy. Among its policy priorities are the introduction of a mixed electoral system, direct election of the heads of local administration, the replacement of Lukashenko, and eventual membership of the European Union. Up to spring 2000 Stanislav Bogdankevich, a former professor and ex-chairman of the National Bank, was party chairman. The party leadership also included Alexander Dobrovol'sky, Gennadii Karpenko, Vasilii Shlyndikov (a former MP and businessman), and finally Anatolii Lebed'ko, a former deputy and chairman of the Association of Young Politicians, who in 1999 succeeded to the position of chairman. The party claims to have 4,500 members and branches in six regions, twenty-eight towns, and sixty-six districts. It also has an established partnership with the British Conservative Party, the Polish Union of Freedom, Russia's Union of Right Forces, and Reforms and Order in Ukraine.

The Parliamentary Elections of 1995 and 2000

The 1995 Elections

Despite an apparent stabilization by 1995, the party system in Belarus remained fragile and unable to withstand the growing pressure of a reactionary parliament and the introduction of the presidency in 1994, which resulted in political stalemate. In January 1994 the parliamentary speaker was removed from office by two-thirds of the deputies and replaced by a politically neutral former KGB officer, Myacheslav Grib. The fragmentation of political forces and a growing distrust of parties in particular facilitated the introduction of a presidential system of government. The election, however, brought in a "new type" politician, Alexander Lukashenko, who immediately put himself in conflict with parliament (see chapter 4). By gradually introducing a presidential "vertical"[19] and giving the presidential administration well-defined rights but vague responsibilities,

Lukashenko steadily consolidated his grip on power and increased his ability to bring "disloyal" parties into line.

After 1994 the configuration of political forces began to acquire a different shape structured around the parties' attitude to the president rather than their ideologies. As a result, a new divide emerged, separating parties into the official opposition to the president on the one hand, and the president and his supporters on the other. This structural cleavage has remained until the present and is one of the most important factors that hinder the emergence of a "normal" party system.

In May 1995, for the first time in the history of the new state, parliamentary elections to the Supreme Soviet of the thirteenth convocation took place, this time on a genuinely competitive basis. The election, however, coincided with a referendum initiated by the president on the day of the election, which diverted public opinion in other directions. The four principal referendum questions were:

- whether to give the president the right to dissolve the parliament;
- whether to approve closer ties with Russia;
- whether to introduce Russian as a second state language; and
- whether to replace postindependence national symbols with those of the Soviet era.

This stirred public nostalgia for Soviet times, and boosted the pro-Russian and pro-Communist vote in the elections. In Belarus one would find it difficult to resist the convincing appearance of the president on the front page of each national paper urging "Do not vote AGAINST, think of your future." As a result, both exercises attracted about 65 percent of the voting population.

For the parliamentary elections 260 constituencies were formed with 2,348 candidates, which represented more than nine candidates per constituency. According to the Central Election Commission, MPs were elected in eighteen constituencies in the first round of voting on May 22. In 216 districts candidates were to compete in a second round, in twenty-four constituencies elections were pronounced invalid, and in one constituency the results were found to have been fraudulent and were annulled.[20] The second round of elections took place on May 28, 1995, and resulted in a 57 percent turnout across Belarus, and in Minsk only 38 percent (which was legally insufficient to validate the results). Another 101 MPs were elected, which made up a total of 119 deputies elected in the two rounds of voting, but was still insufficient for the convocation of parliament, for which two-thirds of all deputies had to be present. By-elections to fill the remaining seats were to take place on November 29, 1995, in 141 constituencies.

In the meantime the parties pressed the twelfth Supreme Soviet, which held legislative power until the new parliament had convened, to pass a law lowering to 25 percent the turnout threshold for the second round of election. The law was passed on September 7, 1995, but was fiercely opposed by the newly elected deputies and the president. The matter was forwarded to the Constitutional Court for resolution, and under pressure the court issued a statement on November 24, recognizing the law but restricting its implementation for the imminent third round of parliamentary elections in 1995.[21]

For the next round of the elections the BNF formed an alliance with four lesser-known nationalist parties, and had twenty-three candidates on the ballot. The liberals formed a "Civic Accord" bloc that brought together the United Democratic Party, the Party of Popular Consent and the Civic Party, nominating twelve candidates. These alliances, however, came to little, and in the event the parties competed against each other. As a result, BNF and the Social Democrats failed to return a single deputy during the first election runoff in November, while the Civic Accord returned only one. Unlike the reformers, the Communists and their allies in the Agrarian Party managed to unite and as a result they were able to win about 38 percent of the seats in the new parliament. The two election rounds later in the year were rather opaque in their administration. According to the authorities[22] during the first round in November 1995 twenty deputies were elected, and another fifty-nine on December 10. The thirteenth Supreme Soviet was finally able to convene after no fewer than four separate rounds of voting.

Table 3.2. Election Results to the Supreme Soviet of 1995

Supreme Soviet: 22/05 and 28/05, 29/11 and 10/12 1995	Seats	Percentage of seats
Communist Party of Belarus	42	21
Agrarian Party of Belarus	33	17
Party of People's Consent	8	4
United Civic Party	5	3
Other parties (PT, Ecological Party, BSDG, Social Sports Party)	15	7
Independents	95	48
Total	*198*	*100*

Source: Based on *Sovetskaya Belorussiya*, 22 December 1995, 2–3.

MPs in the new Supreme Soviet began to organize in factions. By 1996, there were five of them: (1) the pro-presidential "Zgoda" (57 members), headed by Vladimir Konoplev (deputy chairman of the House of Representatives); (2) the Agrarian faction (45), with Mikhail Girut' as leader; (3) the Communist faction (43), headed by Sergei Kalyakin; (4) a faction of social-democrats called the "Labor Union" (18), led by Leonid Sechko; and (5) a liberal faction called "Civic Action" (18), led by Stanislav Bogdankevich. Semion Sharetsky was elected parliamentary speaker. The parliament, however, soon found itself in disagreement with Lukashenko over his moves to concentrate power in his hands at its expense. Even the Communists, however ideologically close they were to Lukashenko's "socialist" policies, soon realized the difference in their positions. As a consequence, political parties and parliamentary factions, from the Communists to the Agrarians and Civic Action, moved closer together. Only fifty-seven members of the "Zgoda" faction and some independents remained loyal to President Lukashenko. "Across-the-board consolidation," it was argued, had "allowed the Parliament to bring forward a remarkable opposition to Lukashenko's efforts to establish one-man rule."[23]

Later in November 1996, in response to the growing power of parliament, Lukashenko initiated a second referendum. He proposed the formation of a bicameral legislature and the transfer of many parliamentary functions (such as the appointment of members of the constitutional court, of the central electoral commission, and of the state control committee) to himself. The parliament opposed these proposals by offering its own questions for the referendum, which included

- the draft of the constitution that had been proposed by the Communist and Agrarian faction;
- the introduction of popular election of the heads of local administrations;
- greater accountability of state expenditure and the rejection of extra-budgetary funding.

A group of oppositional parties was organized to monitor the referendum, and Viktor Gonchar was appointed head of the Central Election Commission.

In violation of the law, voting started two weeks before the due date, which was normally permitted only for itinerants. Gonchar was expelled from the election commission (he subsequently disappeared and is supposedly deceased), and the opposition lost control of the voting process. The final united action by the opposition was to call for impeachment of the acting president. The call was initiated by seventy deputies in accordance with the law and was passed to the Constitutional Court. The impeachment never took place, however, and the decision was renegotiated, with the assistance of the Russian premier Viktor Chernomyrdin, between Semion Sharetsky (speaker), Gennadii Karpenko (deputy speaker) and Lukashenko himself.

The eventual compromise between the president and the opposition was that the referendum result should be accepted and that it should subsequently be considered by a Constitutional Assembly, which was given a mandate to amend the constitution on the basis of the referendum results. In the end, 87 percent of the electorate was reported to have voted in favor of Lukashenko's constitutional revisions, which were signed into law on November 27, 1996.[24] The following day the parliamentary chamber was dissolved, the Constitutional Court was dismissed, and a House of Representatives was invited by Lukashenko to commence its duty. Only 110 members of the previous parliament responded to Lukashenko's proposal—including almost all members of "Zgoda" (fifty-two), twenty-four members of the Agrarian faction, twenty-one Communists, six from the Union of Labor, and another seven independents.[25] Anatolii Malofeev, who had been first secretary of the Communist Party of Belarus in 1990–1991, was appointed chairman of the new parliament.

The 1996 constitutional crisis, as we have seen, had debilitating consequences for all the parties, with a series of divisions opening up between supporters of Lukashenko's increasingly authoritarian system of government and those who continued to insist on parliamentary sovereignty and the 1994 constitution. Still more important was a decline of public trust in parties and interest in party politics as such. Parties began to lose not only their battle against the growing power of the president, but also their public standing as a mechanism through which the mass public could relate to the process of government. In its institutional forms, Belarus gradually moved from being a semi-parliamentary republic in 1990–1994 to becoming a superpresidential state from 1997 onward. The new pro-presidential parliament proved to be compliant and passive, accepting Lukashenko's instructions and his promises of support for the next parliamentary elections, due to take place in late 2000.[26] The antigovernment parties, for their part, became officially known as the opposition to the president, merging their differences into a single political force in their struggle for a democratic future.

The 2000 Elections

As a result of interventions by the Organization for Security and Cooperation in Europe (OSCE), a coordinating council of the opposition was formed in 1999 to unite such parties as the BNF, OGP, PKB, BSDP NG, BSDG, BT, and Hope, with support from the democratic initiative Charter-97 and the Congress of Democratic Trade Unions. Through the initiative of Hans-Georg Wieck of the OSCE, the LDPB and "Yabloko" also joined the council. After a Congress of Democratic Forces had taken place in January 1999, a Coordinating Council of Democratic Forces (KRDS) was elected, which aimed to unite the opposition in their struggle against the growing power of the president. The Council, however, failed to do so, and initiated a farcical alternative presidential election in 1999 that deepened the differences within its own ranks and caused further dissension within the BNF.

In 2000 the Coordinating Council advised the opposition to boycott local and national parliamentary elections, which caused additional friction among its member parties. Some were convinced that participation was necessary in order to improve the declining image of the opposition and propagate its ideas. Nevertheless, the majority of the opposition boycotted the elections, and those who participated on an individual basis were either denied registration or were convicted of violations of the election law during the campaign. Formally speaking, two opposition candidates won seats in the new parliament (one of whom was later suspended), but realistically they failed to represent alternative views in a parliament that remained compliant to the president's wishes.[27]

In advance of the elections a Congress of Soviets was convened at the president's initiative to reinforce the common purpose of representative institutions at all levels. Early voting began six days prior to the election, and was liable to fraud according to the reports of the OSCE monitoring team.[28] Despite the existence of a new electoral code there were many discrepancies found by international observers between the code and administrative laws, the legal provisions for the registration of candidates, and their campaigning and voting procedures. This was quite apart from widespread media censorship and controlled voting for "the right candidate" implemented through the executive control over election procedures, which were common in the course of the campaign and voting.

The first round took place on October 15, 2000, with 562 candidates running in 110 constituencies. The turnout was 61 percent; results were declared valid in ninety-seven districts, and invalid owing to the low turnout (less than 50 percent) in thirteen districts. Some forty-one deputies were elected, and a second round of voting was to take place on October 29 in fifty-six districts.[29] As the official press further commented, the turnout was low in places where oppositional candidates had dared to participate, which clearly reflected "the undisputable support of electors to those candidates who demonstrate their loyalty to the policies of President Lukashenko." There was "no need for the falsification of the election results," in the official view, simply because "the opposition, intimidated by the prospect of losing elections, refused to participate in the vote. As a result, the majority of

Table 3.3. Results of the Parliamentary Elections in 2000

House of Representatives: October 15 and 29, 2000; March 18 and April 1, 2001	Seats	Percentage of seats
Communist Party of Belarus	6	5
Agrarian Party of Belarus	5	4
Republican Party of Labor and Justice	2	2
Liberal-Democratic Party of Belarus	1	Less than 1
Social-Democratic Party of Popular Consent (BSDP NS)	1	Less than 1
Belarusian Socialist Sports Party	1	Less than 1
Independents	81	74
Vacant (constituencies where elections were not valid, and which later elected independents)	13	12
Total	*110*	*100*

Source: Based upon *Sovetskaya Belorussiya*, 3 November 2000, 1, and subsequent press reports.

elected candidates appeared to be respectable citizens of our society."[30] There was a 54 percent turnout in the second round and a further fifty-six deputies were duly returned to the House of Representatives. By-elections were held in thirteen constituencies on March 18, 2001, which returned a further two deputies, and eleven more were elected on April 1, 2001. Turnout in both rounds was higher than usual: 73 and 55 percent respectively, and the number of elected deputies now totaled 110 after four consecutive rounds of elections (see table 3.3).

Problems and Prospects

By the early years of the new century Lukashenko's efforts to concentrate power in his own hands, and the parties' inability to resist this system of personal rule, had given definite shape to a strongly presidential system. At present, parties resemble more a conglomerate of political forces than structured organizations with rules and procedures governing their conduct. Indeed, there can scarcely be said to be a party system at all, at least in the sense of "patterns of competition and cooperation between the different parties in that system."[31] In addition, the established legal and electoral frameworks do not at present encourage party system development in the society. The most obvious obstacles include the continued influence of the Soviet-period management elite, the lack of significant political or economic reform, and an outmoded electoral code. Over time, this has been institutionally reinforced, allowing the presidential system to become one-man rule, with a supportive constitution and a bureaucratic–administrative apparatus based on an extensive network of patronage. International assistance to the political opposition or to a putative "civil society" has at the same time been inconsistent and often clientelistic, in the end creating more problems than solutions.

Changes in the Regulation of Party Activities

At the beginning of the 1990s there was no legal basis for multiparty politics. In 1990 the Council of Ministers introduced a set of "temporary regulations regarding the formation and activity of public organizations in the BSSR," which became the judicial framework for party activities for the following four years. On October 5, 1994, the first law "On Political Parties" was adopted, which defined party rights and sources of finance, procedures of registration, and state control over party activities.[32] In accordance with the law, thirty-four parties had officially registered their activity by the end of the year. However, the introduction of the presidency led to a deepening antagonism between Lukashenko and the parties, in which the president was able to make use of the existing law on parties to his advantage. By 1999, the Ministry of Justice had managed to close many parties on nominally legal grounds, when parties failed, for what were usually trivial reasons, to observe the rules that were specified in their own statutes. The Christian Democratic Party, for example, was closed down on the grounds that it had not held a congress at a certain time, as stated in its statute, and no appeal was allowed.[33] The Ministry of Justice also used the mechanism of a published warning to a party, which if it was followed by another warning within a year resulted in party closure without further formality.

In 1998 the National Assembly, on the president's initiative, made several additions to the electoral law that confined the opposition to an even more limited role on the political stage. First, it did not allow participation in the elections of those who had been convicted of criminal or administrative violations in the previous year, which automatically excluded almost all active opposition candidates. Secondly, those opposition candidates who were eligible to run for election could still be disqualified as the law allowed the denial of registration if a single signature in the candidate's nomination papers was found to be invalid. The law also denied fair access by the opposition to the mass media and adequate conditions for independent observers (who had no right to monitor the count and who could be removed at any time if the electoral commission considered their activity to be interference in their work). Following the intervention of the OSCE Advisory and Monitoring Group and a subsequent series of "opposition–leadership" dialogues, "administrative and criminal convictions" were removed and the process of signature collection for the registration of candidates was eased.[34] Nevertheless, as Silitsky notes:

> Election commissions were still to be filled by the local executive authorities subordinated to the government, the status of independent observers was not raised, and the restrictions on financing the election campaign (each candidate was limited by approximately $100 to pay for a campaign in a 70,000 strong constituency) made it impossible for candidates without administrative resources to effectively spread their message.[35]

At the beginning of 1999 Lukashenko issued a decree on "Regulating the activities of political parties and other public organizations,"[36] according to which every party had to re-register by March 1, 1999, failing which it would lose its legal right to exist. In addition, the minimum requirement for membership was raised to 1,000, with branches in at least four regions of the country. Formally, by the beginning of 1999, forty-three political parties were registered, with twenty-seven of them considered active; however, only five parties (the PKB, Hope, RPTS, LDPB, and OGP) managed to meet the deadline, which was subsequently extended to June 1, 1999, at the request of some pro-presidential parties that had found it difficult to gather the signatures they required. As a result of this re-registration, by the end of 1999 only eighteen parties remained legal on the territory of Belarus.

Electoral Code and Practice of Elections

At the moment of independence Belarus did not possess an electoral code, but operated on the basis of individual laws and the inheritance of the past. Thus, a majority vote system for elections continued to function. New states with majority runoff systems often experience problems in the early stages of their party system formation, advantaging parties that are already in existence (often communist), and making it difficult for newcomers to gain representation.[37] Secondly, such a system also favors individuals over political organizations, motivating voters to cast their preferences for those who are "known" and "reliable" rather than a new and risky alternative candidate. The president dominates the Belarusian system, and accordingly the 2000 and 2001 elections were seemingly a foregone conclusion both to the electorate and to oppositional campaign managers.

By July 1999 an Electoral Code of the Republic of Belarus was finally approved, covering all the procedures that were necessary for electing and recalling candidates, and organizing referendums and elections at all levels.[38] It was drafted with some account taken of the recommendations of the Advisory and Monitoring Group of the OSCE. As mentioned in the report of the Central Election Commission, only a few OSCE recommendations did not find reflection in the law, owing to either their "contradictory legal nature or as not related to the subject of discussion."[39] Thus, OSCE proposals to introduce proportional representation, to drop the procedure for recalling candidates, to reduce the number of signatures needed for the initiation of a referendum, and, finally, to change the selection procedure of the Central Election Commission were found to conflict with the law and were not implemented.

Refusal to implement these recommendations was at the same time of some assistance in securing the return of a special "caliber" of candidate through the mechanism of executive-controlled elections. For example, because of the continuing use of the majority runoff system and state-distributed sums for election campaigns, parties' scarce regional resources do not allow them to canvass extensively outside the large cities, leaving almost 60 percent of the population beyond the reach of the political process—to the considerable advantage of those who can rely on the state and its resources. Another example relates to the procedure for recalling candidates—one of the more opaque provisions in the electoral code. It allows the recall of an elected candidate at any time and on almost any grounds by an election commission at any level. This confusion appears to be helpful in quietly "removing" a few awkward deputies from their elected positions, which naturally encourages loyalty to the incumbent president.

Furthermore, a hidden mechanism of executive-controlled elections is in operation,[40] which may escape the eye of external observers but remains a tangible fact of life in Belarus. This is the *de facto* approval of election outcomes by the head of state, executed by way of involving the "presidential vertical" in the process of the formation and operation of local election commissions during election campaigns and elections.[41] Further powers are available to the president through his control of the levers of employment, including the responsibility he can impose on senior government officials to promote certain candidates among their subordinates, control over food and medical supplies, and the manipulation of salary and pension rights.

One-man Rule

With Lukashenko's accession to the presidency, national-level structures were modified to reinforce his authority, but regional structures remained unaltered—to ensure the loyalty of local administrations through the mechanism of elite recruitment. The presidential vertical, based upon the appointment of the heads of regional executives from above, was intended to control the functioning of local councils, and hence election procedures nationwide. This means that in the regions, when locally elected deputies appoint executive committees to implement regional policies everything takes place under the constant vigilance of Lukashenko's nominees. So does the promotion of candidates to higher decision-making hierarchies, including the elections to the Council of the Republic.[42]

In a further strengthening of central authority, the lower chamber of the National Assembly, the House of Representatives, abandoned many of the practices of its predecessor such as single-ballot voting, which provided for electronic voting on an individual basis with the results reported in parliamentary bulletins at the end of each session. The House also declined the right to organize factions, supposedly for the purpose of "safeguarding" its discipline and efficacy (in the words of one parliamentarian), and lost many rights that before the 1996 referendum had been its sole prerogative. By accepting the constitution in the form in which it had been redrafted by the president in 1996, the voters allowed the formation of a regime of supreme presidential authority.[43]

International Opinion and the Situation in Belarus

One of the most significant influences on democracy building in Belarus has been the policies that have been adopted by the international community. First, the "exclusion" approach of the European Union and the United States between 1996 and 1999 resembled a strategy of ignoring the problem rather than realistically acknowledging it. This was replaced by a clientelist approach toward oppositional and nongovernmental organizations in an attempt to rekindle democracy. Pumping money into these sectors, which by and large were unwilling to take responsibility for actually opposing the regime, did not help to establish a dialogue between the government and the "antigovernment" opposition, and contributed to a more general failure of parties to articulate a political alternative.

Even after the failure of its attempts to influence changes in Belarus, the EU appear still to be convinced that the development of parties and of nongovernmental organizations is the only sensible way to prevent undemocratic practices. Their new motto is to "help Belarus, but not Lukashenko!" One needs, however, to remember that the president was elected with an absolute majority for a second term, and enjoys considerable support from the population even if the election itself was heavily manipulated. It may be that a different strategy would yield greater dividends, one that aimed to raise political awareness of the Belarusian electorate, who still regard strong leadership and governance by decree as more effective than their democratic alternatives. Another may be that to establish a dialogue with Lukashenko and his immediate subordinates rather than continue investing in circles that have no say (or only a limited voice) in decision making in Belarus.

Up to the present, for these and other reasons, parties have failed to establish themselves, and a party system is still in the earliest stages of development. The future role of parties will be affected by many developments, including the extent to which a dialogue can be developed between the presidency and a broader range of political opinion, and the influence that is brought to bear by powerful neighbors, especially Russia and the European Union. For the moment, party politics in Belarus stands as testimony to the extent to which democratization—where it takes place at all—can be a lengthy and disenchanting process.

Notes

1. Comparative survey evidence (1994–2003) suggests that trust in parties has declined from 29 percent in September 1994 to just 12 percent in 2003, reaching its nadir in 1998 (5 percent). This is based on data provided by the Centre for Social and Political Research, Belarusian State University, Minsk, and corroborated by other available evidence; see for instance Oleg Manaev, *Stanovlenie grazhdanskogo obshchestva v nezavisimoi Belarusi: sotsiologicheskie opyty 1991–2000* (Minsk: PhilServplus, 2000); Stephen White and Richard Rose, *Nationality and Public Opinion in Belarus and Ukraine* (Glasgow: Centre for the Study of Public Policy, University of Strathclyde, SPP 346, 2001).

2. Quoted from Yanka Zaprudnik, *Belarus na histarychnykh skryzhavannyakh* (Minsk: Batskayshchuna, 1996), 296.

3. The only highly politicized right-wing organization advocating nation building, and independence. See Jan Zaprudnik, "Belorussian Reawakening," *Problems of Communism*, 8, no. 2 (March–April 1986): 39–57.

4. These organizations were particularly concerned with the consequences of the explosion at the Chernobyl Nuclear Power Station in 1986.

5. *Pragramnyya Dakumenty BNF "Adradzhenne"* (Minsk, 1989), 25.

6. For more details on parties see Mikhail Chudakov, Aleksandr Vashkevich, and

Sergei Al'fer, *Politicheskie partii: Belarus i sovremennyi mir* (Minsk: Tesei, 2002); and Igor' Kotlyarov, *Politicheskie partii Belarusi: mezhdu proshlym i budushchim* (Minsk: MIU, 2003).

    7.   Although Olga Abramova, its leader and currently a member of Belarus's House of Representatives (elected on October 29, 2000), insists that her "Yabloko" is built on the principles and objectives of the Russian association "Yabloko," there is nevertheless very little resemblance between the two. The Belarusian Union "Yabloko," in accordance with its programme, remains a nonpartisan and nonclass organization, and affiliated to the regime (by virtue of being in parliament), which entirely contradicts the principles of its Russian counterpart: see www.belarus.net/minsk_ev/97/english/j8e/abram.htm, last retrieved in October 2003.

    8.   Chudakov et al., *Politicheskie partii,* 63–64.

    9.   Galina and Yuri Drakohrust, and Dmitrii Furman, "Transformatsiya partiinoi sistemy Belarusi," in *Rossiya i Belarus: obshchestva i gosudarstva,* ed. Dmitrii Furman (Moscow: Prava cheloveka, 1998), 106–53.

    10.   For more detailed information see Vladimir Bobkov, Nikolai Kuznetsov, and Vladimir Osmolovsky, eds., *Politicheskie partii Belarusi* (Minsk: BGEU, 1997); and Chudakov et al., *Politicheskie partii.*

    11.   *Belorusskii rynok,* no. 9, 2002, 4.

    12.   See www.charter97.org, last retrieved October 2003.

    13.   See pages.prodigy.net/dr_fission/bpf, last retrieved October 2003.

    14.   After the 1996 crisis Zenon Poznyak went in exile to the United States and later to Poland. He returned to the country to organize and participate in the 2001 presidential election, but failed to meet the selection criteria according to the law.

    15.   See www.bpfs.boom.ru, last retrieved October 2003.

    16.   See www.bsdp.org for more information about the party; last retrieved October 2003.

    17.   *Belorusskii rynok,* no. 9, 2002, 4.

    18.   See www.ucpb.org, last retrieved October 2003.

    19.   From 1996 the heads of regional executive committees at all levels were appointed by the president (constitution, article 85). This phenomenon, known as the "presidential vertical," has in essence deprived the electors of their right to decision making and control of government. Being directly appointed and dismissed by the president, the chairmen of local councils have authority to appoint and dismiss other committee members.

    20.   *Sovetskaya Belorussiya,* 25 May 1995, 1.

    21.   *Sovetskaya Belorussiya,* 24 November 1995, 3.

    22.   There was no official report by the CEC after the first round of elections in November 1995. The total number of elected MPs was reported to be 199 (Election Commission, January 1996), which however diverged from the overall total of 198 that had been registered by the Election Commission in 1995.

    23.   Vital Silitsky, "Explaining Post-communist Authoritarianism in Belarus," in *Contemporary Belarus: Between Democracy and Dictatorship,* ed. Elena Korosteleva, Rosalind Marsh, and Colin Lawson (London: RoutledgeCurzon, 2003), 36–53.

    24.   For details see *Belarus: Pariah or Victim?* by the British Helsinki Committee, at www.bhhrg.org/CountryReport.asp?ReportID=105&CountryID=4, last retrieved October 2003.

    25.   *Sovetskaya Belorussiya,* 30 November 1996, 2.

26. For more information see *Belarus 2000: Parliamentary Elections* by the British Helsinki Committee at www.bhhrg.org/CountryReport.asp?ReportID=14& CountryID=4, last retrieved October 2003.

27. Despite the obstacles created by authorities, a regime-sponsored analysis of the 2000 parliamentary elections insisted that parties were a vital part of national political life and should be supported by all means available. Their failure was attributed to the deficiencies of the Electoral Code, and certain corrections were recommended: "the right to nominate candidates to parliament should belong only to political parties," the authorities should "introduce state sponsorship of those parties whose nominees were elected to parliament," and they should also "increase parliament's powers"; see Mikhail Khurs, ed., *Ozhidaniya, realii i uroki parlamentskikh vyborov v Belarusi* (Minsk: ISPI, 2001), 65–66.

28. OSCE, Technical Assessment Mission, *Statement of Conclusions on Parliamentary Elections in Belarus*, last retrieved October 2003, www.osce.org/odihr/documents/reports/election_reports/by/bel2000_efr_rus.pdf.

29. *Sovetskaya Belorussiya*, 20 October 2000, 3.

30. *Sovetskaya Belorussiya*, 21 October 2000, 5–6.

31. Alan Ware, *Political Parties and Party Systems* (Oxford: Oxford University Press, 1996), 6–7.

32. Ales Piatkevich, "Partyinaya sistema Belarusi," in *Belaruskaya palitychnaya sistema i prezydentskiya vybary 2001 godu*, ed. Pavel Kazanetsky and Valer Bulhakau (Warsaw: CDEE, 2001), 388.

33. Piatkevich, "Partyinaya sistema Belarusi."

34. *Izbiratel'nyi kodeks Respubliki Belarus'*, 2nd edn. (Minsk: Natsional'nyi tsentr pravovoi informatsii Respubliki Belarus', 2001). Alternatively amendments to the Code can be viewed at www.osce.org/odihr/documents/reports/election_reports/bela00-1-assessment.pdf, retrieved October 2003.

35. Silitsky, "Explaining Post-communist Authoritarianism."

36. Piatkevich, "Partyinaya sistema Belarusi," 389.

37. For references see A. Lijphart and C. Waisman, eds., *Institutional Design in New Democracies: Eastern Europe and Latin America* (Boulder, Colo.: Westview Press, 1996); Jon Elster, Claus Offe, and Ulrich K. Preuss, eds., *Institutional Design in Post-Communist Societies: Rebuilding the Ship at Sea* (Cambridge: Cambridge University Press, 1998).

38. *Izbiratel'nyi kodeks Respubliki Belarus'*; alternatively see the Election Commission web site in Belarus www.rec.gov.by, last retrieved October 2003.

39. For additional information, see www.rec.gov.by.

40. See OSCE/ODIHR, *Statement of Conclusions on Parliamentary Elections in Belarus*.

41. For more details see Valer Bulhakau, ed., *Myastsovyya vybary u nainoushai palitychnai historyi Belarusi* (Warsaw: Analitychny hudok, 2003).

42. According to the Electoral Code (article 100), the right to nominate a candidate to the Council of the Republic belongs to the presidiums of local councils and executive committees (whose heads are appointed by the president).

43. The 1996 constitution of Belarus exceeds the 1993 Russian constitution (which was thought to be "strongly presidential") in the magnitude of powers bestowed upon the president compared with parliament, government, and local authorities; see Zaprudnik, *Belarus na histarychnykh skryzhavannyakh*, 296.

4 Lukashenko and the Postcommunist Presidency

Stephen White and Elena Korosteleva

Belarus was the last of the former Soviet republics to adopt a presidential form of rule, under its constitution of March 1994. At the first election under that constitution, in July 1994, Alexander Lukashenko won a convincing mandate with more than 80 percent of the vote in a second-round runoff against the then prime minister, Vyacheslav Kebich.[1] Notwithstanding his runaway victory, Lukashenko was still a relative unknown. He had first entered public life in 1990, when he was elected to the Belarusian parliament in the semi-competitive elections that took place in all the republics of what was still a Union of Soviet Socialist Republics. He became head of the parliament's anticorruption committee and used it to launch a series of attacks on leading officials and in particular on the parliamentary chairman, Stanislav Shushkevich, who was forced to resign in January 1994. This helped to establish a popular perception of the future president as a champion of ordinary people against a corrupt Soviet *nomenklatura*, in much the same way that it had done for Boris Yeltsin in Russia. In December 1991, in another controversial move, Lukashenko had been the only member of the parliament to vote against ratification of the agreement to establish a Commonwealth of Independent States in place of the USSR, a move that was popular with what has always been a broadly pro-Russian electorate.

Within just a few years, Lukashenko became the dominant figure in Belarusian politics; indeed, it was arguably a Lukashenko regime. In part, this was a result of the constitutional changes that he was able to force through, against the opposition of the parliament that had originally brought him to power. A stronger presidency was a much more general trend throughout the post-Soviet republics: in Russia the powers of the presidency had been greatly enhanced by the 1993 constitution; in Ukraine the president initiated a referendum in April 2000 that strengthened his ability to dissolve the legislature, and limited the immunity of deputies from criminal prosecution. In Central Asia, presidents had been able to extend their terms by referendum, or even (in Turkmenistan) to establish a fully fledged autocracy around the figure of its president for life, the former communist party first secretary.[2] A strong presidency was likely, the comparative literature suggested, to inhibit the development of party politics,[3] and a presidency that became increasingly repressive was obviously unlikely to encourage the formation of a civil society that might have helped to defend individual liberties.

The Lukashenko presidency, however, rested on more substantial foundations than the written constitution. There was little doubt, even among his opponents, that the president also commanded widespread popular support, and that he would have won a genuine contest for his office in 2001 if not by so substantial a margin. Lukashenko, for a start, is a figure of considerable presence, even charisma, and an inspiring public speaker. He is relatively young (still in his forties when he was reelected for a second term), and an active sportsman. His administration has avoided ostentation, and it has been relatively free of overt corruption. Not least, it has maintained popular living standards more successfully than elsewhere in the region, even if this has meant postponing unpopular but necessary adjustments. Indeed, as Lukashenko was able to claim during the 2001 election campaign, the people of Belarus lived better—on the evidence of the UN's Human Development Index—than those in all the other countries of the former USSR, and most of Eastern Europe.[4] In this chapter we consider Lukashenko's political career, and then use focus group and survey evidence to explore the bases of his popular support; the following chapter looks in detail at the 2001 election at which the presidential mandate was renewed for a further and, as the constitution now stands, final five years.

The Rise of Alexander Lukashenko

The first Belarusian president was born in a village in the Vitebsk region in August 1954. He graduated from the history faculty of Mogilev Pedagogical Institute in 1975, and took a further degree ten years later at the Belarusian Agricultural Academy. He undertook his military service after graduation, and in the early 1980s served in the border guards. Otherwise, he worked in a variety of capacities in local government and party offices, and then as head of a building materials firm and party secretary of a collective farm before moving in 1987 to the directorship of the "Gorodets" state farm in Shklov district, in the east of Belarus, where he was still working at the time of his election to the national parliament. These were executive positions; but as the president's official biography explained, he was not a product of the party or Soviet *nomenklatura*, or of the existing hierarchy of power, but a member of that "group of leaders whose popularity is explained, above all, by their personal merits and popular support."

Lukashenko was also known for speaking his mind, and although he was a party member, he had received two serious reprimands because of his "inability to keep his mouth shut."[5]

Once elected, Lukashenko lost no time in expanding the powers of his office. This inevitably brought him into conflict with the Belarusian parliament, which began to press for his removal, and with the constitutional court, which overruled a number of the president's decrees. His response, at every turn, was to return to the people for another mandate in the form of a referendum. There was strong parliamentary opposition to the president's plans, particularly from nationalists; Lukashenko, however, insisted that he would call a referendum whether they liked it or not, and warned that those who resisted would be dismissed from their positions. Opposition deputies, in an attempt to prevent the referendum taking place, declared a hunger strike and locked themselves into the parliament building, but were removed by soldiers on the pretext of a bomb scare, and the parliament, in the end, accepted all the proposals that the president wished to put to the electorate. There was overwhelming popular support, when the vote took place in May 1995, for the four propositions that appeared on the ballot paper: for the Russian language to have the same status as Belarusian, for a return to the state symbols of the Soviet period, for economic integration with Russia, and for the president to be entrusted with the power to suspend parliament if it was held to be acting unconstitutionally.[6]

The parliamentary elections that were conducted on the same date offered the president another opportunity, when complicated rules and a low turnout meant that there was difficulty filling all the seats (see chapter 3). The new Supreme Soviet, as a result, was unable to gather the votes it needed for a quorum until December 1995. Lukashenko, in the interim, was able to use powers of decree to extend his control over the security services, the state-owned media and the central electoral commission, and the confrontation between president and opposition became increasingly bitter and uncompromising. When the new session began, both sides sought to advance their position by amending the constitution in their favor: Lukashenko's draft significantly increased his own powers, while the parliament proposed an alternative that would have taken the appointment of the heads of local administrations out of presidential hands, and ensured that state institutions were funded directly rather than from extrabudgetary sources that were controlled by the president. In the event, it was Lukashenko's version that secured popular approval, at a referendum that took place amid considerable controversy on November 24, 1996. On a turnout of 84 percent, 70.5 percent of those who took part approved the presidential draft, and only 7.9 percent voted in favor of the parliamentary alternative.[7] This was effectively a constitutional coup, and it paved the way for the establishment of an increasingly authoritarian regime.

Under the Belarusian constitution, as modified by the 1996 referendum, the president is head of state and guarantor of the constitution itself. He enjoys immunity, and his honor and dignity are protected by law. He can call referendums, in appropriate circumstances, and regular and extraordinary elections to the national parliament and local councils; where the constitution allows him to do so, he can also dissolve parliament. He appoints the prime minister "with the consent of the House of Representatives," and appoints and dismisses deputy premiers and individual ministers; he can also dismiss the government as a whole. In addition, he appoints the members of the Supreme and Economic Courts, subject to the consent of the Council of the Republic; the chairman of the Constitutional Court—subject again to the consent of the Council of the Republic—and six of its individual members; the chairman and six members of the Central Electoral Commission; the Procurator-General; and the chairman and board members of the National Bank (he can also dismiss any of them provided the Council of the Republic is notified accordingly).

The Belarusian president delivers addresses to the entire population on "the state of the nation" and the broad outlines of domestic and foreign policy, and he presents annual messages that "are not open to discussion" to a joint session of parliament. He can preside over meetings of the government, and appoints his own administration as well as the most important state officials. In addition, he has a wide range of ceremonial powers, including the granting of citizenship, the conferment of awards, and receiving the credentials of foreign ambassadors. In certain circumstances he can declare a "state of emergency," or martial law. He can veto legislation and overrule the decisions of government; and he can issue his own decrees, which have the force of law although they must themselves be consistent with the constitution. There are procedures for the president's removal from office on grounds of persistent ill health, and for his impeachment in the event of treason or other grave crimes, but only when at least two-thirds of the full membership of both houses vote in favor. In addition, the Belarusian president has the power to appoint and dismiss the heads of local executive and administrative bodies, subject to the approval of local councils of deputies; this provides the basis for the mechanism of central regulation of the affairs of the entire nation that is known as the "presidential vertical."[8]

Compared with the 1994 constitution the president's powers had been widened considerably, including the right to call referendums, to dissolve parliament in specified circumstances, to overrule the decisions of government, and to appoint members of the upper house and of the constitutional court in a manner that is scarcely consistent with the separation of powers. Equally, he no longer needs parliamentary approval for the appointment and dismissal of deputy premiers, or of the ministers of finance, foreign affairs, defense, and internal affairs, or the KGB chairman. The Belarusian parliament suffered a corresponding reduction in its powers. The old parliament, the Supreme Soviet, was the "highest representative" and "sole legislative body of state power of the Republic of Belarus"; it was directly elected, and had the power to adopt and amend legislation, including the constitution itself. The new parliament, the National Assembly, is simply a "representative and legislative body." It consists of two chambers: a House of Representatives, which is directly elected, and a Council of the Republic, which is elected by the regions and the city of Minsk, with a further eight that are appointed by the president himself. The House of Representatives does have the right to reject nominations to the premiership, and it can pass a vote no confidence in the government itself; if it votes by a sufficiently large majority, it can override a presidential veto. Unusually, however, the powers of either chamber can be terminated by the Constitutional Court if they are held to be in serious and systematic violation of the powers with which they have been entrusted.[9]

Several attempts have been made to develop a scale against which the strength of presidential powers can be evaluated. The most influential of these formulations has identified a set of relevant variables that extend across an elected president's legislative and extralegislative powers.[10] Measured in this way, the powers of the Belarusian president are certainly extensive. The Belarusian president can veto legislation, although his veto can be overridden by a two-thirds majority in both chambers (this would approximate to a 2 on Shugart and Carey's five-point scale, the same as in the United States). He can veto part of a piece of legislation, as well as the entire bill (a score of 3 would seem appropriate in this case). The Belarusian president can issue decrees on his own authority, but is bound to remain within the framework of the constitution (perhaps a 2). And he has no monopoly of the right to initiate legislation, although he must give his agreement to proposals that would reduce state resources or increase public expenditure (a score of 1). The president does not introduce the annual budget—this is the responsibility of government, although it requires presidential approval (0); and although he can call a national referendum on his own authority, he shares this right with the houses of the Belarusian parliament and with a specified number of ordinary citizens (a score of 2 would once again appear appropriate).[11]

The president's other powers are also relevant to an assessment of the relative strength of his office. The Belarusian president appoints members of the government, although his nomination to the premiership requires the approval of the lower house (a 3 in terms of the Shugart–Carey scale), and he can dismiss individual ministers or the government as a whole without reference to parliament, which is a power as extensive as any that at present exists (a score of 4). Parliament can express its lack of confidence in the government, in which case the president must either accept its resignation or call new elections (in such cases a score of 2 is suggested). The president, finally, has the right to dissolve the legislature, but can do so only if parliament has twice refused to accept his nomination to the premiership or if the lower house approves a vote of no confidence in the government, and not during a state of emergency or martial law or in the course of impeachment proceedings (a score of 1). This places the Belarusian president well above, for instance, the Mexican or American president in terms of legislative powers, but below them both in terms of his extralegislative authority.

There has been some criticism of mechanical exercises of this kind: a president who looks powerful on paper may be "quite weak in reality (and vice versa)," and in any case the powers of the presidency are difficult to distinguish from the "exceptional personalities" that have held this office during the relatively short period of postcommunist rule.[12] The Shugart–Carey scale certainly misses some important variables. The Belarusian president, for instance, enjoys very far-reaching powers of appointment within the judiciary, including the constitutional court that is formally supposed to monitor his own actions (and which had caused Lukashenko considerable inconvenience before the adoption of the constitutional amendments of 1996). The Belarusian president also enjoys considerable powers in the formation of the upper house of parliament, which are difficult to reconcile with the principle of the separation of powers on which the Shugart–Carey scale is premised. On the other hand, the scale makes no direct reference to the possibility that the president himself may be forced out of office by a process of impeachment; the Belarusian constitution does provide for a procedure of this kind, even if it is extremely difficult to initiate and in present circumstances inconceivable that any serious attempt might be made to do so.

The outcome was a distinctive type of regime that was often described as "superpresidential,"[13] but which had many of the characteristics of a system of a personal authoritarianism. Under a regime of this kind, the rule of law largely ceased to operate, as the higher courts were staffed by presidential appointees who were in no position to resist the president's directives. Opposition parties continued to exist, but were not represented in the National Assembly, and their activities were restricted by a variety of means both within and outside the law, including the forcible disruption of public meetings. State television was subject to heavy government control, and independent newspapers operated under a series of handicaps: printing presses refused to produce them, advertisers were reluctant to use them in case they suffered consequences, and they could be suspended or closed down at any time for reasons that included real or imaginary attacks on the "honor and integrity" of members of the government. Opposition politicians, for their part, were forced into exile, or more alarmingly, they simply disappeared—among them the opposition leader Viktor Gonchar and the interior minister Yuri Zakharenko in 1999, and Dmitri Zavadsky, a Russian television cameraman, in July 2000. It was for reasons such as this that Freedom House classified Belarus as "unfree" at the start of the new century, with a score that placed it alongside Burundi, Haiti, Tajikistan, and Zimbabwe.[14]

The President and His Voters

The accumulation of authority in the hands of a single person is no more remarkable than the extent to which Lukashenko has enjoyed a high level of public support throughout the years of his presidency. His popularity has continued in spite of the growing political consciousness of the electorate,[15] rising prices, and the controversy that has surrounded the regime itself (including the enhanced authority of KGB, the "disappearances," and alleged state-sponsored "death squads"). The presidential election in September 2001 once again demonstrated the depth of public trust by returning the president with a 76 percent majority (see chapter 5). Even if this victory is considered in the context of alleged electoral violations attested to by the international community, the situation remains barely altered: Lukashenko is the only credible political player in present-day Belarus. To highlight this fact, in the following section we will focus on the profile of Lukashenko's supporters who are the foundation of his remarkable popularity.

According to the survey data, in October 1994 39 percent of the population believed that President Lukashenko was capable of leading the country out of its crisis, and 52 percent regarded him as a man of authority.[16] This was three months after his election to the presidency, when he was still relatively unknown to the majority of the population. This level of electoral confidence persisted remarkably over the years that followed. In 2000 39 percent again believed that Lukashenko was the only one who could resolve the country's problems, and 42 percent considered him a man of authority.[17] Similarly, there has always been a high proportion of electors—about one third of the electorate—who have said they are ready to vote for Lukashenko if an election were to take place "next Sunday" (figure 4.1).

According to figure 4.1, Lukashenko's rating—an unprompted response to the question "Whom would you vote for if an election were to take place next Sunday?"—has never been lower than 26 percent, which is still 20 percent higher than that of any other politician in the country, and is currently rising once again. His popularity enjoyed two distinct peaks, which coincided with his signing of several Union Acts with Russia in 1998 (see chapter 7) and his reelection campaign in 2001. The period after September 2001 witnessed a downturn in his popularity, reaching a nadir of 26 percent in April 2003. This was the lowest score Lukashenko had received in the course of his eight years of presidential rule. However, as the data further suggest, by September 2003 he seemed to have recovered his public standing, gaining 32 percent of the votes in a hypothetical election the following Sunday.[18]

How do these tendencies correspond to the voting behavior of Lukashenko's core supporters and opponents? If we look at table 4.1, a positive rise in Lukashenko's core supporters can be observed after 2002, which may have something to do with his insistence on the sovereignty of Belarus within the proposed

Figure 4.1. The Dynamics of Electoral Preference for President Lukashenko, 1997–2003

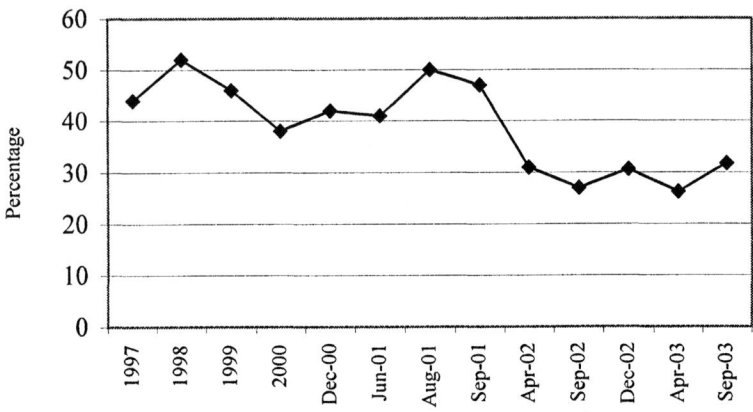

Source: Derived from Oleg Manaev, "Obval," in *Narodnaya gazeta*, 4 May 2002, based on a survey conducted by the Independent Institute of Socio-Economic and Political Research (NISEPI) in April 2002 (*n* = 1464); Manaev, personal communication, November 2002; and *Novosti NISEPI*, no. 3 (29), September 2003, 24. The graph indicates the percentage of those who chose Lukashenko in response to the question "Whom would you vote for if an election were to take place next Sunday?"

Table 4.1. The Dynamics of Lukashenko's Electoral Support, 1997–2003 (percentages)

Electoral groups	11/97	09/98	06/99	04/00	08/01	04/02	09/03
Core supporters	26	29.3	21.8	15.5	21.8	10.4	14.9
Undecided	53.2	53.3	52.1	54.2	46.1	42.7	42.4
Core opponents	20.8	17.4	26.1	30.3	32.1	46.9	47.8

Source: Adapted from *Novosti NISEPI*, no. 3 (29), September 2003, 3.

Russia–Belarus Union, a position that reflects the views of a majority of the Belarusian electorate. Relatively stable (on average 23 percent up to the end of 2001), his popularity among his core supporters seems to have suffered losses in 2000 and then again in 2002,[19] a year before and after his reelection. By contrast, the number of his core opponents has steadily grown, reaching nearly half of the electorate by September 2003. "Undecided" voters have meanwhile contributed recruits to both supporters and opponents of Lukashenko. From 2000, in one year, their numbers fell by 8 percent, providing an additional 6 percent growth among Lukashenko's core supporters and 2 percent amongst his opponents. The balance, however, swung in the opposite direction a year later, in changes in voting intentions that added an extra 14 percent to Lukashenko's opponents. This time the shift was based more upon defecting Lukashenko supporters (10 percent) than upon the "undecided" part of the electorate (4 percent). In 2003 seems to have been a slow recovery (up 5 percent) in the president's standing amid his core supporters, whereas the numbers of his opponents have barely altered (up just 0.9 percent).

The level of trust in institutions is another means of registering the changes that have been taking place in Belarusian political culture. Since 2001 the general level of trust in institutions has been slowly declining (see figure 4.2), with the most dramatic change in the level of trust in the president, which fell by 15 percent over the two following years. This may suggest that although popular allegiances are still strongly supportive of the president—who indeed, both politically and "institutionally," remains the only realistic alternative—the true picture of despondency and distrust is revealed by the continuously declining level of trust by voters in all aspects of the political system, and most of all in the president (down 15 percent), his government (down 12 percent), and parliament (down 12 percent).

Figure 4.2. Trust in Civic and Political Institutions, 1997–2003 (percentages)

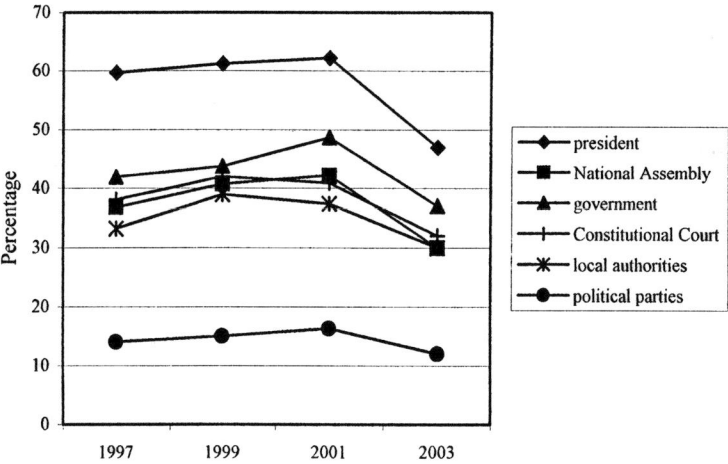

Source: Adapted from 1997–2003 surveys conducted by the Center for Social and Political Research under the guidance of David Rotman, based on a stratified nationwide sample of at least 1,000 members of the adult population.

Figure 4.3. The Lukashenko Electorate, 2003

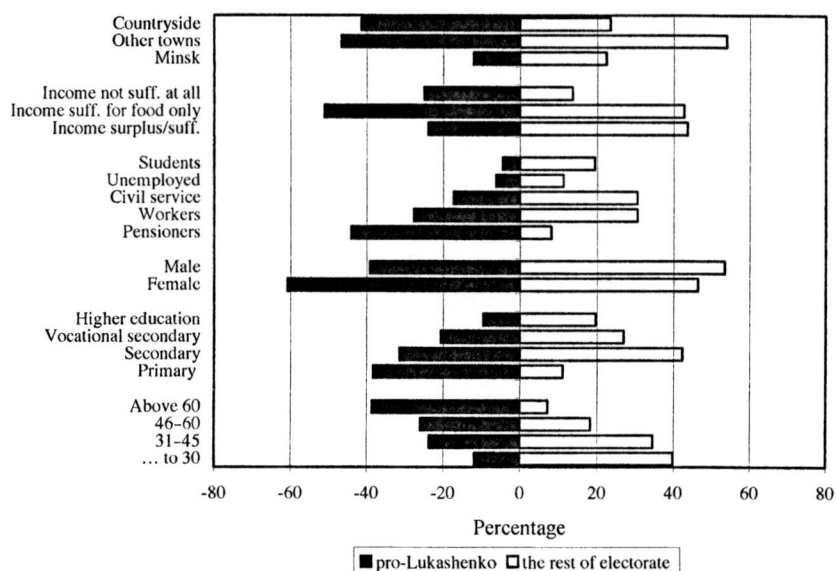

In order to obtain a better understanding of the still somewhat mysterious origins of Lukashenko's popularity, we shall now examine the characteristics of Lukashenko's supporters, from their socio-demographic profile to their hopes and beliefs. This may help us more easily to identify the nature of the linkage that binds the president and his voters and the patterns of opinion that sustain it (see figure 4.3).

Over time, the Lukashenko electorate has acquired a number of features that allow it to be distinguished from the electorate as a whole and from that of his opponents. Data collected in the course of our INTAS research project in December 2000[20] indicate that Lukashenko's voters were largely over 60 years of age, with lower levels of education than the average. They were more likely to be retired and to live in small towns and villages, and they were more likely to perceive their personal income as sufficient for food purchase only or not sufficient at all. By contrast, the rest of the electorate were dominated by younger voters with higher levels of education, working in the private sector or in full-time education, resident in a large city, whose income was sufficient or surplus.

The 2003 evidence suggests that Lukashenko's electorate has not much altered, with only a slight increase of supporters among state employees and those who believe their living standards have improved.[21] The gulf between his followers and opponents continues to widen, and real differences in the expectation of economic and political hardship can be observed in each case. The majority of Lukashenko supporters appear to feel safe and less concerned about such issues as delays in wage payments or the threat of unemployment. Only 18 percent of Lukashenko's supporters regard these as of great importance, against 74 percent of his opponents. Lukashenko's supporters also feel less concerned about the prospect of dictatorship, or a fall in living standards.

Lukashenko's supporters are less likely than the rest of the electorate to suggest any particular course of action when asked what they would do personally in a situation of hardship and economic decline. Furthermore, they tend to blame "politicians" and the "corrupt bureaucracy" for the country's various difficulties more than others. By contrast, other members of the electorate are ready to explore any opportunities or even work abroad; they also believe that private ownership is more effective, and blame Lukashenko and his government for the continuing national impoverishment.

When one compares the ideological orientations of Lukashenko's supporters with the electorate as a whole and with his opponents, a considerable gulf emerges between the first two and the latter. The Lukashenko electorate, as if mirroring the nation, disproportionately includes those who favor a state-controlled economy (82:61:22 percent respectively in the three groups), and a union with Russia (82:59:25 percent respectively). They also believe that Lukashenko's administration caters for human rights (58 percent), that his election in 2001 was not fraudulent but honest (94 percent), and that he will be able to deliver his pledges (64 percent), all of which forms the basis for their unconditional support of the president in the next election (88 percent).[22] Lukashenko supporters, in fact, entertain quite inconsistent views. A majority favor a closer relationship with both Russia and the West, and democratic as well as authoritarian forms of leadership.[23] They also strongly believe that a national leader should be given the power to act as he deems necessary, and that governance by decree is more effective than the politics of compromise. On our evidence, Lukashenko's core voters may best be characterized as the "socially vulnerable" —that is, those who believe they need the protection of the state and look to a politician like Lukashenko to be their guardian.

Lukashenko's Supporters: The Qualitative Evidence

In addition to the evidence of opinion surveys, semi-structured group interviews conducted under our auspices in December 2001 and April 2003 allowed Lukashenko supporters to express their feelings in their own words. Although there are obvious limits to the extent to which this evidence can be compared with the nationally representative findings that are made available by surveys, it none the less allows us to explore some parallels in public attitudes.[24] The findings of our focus groups confirm a tendency by which support for Lukashenko is emotionally "unqualified" and driven by hope, especially when uncontested. Some respondents noted that their attitudes to the president had become more positive over the years, but others mentioned that they had only recently returned to the president's support as they witnessed the effectiveness of his leadership and the incompetence of his opponents.

> I believe that our President is the most exceptional leader. I voted for him in the first election, and will vote again, if necessary. My sons, and my grandsons, are all in his favor. I have relatives in Siberia, who say that, if Alexander Grigor'evich were to run for election in Russia, they would support him with no doubts. He is an outstanding man. [Vasilii Ivanovich, 75 years, December 2001]

> You could see that this man was taking all the problems too close to his heart and wanting to help people. He was not speculating about immediate effects, but asking for our support, which could make his actions more effective. He managed to touch something deep inside me, some kind of sacred chord in my soul, which I could not resist. [Alla Ivanovna, 48 years, December 2001]

Some bore out the president's claim that he would facilitate "freedom and peace," so that (in his own words) "people can live safely and look into their future. Those who would like to live well; they can and will live well in Belarus."[25]

> Relatives from Ukraine say that we should worship our president, as we live in a free country, and have everything we need. . . . [Vasilii Ivanovich again]

> My aunt from Latvia phoned up being concerned about the situation in Belarus, as the media reported. They all say he is a dictator, and we are at the brink of starvation. I suggested her to come and visit us, and see for herself how these repulsive journalists can lie! . . . I met a man with a family from Chechnya who settled in Belarus. He says it is safe here and one can get a job everywhere, even in the Chernobyl zone. [Anna Vladimirovna, 56 years]

> On holiday in Crimea I noticed that 50 percent were Belarusians, which means they have the means to travel and enjoy life within limits. Can the Ukrainians afford this? No. [male, 44 years, higher education]

Often motivations to vote for Lukashenko echoed the president's election manifesto and the promises he had made when he was conducting his campaign for reelection in September 2001, even though our focus groups were conducted some months before the election campaign had formally begun. There was support for the president in person, and for the policies with which he was associated:

> I remember Lukashenko since he made his famous report on corruption. . . . [female, over 60 years, incomplete secondary education]

> I would vote for him because he is for the union with Russia. . . . He also promised to raise pensions, and what is more important, to keep higher education free. . . . [Svetlana, 34 years]

> Lukashenko made our normal life possible; he reduced crime and gave us the opportunity to work. . . . [Dima, 25 years, student]

> Just look how multinational our country is. And we all live in peace and there are no humiliations. [Polina Mikhailovna, 70 years]

> He was the only one to stand up against the dissolution of the USSR. They threatened him, but he fears no one! [Alla Ivanovna, 48 years]

> I grew up on ballet and opera, and free access to culture. I want my children have this too. . . . [Anna Vladimirovna, 56 years]

> I am for the implementation of death sentences, and for the noninterference of all these OSCE, UN, and America into the life of our nation! [Dima, 25 years]

Together with these statements of general support, there were obvious discrepancies in people's attitudes toward their "chosen one." On the one hand interviewees revealed a high degree of emotional attachment to their leader, almost reaching adulation. On the other hand, the interviewees tended to justify and give their own explanations for Lukashenko's failures to deliver his pledges. Most often they mentioned unfavorable economic and political circumstances, plus the lack of a reliable team and a number of unfortunate appointments:

> He is in a difficult situation. Without absolute support one can do little, especially when some are too eager to discredit his achievements. . . . [female, over 60 years, incomplete secondary education]

> He is a real hero, trying to bring the two epochs together! In addition, he is left with a multiparty system, not something to envy. . . . [Anna Vladimirovna, 56 years]

> In 1994 he received a ruined economy, which he, bit by bit, managed to put together and make it work for his people! [Svetlana, 34 years]

> The state is like one big family. Until we all have different opinions, our president won't be able to help us. . . . [Alla Ivanovna, 48 years]

An obvious tension can be observed in respondents' description of their image of an ideal leader, and that of an "actually existing" Lukashenko. In their understanding the ideal leader must possess outstanding managerial skills (the ability to organize and lead people, and to explain ideas and deliver promises); he must also have competence and experience, and he should have shaped his own career. The ideal leader need not be from any particular social group, but must be broadly educated and multilingual. He (or she) must be honest, determined, and a patriot; he or she must never lie, must be consistent, should avoid populism, and should be tactful, sociable, and (if possible) charismatic. An ideal leader also "must not paint their opponents black on the eve of an election. He would not be then an amicable and constructive leader." The leaders that were most often cited as representing these attributes were Joseph Stalin, Fidel Castro, and the still revered Brezhnev-era Belarusian party leader Petr Masherov.

These expectations, paradoxically, do not correspond with what the president has actually provided, and the same images often appear contradictory, even in voters' own words. Lukashenko, it is acknowledged, lacks a broad education and wide experience, and he is neither multilingual, reticent, nor diplomatic—quite unlike the ideal leader. He is often referred to as overly emotional and domineering, or as one of our interviewees described him:

> He emitted so much energy that I felt suppressed. Each time when I watched him on TV, I had an impression that he was trying to crush me directly out of the screen (leaning forward, and ominously gesticulating). [male, 40 years, higher education]

Lukashenko's credentials were seriously weakened during the 2001 election campaign by the allegations of "disappearances" and state-sponsored "death squads," which entered the public domain and stimulated an international discussion. Nevertheless, neither these nor any other negative references dramatically reduced the popular trust he enjoyed—they may even have increased his chances of reelection. Many respondents, certainly, remarked that aggressive and unsubstantiated attacks upon the president by the opposition had quite the opposite effect to what was intended. People particularly noted Lukashenko's qualities as a fighter "who [did] not fear anyone, and who [would] always fight for truth, freedom, equality, and us, the common people" [female, 70 years]. One respondent insisted that "if Lukashenko were less forceful or authoritarian he would have been buried and fed to the opposition a long time ago" [male, 40 years]. Lukashenko was even compared with Don Quixote and Joan of Arc.

Among the president's most serious shortcomings, in the view of our participants, was the lack of a supportive group of colleagues, and a surplus of emotions:

> I believe that in many cases he is simply misinformed. He cannot control everything himself. And his entourage always plays dirty tricks on him. . . . [female, over 60]

> It is a pity that he cannot choose his own team . . . which he can absolutely trust. [female, 70 years]

These sentiments return us to the traditional belief in a "benevolent Tsar, who is surrounded by a court of fools and schemers," or what the social scientist might define as charisma,[26] and were reinforced by the lack of any serious criticism of the leader or even of the belief that comment from ordinary citizens might be appropriate. When asked what kind of advice one could give to the president, the majority of the respondents merely stated:

> You know it is inappropriate for us to advise him. What we can see here below is different from his broad vision. He can see everything from top to bottom, and make the right decisions himself. We only wish him strength and good health, to continue what he has begun. . . . [female, 69 years]

It is clear from both opinion poll and focus group interviews that Lukashenko continues to maintain the image of a popular leader, for whom the *emotional* support of the voters has never been challenged—after eight years of presidential rule, and without necessarily living up to his promises.[27] He enjoys public loyalty through his personal presence and through the lack of an alternative, which in turn is reinforced by a stable but unreformed economic system, supportive institutions, and stereotypes of a tsar–people relationship. Our study reveals that voters' support for Lukashenko is an emotional and undifferentiated one, which is buttressed by rational considerations in a situation of a limited choice. In the course of a postcommunist transition, in which public identities are changing and economic uncertainties alarming, there is a clear propensity to support a strong and forceful leader who can offer stability and speak to ordinary voters in terms they understand.

Cultural traditions of this kind have long been prevalent in the Slavic world; they have been sustained in the postcommunist period by a favorable institutional environment, including a weak party politics.[28] Lukashenko's supporters are clearly in favor of a strong leadership, to whom the full range of powers and responsibility for national destiny may be unquestioningly delegated. In fact, and in the words of one of our interviewees, this transfer of trust has already taken place in the form of "democratic authoritarianism," when an authoritarian leader follows a majority's opinion, a development that is seen by many of our interviewees as a very welcome one. Additional evidence of the public longing for a strong leader and a more general stability is reflected in the desire to have a successor to Lukashenko's presidency, which is reflected in statements such as the following:

> If Lukashenko were to advise us of his successor, we all would support him at once. He is a trustworthy man . . . different from Yeltsin and Putin [male, 75 years]

The findings of focus groups in 2003 revealed little change in popular attitudes to the president, except for a modest shift toward a more critical evaluation of his policies, which associates somewhat with his "critical acclamation" than real criticism:

> I understand it is difficult. . . . But he did not fulfill what he pledged, we now can see more bureaucracy around, the militia grew by three times, and the cost of housing doubled. I understand he needs a good team, but no one forced him to choose a bad one. . . . [male, 65 years, April 2003]

> I still believe in him, and his promises and statements. However, I do not hope for anything better. It's just the hope that is left . . . and yourself [female, 48 years, April 2003].

In summary, President Lukashenko remains the only realistic alternative for a considerable part of the Belarusian electorate, which in a situation of weak parties and institutionally limited pluralism makes any form of liberal democracy difficult to realize. There are, of course, many other forms of government that are at present being tested by transitional states, including a delegative leadership, but none of them seems yet to have achieved a sustainable balance between *demos* and *kratos*, or between mass electorate and political regime. What has become evident is that under ostensibly free and regular elections, liberties that are guaranteed on paper, and the nominal presence of a rule of law, the Belarusian president has successfully managed to engineer a system of personal rule that takes particular strength from his personal commitment to its maintenance and that enjoys continuing public support.

Notes

1. According to the preliminary results, Lukashenko won 45.1 percent of the vote in the first round, ahead of Kebich with 17.4 percent; Zenon Poznyak of the Belarusian Popular Front won 12.9 percent, former parliamentary chairman Stanislav Shushkevich took 9.9 percent, Alexander Dubko of the Peasants' Party won 6.0 percent, and Vasil Novikov of the Communist Party of Belarus took 4.6 percent (spoiled ballots accounted for a further 3.6 percent; *Sovetskaya Belorussiya*, 25 June 1994, 1). In the second round Lukashenko won more than 4.2 million votes or "just over 80 percent," leaving Kebich with an ignominious 14.2 percent (*Sovetskaya Belorussiya.*, 12 July 1994, 1).

2. See John Anderson, "Authoritarian Political Development in Central Asia: The Case of Turkmenistan," *Central Asian Survey* 14, no. 4 (December 1995): 509–27; rulers of this kind were described as "emirs" in other writings: L. A. Okun'kov, *Prezident Rossiiskoi Federatsii. Konstitutsiya i politicheskaya praktika* (Moscow: Infra.M-Norma, 1996), 27. For a more general study, see *Postcommunist Presidents*, ed. Ray Taras (Cambridge: Cambridge University Press, 1997).

3. See for instance Alfred Stepan and Cindy Skach, "Constitutional Frameworks and Democratic Consolidation: Parliamentarianism versus Presidentialism," *World Politics* 46, no. 1 (October 1996): 1–22; and *The Failure of Presidential Democracy: Com-*

parative Perspectives, ed. Juan J. Linz and Arturo Valenzuela (Baltimore, Md.: Johns Hopkins University Press, 1994). Easter broadly concurs with Linz, but for different reasons, seeing presidentialism as the "preferred strategy of those actors who calculate that they have the most to gain by limiting the access of others to the state's power resources": Gerald M. Easter, "Preference for Presidentialism: Postcommunist Regime Change in Russia and the NIS," *World Politics* 49, no. 2 (January 1997): 184–211 (211). This proposition has not been uncontested; see for instance John T. Ishiyama and Matthew Velten, "Presidential Power and Democratic Development in Post-communist Politics," *Communist and Post-Communist Studies* 31, no. 3 (September 1998): 217–33, which argues that the electoral system has a more substantial impact on democratic consolidation than socioeconomic or institutional factors; and John T. Ishiyama and Ryan Kennedy, "Superpresidentialism and Political Party Development in Russia, Ukraine, Armenia and Kyrgyzstan," *Europe–Asia Studies* 53, no. 8 (December 2001): 1177–91, which finds that presidentialism does not necessarily inhibit party development.

4. *Vmeste za sil'nuyu i protsvetayushchuyu Belarus'. Predvybornaya programma Prezidenta Respubliki Belarus'* (Minsk, 2001), 2.

5. See *Kto est' kto v republike Belarus'* (Minsk: Zivigar, 1999), 170–71; and for the official biography www.president.gov.by/rus/president/profile.shtml. Lukashenko's rise to power is examined in Valerii Karbalevich, "Put'Lukashenko k vlasti," in *Belorussiya i Rossiya: obshchestva i gosudarstva*, ed. D. E. Furman (Moscow: Prava cheloveka, 1998), 226–58.

6. The results of the vote were reported in *Sovetskaya Belorussiya*, 16 May 1995, 1; all the propositions were approved by more than 75 percent of those who voted. The background to this period is considered in Margery McMahon, "Aleksandr Lukashenka, President, Republic of Belarus," *Journal of Communist Studies and Transition Politics* 13, no. 4 (December 1997): 129–37; and in David Marples, *Belarus: A Denationalized Nation* (Amsterdam: Harwood, 1999), chapter 4.

7. *Sovetskaya Belorussiya*, 27 November 1996, 1. The proposal to move Belarusian independence day to July 3—the end of the Nazi occupation of Minsk—was overwhelmingly approved, but there was little support for the buying and selling of land, or for the abolition of the death penalty.

8. The entire text of the constitution in its revised form appeared in *Sovetskaya Belorussiya*, 27 November 1996, 3–4; it was published as *Kanstytutsyya Respubliki Belarus' 1994 hoda (sa zmyanennyami i dapaunennyami). Prynyata na respublikanskim referendume 24 listapada 1996 hoda* (Minsk: Belarus', 2000). The references here are to articles 79, 84, 85, 88, and 129.

9. The entire texts of the 1994 constitution and of its amended 1996 version are conveniently reproduced in *Transition to Democracy. Constitutions of the New Independent States and Mongolia* (Strasbourg: Council of Europe Publishing, 1997).

10. See particularly Matthew Shugart and John M. Carey, *Presidents and Assemblies: Constitutional Design and Electoral Dynamics* (Cambridge: Cambridge University Press, 1992), chapter 8. Another attempt to construct a "constitutional power score" is presented in James McGregor, "The Presidency in East Central Europe," *RFE/RL Research Report*, 3, no. 2 (14 January 1994): 23–31. Frye bases his scale on a list of twenty-seven presidential powers, but it is very highly correlated (more than 0.8) with the Shugart–Carey index (Timothy Frye, "A Politics of Institutional Choice: Post-communist Presidencies," *Comparative Political Studies* 30, no. 5 (October 1997): 523–52 (547–48).

A recent survey, which does not directly cover Belarus, is available in "Post-communist Leadership: Individuals or Institutions?," a special issue of *Problems of Post-Communism* 50, no. 5 (September–October 2003).

11. At least 450,000 electors are required to call a referendum, at least 30,000 from each of the regions and the city of Minsk; detailed regulations are included in chapter 7 of the electoral code (*Izbiratel'nyi kodeks Respubliki Belarus'*, 2nd edn. (Minsk: National'nyi tsentr pravovoi informatsii, 2001).

12. See John Elster, "Afterword," in Taras, ed., *Postcommunist Presidents*, 226. The same point is made in Lee Kendall Metcalf, "Measuring Presidential Power," *Comparative Political Studies* 33, no. 5 (June 2000): 660–85 (683).

13. *East European Constitutional Review* 7, no. 3 (Summer 1998): front cover.

14. Adrian Karatnycky, "The 2001 Freedom House Survey," *Journal of Democracy* 13, no. 1 (January 2002): 99–112 (108–9).

15. See Christian Haerpfer, "Electoral Politics of Belarus Compared," in *Contemporary Belarus: Between Democracy and Dictatorship*, ed. Elena Korosteleva, Rosalind Marsh, and Colin Lawson (London: RoutledgeCurzon, 2003), 85–99.

16. David Rotman et al., *Kakoi my vidim nashu Belarus': dannye sotsiologicheskikh oprosov 1994–1995 gg*. (Minsk: BSU, 1996).

17. We draw here on data collected for the INTAS Project "Charismatic political leadership in Russia, Belarus and Ukraine," commissioned by the University of Bath in collaboration with Sciences-Po (Paris), Moscow State University, the Belarusian State University (BSU), and Gallup-Socis of Kyiv (see www.intas.be).

18. *Novosti NISEPI*, September 2003, no. 3(29): 3–4.

19. Here could be mentioned an alternative presidential election organized by the opposition to denounce Lukashenko's presidency as illegitimate (May 1999), the boycott of the parliamentary elections in 2000 to demonstrate their fraudulent nature, the campaign begun by the opposition in 2001 to draw greater attention to the disappearances and "death squads," and finally, his seeming inability to deliver campaign pledges in the aftermath of the 2001 election.

20. National survey in Belarus was part of the INTAS project (99-245), carried out by the Centre for Social and Political Research of the BSU under the direction of David Rotman in December 2000. The survey was nationwide and included 1,000 people aged 18 and over, representing the principal socio-demographic groups of the population. The survey resulted in a 99.47 percent coefficient of probability.

21. Oleg Manaev, "Presidentskie vybory: chto bylo na samom dele," *Analiticheskii byulleten'*, 2002, no. 1(15): 5–14, and Elena Korosteleva's own research in Belarus (SG-13350, British Academy), March–April 2003.

22. Manaev, "Prezidentskie vybory": 11–13.

23. Pro-presidential respondents had equally positive answers to such questions as "would you support a candidate for the president who . . . believes that governance by decree can be more effective than the politics of compromise, and . . . who believes in dictatorship of law; who favors fixed prices and small but regularly paid wages, as well as . . . [one who] thinks that liberalization and marketization are necessary steps to the welfare future," etc.

24. The focus groups were part of the INTAS project, conducted in December 2001. The focus groups were designed to examine the attitudes of the supporters of the three leading politicians in Belarus—Alexander Lukashenko, Vladimir Goncharik, and

Zenon Poznyak. Two groups of supporters were interviewed for each chosen leader, and the sample of respondents reflected the general socio-demographic profiles of leaders' followers as evidenced by opinion polls. Each focus group included 7–9 people, who were selected on the basis of positive answers to the following questions: (1) do you support this leader, and (2) did you vote for this leader in the recent election? Interviews were conducted in Minsk, and participants were selected by a snowball method.

25. Quote from Alexander Lukashenko's speech at a press conference in Minsk on 17 September 2002, available at http://www.president.gov.by (retrieved October 2003).

26. R. Itvel [Roger Eatwell], "Vozrozhdenie kharizmy? Teoriya i problemy operatsionalizatsii ponyatii," *Sotsiologicheskie issledovaniya*, no. 3 (2003): 9–19. Rotman and his colleagues, on the basis of a December 2001 survey, found Lukashenko eight times more charismatic than the next-placed Belarusian leader and more charismatic than he had been in 1994 (D. G. Rotman et al., "Belorusskii variant kharizmy," *Sotsiologicheskie issledovaniya*, no. 3 (2003): 29–38 (35–36).

27. See a critical review of his activities over the years of his presidency in *Belorusskaya gazeta*, 9 September 2002, 2.

28. For a full discussion of structural and institutional constraints see Elena Korosteleva, "Party System Development in Post-communist Belarus," in Korosteleva et al., eds., *Contemporary Belarus*, 68–84; and Korosteleva, *Explaining Party System Development in Post-Communist Belarus* (Ph.D. thesis, University of Bath, 2001).

5 The Dynamics of the 2001 Presidential Election

Uladzimir Padhol and David R. Marples

Many observers perceived the September 2001 presidential elections as a pivotal event in Belarusian politics. It was only the second presidential election in the life of the independent state.[1] That it was delayed until 2001 was a result of amendments made to the Belarusian constitution by Alexander Lukashenko following the referendum of November 1996, which considerably enhanced the powers of the president *vis-à-vis* the parliament and the Constitutional Court. For the opposition, which has abided by the original 1994 constitution and recognized until recently the authority of the dissolved Supreme Soviet of the thirteenth convocation, Lukashenko ceased to be a legal president when his mandate expired on July 20, 1999. In the late summer of 2000, as we saw in chapter 3, new parliamentary elections were held under highly restricted conditions; more than a hundred candidates were removed from electoral lists for alleged misstatements about their financial situation, and access to the media was also limited. The result was a compliant legislature with only a few individual deputies elected on an independent ticket. Thus neither the president nor the parliament possessed international recognition at the time of the election.

Lukashenko, though firmly in power, had come under some pressure by this time. Over the previous seven years, Belarus had evolved into a dictatorial regime in which individual freedoms had been curtailed, the media had been subordinated to the interests of the government, and opposition leaders had frequently been harassed and in some cases had disappeared in suspicious circumstances. Belarus paid lip service to the demands of the OSCE, including its Advisory and Monitoring Group in Minsk, to enter a dialogue with the opposition, to provide equal access to television and other media, and to cease the infringements of human rights and the arrests and beatings of demonstrators. The

United States had emerged as a forthright critic of Belarusian internal policy. Conversely, Russia remained a supporter of Belarus through the Russia–Belarus Union, but President Putin appeared unwilling to support the Lukashenko regime openly. Indeed, the Belarusian president had expressed his dissatisfaction at the sluggishness of the Russian side in bringing about the integration of the two states.[2]

Lukashenko had certainly faced some significant international criticism. The then–US ambassador to Belarus, Michael Kozak, had described the country publicly as the "Cuba of Europe."[3] Lukashenko had himself supported the regime of Slobodan Milošević of Yugoslavia when the Yugoslav leader had become isolated internationally, and had even offered Milošević asylum in Belarus should that become necessary.[4] The Belarusian president has often expressed his fears that Belarus will be the next target of the United States, and has raised the prospect of NATO intervention in order to remove him from office.[5] The image is used for convenience, to bolster the projection of the president as a man who can stand up to the West. Often, for Lukashenko, rhetoric is not matched by deeds. In theory, he has created a Soviet-style state in central Europe, and his speeches often refer wistfully to the former Soviet Union. That he held ambitions broader than the confines of his own small country seems plain. At one time the Russia–Belarus Union appeared a means to his entering the stage of Russian politics. However, not all political circles in Russia took his candidacy seriously and, with the advent of Putin, Lukashenko's prospects of a future in Russian politics disappeared. The presidential election offered him a chance to regain international credibility, but it appears to have been more about the consolidation of power, and less about the restoration of a "Soviet utopia."

Nominating the Candidates

Elections in Belarus are governed by the 1994 constitution, as modified in 1996, and by an electoral code that was adopted in February 2000.[6] Any citizen who is more than thirty-five years old, who enjoys electoral rights and has been resident in the republic for at least ten years may seek nomination as a presidential candidate. The president is directly elected for a five-year term, and may not serve more than two terms in total. Candidates must obtain the signatures of at least 100,000 electors in order to register their nomination, and are elected if they secure the support of more than half of those who take part in the ballot provided at least half of the electorate has voted. If no candidate has an overall majority, a second round is held within two weeks between the two candidates with the largest numbers of votes. The candidate who secures more than half the vote in this second round becomes the new president, and is inaugurated after swearing the presidential oath "faithfully to serve the people of the Republic of Belarus, to respect and safeguard the rights and liberties of man and citizen, to abide by and protect the Constitution of the Republic of Belarus, and to discharge strictly and conscientiously the lofty duties" of that office.

Under the Belarusian constitution presidential elections are called by the lower house of parliament, the Chamber of Representatives, not less than five months before the date of expiry of the serving president's term of office, and must take place not less than two months before that date. The Council voted accordingly on June 7, 2001, and set the election date for the following September 9. Prospective candidates had eight days to declare their intentions, and then a further five days to register "initiative groups" of not fewer than a hundred supporters, which had until July 20 to collect the signatures that were needed. The final registration of candidates was to be completed by August 9, a month before polling day, and after that campaigning proper could begin. By June 15, when registrations ended, there had been twenty-five applications to register an initiative group; on June 19 it was announced that twenty-two of these initiative groups had been registered, and on June 21 they began to collect signatures in support of their various candidates.

In order to concentrate their otherwise disparate forces, opposition parties had agreed to choose a candidate that would be acceptable to most of them and to other groups, such as the trade unions. Eventually, two separate groups emerged. The first was the Coordinating Council of Democratic Forces, which combined the BNF of Vintsuk Vecherka, the United Civic Party under Anatolii Lebed'ko, and a separate group that supported the candidacy of Semion Domash, the former governor of Grodno. The second group, the Federation of Trade Unions led by Vladimir Goncharik, combined the Communists and a portion of the Social Democratic Party led by Nikolai Statkevich. The first group attracted a broadly pro-Western coalition of supporters, while the second was more Moscow-oriented. By the end of 2000 a further coalition came into existence, consisting of Domash, Goncharik, and former prime minister Mikhail Chigir; two names were later added: those of former defense minister Pavel Kozlovsky and Communist leader Sergei Kalyakin.[7] However, the coalitions existed more on paper than in reality, as each leader created his own headquarters and began to organize a separate election campaign; both groups, moreover, took pains to emphasize that the leadership of the Russian Federation would support their own campaign rather than that of the Belarusian president. As the deadline for registration for the election campaign approached it was still unclear whether the opposition would be able to agree a single choice.

In the event, the five leaders met again on the evening before the deadline[8] and agreed to nominate Goncharik as a "unified candidate" on behalf of the entire opposition. Domash, in fact, did not withdraw immediately; sufficient signatures had been collected on his behalf and he was duly registered as a candidate, appearing on television on August 21 with a prerecorded appeal for a change of regime as a "national salvation task" (he formally withdrew the following day, apparently under pressure from the American ambassador, on the understanding that he would be Goncharik's prime minister).[9] Western governments had certainly encouraged the attempt to find a single opposition candidate, and they reportedly made $50 million available to assist his election campaign.[10] Goncharik, in a press statement, promised to restore democracy in Belarus, to pursue market reforms, and to organize new parliamentary elections in the event of his victory. "Today we made one step . . . towards building a new, democratic Belarus," Goncharik commented after the signature of the agreement. "At last a choice has appeared for the Belarusian people."[11]

Several other candidates featured in the preliminary campaign. They included several that were broadly pro-Moscow: Chigir; General Kozlovsky; businessman Yuri Dan'kov; the head of the agricultural workers' union, Alexander Yaroshuk; Leonid Sinitsyn, a former close aide to Lukashenko and a member of the Supreme Soviet of the twelfth convocation; Viktor Tereshchenko, a former member of the Lukashenko administration now operating a private management institute; Mikhail Marinich, a former economics minister in the government and more recently Belarusian ambassador to Latvia; and Natal'ya Masherova, the daughter of the popular communist leader who had ruled for fifteen years during the Brezhnev period. On the right of the political spectrum were Zenon Poznyak, who adopted a strongly nationalist platform, and Sergei Anton'chik, the leader of an unregistered movement called "Workers' Self-Reliance."[12] The government focused its attention on Masherova, as the candidate most likely to draw votes from Lukashenko. Masherova herself focused on the leadership of her father, comparing him to the Belarusian president, and describing her own role as that of heir to the country's two great leaders; she insisted several times that the car crash that had killed her father in 1980 had been a political murder rather than an accident.[13] The presidential administration clearly exercised its powers of persuasion, as Masherova suddenly withdrew her candidacy during the period of signature collection.

On August 14 the chairman of the Central Election Commission, Lidiya Ermoshina, announced that four initiative groups had in the end gathered sufficient signatures: those of Lukashenko (395,821), Domash (160,077), the Liberal Democratic chairman Sergei Gaidukevich (133,066), and Goncharik (121,041).[14] The others had all reportedly fallen short, generally because a number of their supporting signatures had been declared invalid, including the groups that had sought to further the candidacies of Kalyakin, Marinich, Sinitsyn, Chigir, and Poznyak. Sinitsyn claimed a week later that tens of thousands of his signatures had mysteriously been "lost" in the regions of Mogilev and Brest. Dan'kov also claimed to have gathered 130,000 signatures, but rival groups had pressured his supporters into leaving these names off their list.[15] Gaidukevich, whose Liberal Democratic Party was only loosely associated with its Russian namesake, remained in the contest as a fringe candidate. So far as the antigovernment lobby was concerned, the goal was to support Goncharik and help him to overcome the formidable apparatus of President Lukashenko.

The Election Campaign

Lukashenko's program drew attention to what had been achieved during his first term, and set out the tasks that would form his main priorities if reelected. Belarus, Lukashenko claimed, had recovered from the economic collapse that was taking place at the time of his original election, and it had avoided the national and political divisions that had undermined so many of its postcommunist counterparts. Like other candidates, Lukashenko's aims for the future centered on a "sharp improvement" in living standards, but he placed particular emphasis upon the need to use evolutionary rather than more radical methods, and to maintain the country's social and political stability. Exports, housing, the food supply, science, and public health were all identified as priorities; salaries, he promised, would increase over the coming five years to an average of $250 a month, and pensions would double. At the same time there would be fewer restrictions on business, and more encouragement would be given to small and medium enterprises. Internationally, the union with Russia would continue to be the country's "main priority," but the program also called for the broadest possible cooperation with other countries on the basis of equality and mutual respect.[16]

Lukashenko's main challenger was the opposition's "unified candidate," Vladimir Goncharik. Goncharik, at sixty-one, was substantially older than both the other candidates and had served in various Young Communist League and Communist Party positions up to his appointment, in 1986, as head of the republic's trade unions. All of this allowed opponents to represent him as a Soviet-period holdover. Goncharik's own publicity took a rather different view, identifying him as a candidate of experience and proven competence, whose age had allowed him to share the formative experiences of modern Belarus including the war and the difficult years of reconstruction. Goncharik, in the words of his campaign flyer, was the candidate who could most reasonably be seen as "one of us." His family was "large, simple, and kind," made up of people "who love the land and know how to work." His father, a country schoolmaster, had fought in the Second World War; his mother was a collective farmer; and of the four children, one had become a bookkeeper and the other two were ordinary workers. An economics graduate who had been a deputy in both the Soviet and the Belarusian parliaments, Goncharik was presented by his campaign literature as a candidate who was "able to define exactly the main directions of the [country's] economic and cultural development."[17]

Goncharik's official program consisted of seven points, none of which was particularly novel—a reflection, among other things, of his wish to compete for Lukashenko's traditional electorate. First of all, there must be a "strong state and prosperous citizens," with guaranteed employment, decent pay, and stable pensions. Only professional economists and managers—like Goncharik himself—should be allowed to take part in the work of government. There must be a greater effort to support domestic producers, and to encourage an inflow of foreign investment and the revival of agriculture. Education, housing, and medicine must be accessible to all citizens, and benefits for veterans and the handicapped must be restored. All would be equal before the law, within courts that would be independent. Meanwhile, parliament, the central government, and local councils would all be given greater powers, at the expense of the presidency. And in foreign policy there would be a search for "friends throughout the world," including an end to the country's "international isolation" and "the entry of Belarus into common European structures"—in other words, eventual EU membership.[18]

The third candidate, Sergei Gaidukevich, was a successful businessman who had served in the armed forces, and then headed a department of the newly independent republic's Council of Ministers. In 1992 he had been influential in the formation of the Liberal Democratic Party out of a couple of dozen smaller parties and movements, and was elected president of the party in 1995. The Liberal Democrats saw themselves, in the words of their statute, as a "centrist democratic party" that sought to advance the rights and security of all citizens, and the "only party that [was] against the abstract 'market' or communist ideals." Gaidukevich, however, made little headway during the campaign; Goncharik supporters claimed that his nomination had actually been inspired by Lukashenko, who was anxious to make sure there was at least one opposition candidate he could easily defeat.[19]

The campaign itself was relatively low-key, with relatively few meetings and public advertising. It was dominated by the incumbent, even though Lukashenko (like Putin in the Russian presidential contest a year earlier) refused to campaign directly and relied instead upon the overwhelming advantages enjoyed by the possessor of that office in a strongly presidential system. Each candidate was entitled to the equivalent of approximately $12,500 in funds provided by the state. In addition, citizens could contribute to a common election fund that was then distributed equally among the candidates—which was hardly an encouragement. In practice, Lukashenko could also draw upon the resources of the state machine, and upon the prominence he was able to enjoy as he continued to perform the official duties of his office. Lukashenko enjoyed a further advantage in the disproportionate attention he received on Belarusian television, with 58 percent of the coverage devoted to all candidates and 84 percent of the time devoted to all candidates on news programs. Lukashenko's advantage on Russian television channels, which attract a majority of prime-time viewers, was even more pronounced.[20]

In theory, the Goncharik campaign also had access to a wide variety of media resources, including Belarusian state television. However, the candidates were not permitted live interviews: there was no unedited public debate, for example, between Lukashenko and his various challengers. At the same time, virtually each day of the campaign Belarusian television depicted the president carrying out his presidential responsibilities—opening a new bridge or apartment building, inaugurating a new underground station in the capital, meeting foreign statesmen, checking the reserves of the state bank, or conversing with expectant mothers. State-sponsored newspapers reflected the same emphases.[21] Curiously, the incumbent president elected not to use the airtime allocated to him during the election campaign. The impression given was that the president had no need to defend his record or to persuade the public to vote for him. Nonetheless, television viewers were still subjected to a daily round of Lukashenko's activities in various capacities. It was a subtle approach befitting an astute politician. By contrast, Gaidukevich in particular proved a poor performer in front of a television camera.

The Goncharik campaign did have some potential weapons at its disposal. Three in particular stood out: first, an economic situation that (in their view) had deteriorated markedly during the seven years of the Lukashenko presidency; secondly, the disappearance and alleged execution by death squads of prominent Lukashenko adversaries, notably the former minister of internal affairs, Yuri Zakharenko, and the former chairman of the Central Election Commission and deputy chairman of the Supreme Soviet of the thirteenth convocation, Viktor Gonchar.[22] This was related to the third issue, namely the attitude of Russia, and particularly of President Vladimir Putin, toward the Belarusian presidential race. Initially, Putin appeared uncommitted and unwilling to endorse any of the candidates. In itself, that position seemed to work in favor of the opposition candidates. Lastly, there was the isolated position of Belarus in international affairs, and the complete failure of the nation to move closer to Europe or to integrate itself within European structures.

The president was able to deflect the first question quite easily because it was far from evident that his opponents possessed a credible economic reform program. Both his rivals promised a large rise in minimum wages and average salaries. Lukashenko, however, managed to raise the average salary to US$100 by the time of the election, thereby undermining the financial incentives offered by his opponents and one of the campaign slogans of Chigir in the earlier stages of the election. Goncharik, by contrast, headed an organization that reputedly had frittered away the automatic deductions taken from the salaries of workers. Though the quality of life in Belarus was decidedly low, the Belarusian economy had not collapsed. Lukashenko's argument was that it reflected a specifically Belarusian way of dealing with problems. He had avoided the Western model of shock treatment that had brought impoverishment to so many residents of Russia and Ukraine. He had paid pensions on time, and a system of state intervention could be perceived as more humane and closer to the model of the Soviet period.

The matter of kidnapping and executing opponents was less easy to dismiss. Rather like the Gongadze case in Ukraine,[23] the exposure of the shooting of opponents threatened to unhinge the presidency. Goncharik played a pivotal role, releasing to the news media an interview with the head of the prison in which Gonchar and Zakharenko had been held, and sending relevant documents directly to the president.[24] The prison chief maintained that his "execution pistol" had been taken from him and used on the day that the two men disappeared. Two KGB officers also revealed the alleged burial ground of the executed oppositionists. Goncharik demanded that the president conduct an independent investigation into the deaths. It was noteworthy that the "whistle-blowers" in the cases of Gonchar and Zakharenko had made their way to Moscow immediately afterward. The likelihood is that the Russian FSB had become involved, on the instructions of President Putin. If this was the case—and it is supported implicitly by the long period of silence of the Russian president concerning the Belarusian elections—then Putin at some point changed his mind. The evidence concerning these deaths was far less clear-cut than in the Ukrainian case, in which a headless corpse had actually been discovered. Moreover, and perhaps critically, Putin evidently had little faith in Goncharik as a possible alternative to Lukashenko. Belatedly, the Russian regime began to laud Lukashenko for his contributions to the Russia–Belarus Union.[25] Later in the campaign Aleksii II, head of the Russian Orthodox Church, visited Belarus and together with the Belarusian church leader Filaret demonstrated the support of the ecclesiastical hierarchy for the incumbent president.[26]

A subsidiary issue to the question of internal politics was the alleged disaffection of several members of the Lukashenko team from the president. The president regularly changed the ruling bureaucracy, and appeared to favor certain organizations, such as the KGB, over others when making appointments. The Goncharik team used intermediaries to approach the prominent state official, chairman of the presidential administration (and later head of the Belarusian Academy of Sciences), Mikhail Myasnikovich. The attempt also resulted in failure. Lukashenko soon discovered the approach but expressed his faith in Myasnikovich in a public meeting with officials on July 31, 2001.[27] The member of the president's own staff could hardly ignore such a veiled warning, and soon afterward he ended his contacts with opposition leaders. The significance of this approach is that it represented an authentic attempt to unseat the president from within the administration. The outcome indicated either that the extent of the dissatisfaction with the president was less than expected, or that government bureaucrats were too timid to take such a bold step without any clear guarantees that it would not endanger their position.

The fourth electoral issue, that of the country's isolation, was turned by Lukashenko to his electoral advantage. He skillfully blended monitoring activity with external politics to demonstrate that attempts to scrutinize the election were in fact a form of interference in internal politics. The first area of focus was the existence and role of the OSCE Advisory and Monitoring Group in Belarus, headed by the German diplomat, Ambassador Hans-Georg Wieck. From being a scourge of the opposition (at least to people like Poznyak) Wieck had come full circle, and was now regarded as a menace by the administration. Television programs depicted him as an ally of the opposition who was working covertly to remove Lukashenko from power, the main government newspaper *Sovetskaya Belorussiya* made a series of detailed allegations to this effect in its issue of September 5, and Lukashenko himself hinted strongly that the office would be closed immediately after the election campaign. Over the previous two years Wieck had endeavored to develop a dialogue between the government and the opposition. Though partly successful, its results had been limited by the government's failure to adhere to certain conditions, such as an end to harassment and arrests of oppositionists and journalists, equal access to the media, and a viable and autonomous parliament. The government refused permission for the Russian TV network ORT to interview Wieck, who had to travel to Warsaw before his views could be aired.[28]

During the election campaign the OSCE's role was heightened because of its part in monitoring the elections. However, the Belarusian government delayed permission for international observers to oversee the election campaign, so that full monitoring was possible only during the final three weeks. Ultimately the International Monitoring Mission included representatives of the Bureau on Democratic Institutions and Human Rights of the OSCE, the Parliamentary Assembly of the European Council, and the European parliament. The Belarusian foreign ministry refused visas for two key members of the group of long-term observers.[29] The monitors noted that opposition members were not permitted to join Election Commissions for the election, and observers often could not see the ballot boxes from their positions at polling stations. If they complained about this problem, they were removed from the building. The head of the Election Commission took away the ballot boxes after the voting and looked through them in a private room with a member of the local government. They then emerged from the room to announce the results. Internet and cell-phone connections from polling stations did not work, and thus observers could not communicate their findings initially.[30] Plainly there were numerous infringements of the democratic process and the team of observers noted this in their official report. The president regarded the missions as a foreign intrusion on Belarusian territory and the concessions made to observation were minimal.

Patterns of Electoral Support

Lukashenko had led national opinion polls even before his election campaign began. In April 2001, for instance, 39 percent of the mass public were intending to support him, compared with 10 percent who proposed to support Goncharik, 8 percent who favored Domash, 6 percent who preferred the BNF leader Poznyak, 5 percent who favored General Kozlovsky, and 3 percent who favored the Communist leader Kalyakin. Only the former prime minister Chigir (18 per-

Table 5.1. *Voters' Attitudes to the Two Leading Candidates during the Presidential Electoral Campaign, July–September 2001 (percentages)*

	8 Jul	16 Jul	24 Jul	1 Aug	9 Aug	17 Aug	25 Aug	31 Aug	8 Sep
Lukashenko									
positive	51	52	51	51	51	49	49	53	52
negative	38	37	38	37	40	41	42	39	40
difficult to say	11	11	11	11	9	10	9	8	8
Goncharik									
positive	20	19	21	26	30	28	31	33	37
negative	18	16	20	21	21	28	31	37	39
difficult to say	62	64	60	53	40	44	38	30	24

Source: Derived from Oleg Manaev, "Presidentskie vybory," p. 7.

cent) could have presented a viable alternative to the president had his candidature been validated.[31] Vladimir Goncharik emerged relatively late as the "unified candidate" of a now-united opposition, and had less than a month to develop a viable challenge. It was unrealistic to believe that Lukashenko's commanding lead could be overtaken within such a period, given that he was starting with more than twice as much popular support as all his possible opponents (see table 5.1).

Figure 5.1. *Voters' Readiness to Support Candidates of Their Choice, July–September 2001*

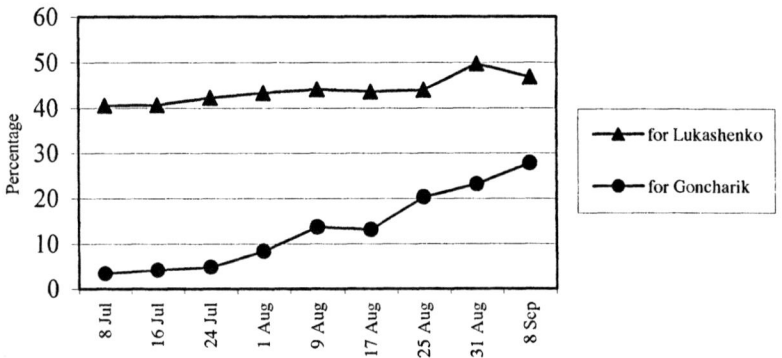

Source: As table 5.1, p. 8.

As table 5.1 makes clear, voters' attitudes to the incumbent president changed very little in the course of the election campaign, either positively or negatively. Goncharik's support, however, moved in both directions. His positive evaluations almost doubled between mid-July and early September. Unfortunately for Goncharik, however, negative assessments increased even

Table 5.2. Voters' Attitudes to the 2001 Presidential Election (percentages)

Questions	Lukashenko's electorate	Goncharik's electorate
Did the candidates have equal conditions in the election?		
Yes	63	7
No	21	88
Did opposition candidates have equal access to the mass media?		
Yes	55	6
No	27	89
Was the election fair and did Lukashenko indeed gather the majority of votes?		
Yes, certain/hope it was	94	13
No, I doubt/certain it wasn't	3	85
Were there any manipulation of the law, as the opposition asserts?		
Yes, plentiful	4	55
Yes, occasional	20	19
No	57	7
Can one trust in the outcomes of the election produced by the Election Commission?		
Yes	92	8
No	3	77
The Election Commission is an:		
Unbiased organization, governed by the law	64	6
Organization that looks up to the president's orders	13	81
Your attitude to the fact that the OSCE did not recognize the election as free and fair?		
Yes, it is just	9	66
No, it is unjust	46	9
Will Lukashenko be able to ensure the pledged increase in living standards?		
Yes	64	1
No	7	93
If an election was tomorrow, would you vote for:		
Lukashenko	88	0
Goncharik	0	47

Note: Cells do not round up to 100 percent as "don't know" and "no answer" were omitted.

Source: As table 5.1, pp. 12–13.

more rapidly. It remains remarkable that Goncharik, despite a short and poorly managed campaign, was able to persuade about two-thirds of the undecided electorate to support his campaign, and it would evidently have gained an even larger proportion if the election campaign had begun earlier.[32] Voters' readiness to cast their votes for Goncharik had meanwhile grown steadily from July onward (figure 5.1), and the electoral distance between the two leading candidates was beginning to diminish.

What were voters' attitudes to the election procedure and results? A striking difference in voters' evaluation of the election outcomes and fairness of procedures can be observed on the basis of the survey evidence. As table 5.2 shows, even if the election results were fraudulent, as his opponents alleged, Lukashenko's electorate nevertheless displayed a loyalty to their leader that was paralleled in their belief in the fairness of the election procedures and the justice of the Central Election Commission. The president's supporters also shared the belief that he would win, and that he would be able to deliver his electoral pledges. Overall, it was clear that the incumbent president remained the only credible choice for the larger part of the Belarusian electorate in the election, in spite of the efforts of the opposition to develop a serious alternative.

The Outcome

Within an hour of the close of polling, the Central Election Commission was in a position to announce the preliminary results. Lukashenko was the clear winner with nearly 76 percent of the vote, well ahead of Goncharik with 15 percent and Gaidukevich with just over 2 percent on what was stated to be an 84 percent turnout. The Commission chairwoman, who had already told the press that she would regard Lukashenko's defeat as a "personal tragedy," insisted that the ballot had been conducted "irreproachably"; the presidential newspaper, in its first reports, hailed a "triumphant victory" that—it added without apparent irony—had been "predetermined."[33] The victorious president, in a press conference that was called as soon as the outcome had become clear, called it an "elegant victory" in which the people had shown their "wisdom and consistency," and promised to work for the support of those who had supported other candidates, including many young people.[34] When the full results were announced on September 14, it emerged that Lukashenko had secured an outright majority throughout the country, but with considerable variations between the city of Minsk, where 57 percent had voted in his favor, and his home region of Vitebsk, where 85 percent had done so. He was formally inaugurated on September 20.

How genuine were these results? Opinion polls conducted prior to the vote had certainly suggested the figures would be much closer. In June, before the candidates had been registered, 42 percent intended to vote for Lukashenko, with Natal'ya Masherova in second place (22 percent) followed by Chigir (19 percent), Domash (13 percent), and Goncharik (11 percent). Masherova, however, had the largest number of positive ratings, ahead of the Belarusian president.[35] By late August, after the campaign had formally started, the Belapan news agency reported that a poll in Minsk—admittedly, not an area in which Lukashenko would have expected to poll most strongly—had found that 38 percent intended to vote for Goncharik, ahead of the 32 percent that intended to vote for Lukashenko, with Gaidukevich lagging far behind with 8 percent. A nationwide survey conducted at the same time by the Independent Institute for Social, Economic and Political Studies, however, found a rather different picture: 47 percent intended to vote for Lukashenko, 12 percent for Domash (who was still a candidate at the time of the survey), 11 percent for Goncharik, and just 4 percent for Gaidukevich.[36] Thus, although Lukashenko was clearly the front-runner, he was not expected to win an overall majority in the first round of voting. That he had done so, and claimed to have received as much as 75 percent, appeared to the opposition to be outright fraud.

Goncharik and other opposition leaders responded to the declaration by calling a protest in front of the presidential palace on the night after the elections, at which he claimed to have received 40 percent of the vote compared with Lukashenko's 46 percent. However, only a thousand people joined the protest on a cold and rainy evening, a reflection of the failure of the "unified candidate" to win over a large body of the electorate. These claims, moreover, did not tally with the unofficial results that were provided by the Independent Institute for Social, Economic and Political Studies, which estimated that Lukashenko had received slightly more than 50 percent of the vote and Goncharik about 40 percent.[37] Lukashenko's other opponent, Gaidukevich, conceded immediately, telling reporters it was "no disgrace to be defeated by such an opponent."[38] At the other extreme the monitors who had been sent by Russia and the other CIS states expressed their entire satisfaction—the election, they declared, had been "free, open [and] in compliance with all universal democratic procedures"[39]—and President Putin was among the first to offer his congratulations.

Western monitors, for their part, concluded that the balloting on September 9 had taken place with very few irregularities, but were not prepared to approve the exercise as a whole. One of their concerns was the substantial vote that had taken place over the five days before the poll, without proper supervision (the Central Election Commission reported that 14 percent had voted in this way; newspaper reports suggested that early voting had been particularly characteristic of potentially unreliable groups of voters, such as students, and it was certainly more difficult to ensure the secrecy of the ballot in such circumstances).[40] The OSCE complained, in its final report on September 10, of "fundamental flaws" in the entire process, including a legislative framework that failed to ensure the independence of the election administration, a campaign environment that seriously disadvantaged the opposition, and a "smear campaign" against international observers themselves.[41]

Table 5.3. Results of the Belarusian Presidential Election, September 9, 2001

Candidate	Votes	Percentage
Alexander Lukashenko	4,666,680	75.65
Vladimir Goncharik	965,261	15.65
Sergei Gaidukevich	153,199	2.48
Invalid	138,706	2.20

Source: Communique of the Central Election Commission, *Sovetskaya Belorussiya*, September 15, 2001, 1. The total electorate was reported at 7,356,343 and the total ballots cast were reported at 6,169,087, or 83.86 percent of the registered electorate. Votes "against all candidates" were not reported.

The official results that were announced by the Central Election Commission are accordingly highly suspect (table 5.3). They indicate that Lukashenko received more than 75 percent of the vote, Goncharik more than 15 percent, and Gaidukevich just under 2.5 percent, which was hardly more than the total of invalid votes. At the level of individual regions, only the city of Minsk offered substantial support to Goncharik (30.5 percent), and Lukashenko reportedly received over 80 percent in Mogilev and Gomel, his political base and the regions closest to the Russian border.[42] What then can one deduce from this conglomeration of figures and highly disparate results? Did the elections consolidate the Lukashenko regime or did they offer some hope to the opposition? Did the latter miss its great opportunity to unseat the man who is sometimes referred to as the last dictator in Europe?

The answer is, first, that there are some apparent weaknesses in the Lukashenko administration, and not least its lack of popularity in the national capital. The city of Minsk represents about one-fifth of the population of Belarus, its government and educational centers, and it is home to the country's intellectual elite. Outside Minsk, on the other hand, the opposition has manifestly failed to attract the interest or support of the electorate. Brest and Grodno offered the most votes to opposition candidates, but they do not appear to have rejected Lukashenko. The president played the "foreigner" card more skillfully than his rivals. Thus he played on fears of a Yugoslavia-style resolution to the country's differences, led by the Americans. The United States had hardly acted in a subtle manner toward Belarus: the Helms Bill had been widely publicized,[43] and, as noted above, the US ambassador had made disparaging comments about the Belarusian president in an opposition newspaper. The population's fears of some sort of NATO or American intervention in Belarus cannot be dismissed lightly; NATO's attack on former Yugoslavia in 1999 made a profound and very adverse impression. Fear of the West is likely to have outweighed concern about the unpredictable and authoritarian nature of the regime itself. Furthermore,

Goncharik had hardly endeared himself to the electorate, and there was little confidence that a trade union leader in power would bring about a substantial improvement in living standards.

On the other hand, after seven years of repressive rule, Lukashenko had hardly quelled opposition, even with virtually complete control over the media and harsh measures applied to his opponents. For the first time, the opposition was able to choose a united candidate, the failings of this particular selection notwithstanding. Ultimately, however, the populace was faced with a grim fact: of the two major players in the foreign affairs of Belarus—the West and Russia—only the latter has offered assistance and shown an extended interest in Belarusian affairs. Most of the new businesses opening in Minsk, for example, are of Russian origin and based on Russian finance. The adversarial stance of the United States, and to a lesser extent the European Union, toward the Lukashenko regime may or may not represent the wisest policy toward a dictator. It does, however, limit the choice, real or imagined, of Belarusian voters. Had Russia turned against the Lukashenko regime, or had it supported Goncharik's challenge, then the situation would have been fundamentally different. For Putin, evidently, a pro-Russian dictator is preferable to an ambivalent democrat. Overall, the electorate of Belarus was inclined to agree with him, thereby ensuring that the Lukashenko regime, anachronism or otherwise in twenty-first century Europe, will continue for the immediate future.

Notes

1. For more details, see the official commentary in Evgenii Dmitriev and Mikhail Khurs, eds., *Belarus: itogi i uroki prezidentskikh vyborov* (Minsk: ISPI, 2002); and alternative commentary in Valer Bulhakay, ed., *The Political System of Belarus and the 2001 Presidential Election* (Minsk: Analytical Group, 2002).
2. Belarusian Television, 5–6 June 2001.
3. *Narodnaya volya*, 16 December 2000; Kozak's term as ambassador ended in late 2003; his successor was George A. Krol.
4. Belarusian Radio, 14 April 1999; see also A. Starevich, "Slobodan pakuet chemodan," *Narodnaya volya*, 14 October 2000.
5. Belarusian Radio, 8 May 1999; for a general summary of Lukashenko's fears about NATO intervention, see also http://belta.press.net.by/archive/1999/04/16/7.htm.
6. See respectively *Konstitutsiya Respubliki Belarus 1994 goda (s izmeneniyami i dopolneniyami)* (Minsk: Amalfeya, 2001); and *Izbiratel'nyi kodeks Respubliki Belarus*, 2nd edn. (Minsk: Natsional'nyi tsentr pravovoi informatsii Respubliki Belarus', 2001). For other assessments of the 2001 presidential elections see, for example, Kimmo Kiljunen, "Belarus 2001 Presidential Election: Somewhat Free but Not Fair," in *The EU & Belarus: Between Moscow and Brussels*, ed. Ann Lewis (London: The Federal Trust, 2002), 71–74; Ronald J. Hill, "Belarus's Presidential Non-election," *Journal of Communist Studies and Transition Politics* 18, no. 2 (June 2002): 126–38; Stephen White,

"The Presidential Election in Belarus, September 2001," *Electoral Studies* 22, no. 1 (January 2003): 173–78; and Joe Price, "Belarusian Presidential Election in 2001 and its Aftermath: An Overview," *Belarusian Review* (Summer 2003): 31–32.

7. *Nasha svaboda*, 27 April 2001.

8. *Belorusskaya gazeta*, 13 and 20 August 2001.

9. Belarusian Television, 21 August 2001, 19:00 hours; and for the American ambassador's presumed role, *RFE/RL Newsline*, 15 August 2001.

10. *The Guardian* (London), 14 September 2001, 20.

11. *RFE/RL Newsline*, 14 August 2001.

12. This organization is made up mainly of relatively poor members of the workforce who rely on charitable donations from the business sector, particularly those with political ambitions. Anton'chik supported the principle of workers' solidarity and the unity of the workforce in the forthcoming political struggle.

13. One such occasion was on NTV (Moscow), 4 July 2001; see also the interview with Masherova cited in Belapan, http://election.by.narod.ru/13.htm.

14. *Sovetskaya Belorussiya*, 15 August 2001.

15. See www.ilhr.org/ilhr/regional/belarus/updates/2001/30.htm.

16. Vmeste za sil'nuyu i protsvetayushchuyu Belarus'. Predvybornaya programma Prezidenta Respubliki Belarus' (Minsk, 2001). Lukashenko's program was also printed in Sovetskaya Belorussiya, 21 August 2001, 1, and again on 5 September 2001, 1.

17. Edinyi kandidat v Prezidenty Respubliki Belarus' (campaign flyer, 2001).

18. Edinyi kandidat; Goncharik's program also appeared in *Sovetskaya Belorussiya*, 31 August 2001, 1.

19. *Programma Liberal'no-demokraticheskoi partii* (Minsk: Vysshii Sovet LDP, 2001). Gaidukevich's program also appeared in *Sovetskaya Belorussiya*, 22 August 2001, 1.

20. Monitoring the Media Coverage of the September 2001 Presidential Election in Belarus. Final Report, December 2001 (Dusseldorf: EIM, 2001), 2.

21. For example, on 6 September 2001, *Sovetskaya Belorussiya* ran an article about the president opening a new metro station in the capital, and on 25 September it published an article about Lukashenko opening a new bridge over the Berezina River.

22. The alleged execution was discussed in *Naviny*, 11 May 1999, and *Zvyazda*, 24 September 1999.

23. For details of this case, see www.bhhrg.org/ukraine/ukraine2001/kuchmagate/chapter1.htm.

24. Natal'ya Kulagina in *Belapan*, 15 July 2001.

25. See, for example, http://elections.belapan.com/analyses/010.shtml and *Sovetskaya Belorussiya*, 9 August 2001.

26. The meetings were shown on the program Panorama, *Belarusian Television*, 23–27 June 2001.

27. According to a report in *Narodnaya gazeta*, 1 August 2001, the president also ordered the arrest of several high officials from the special services.

28. The interview aired on 7 June 2001 on ORT on the program "Vremya."

29. The authorities refused to issue visas for Andrew Bruce of the United Kingdom and Brian Bonner of the United States.

30. For a detailed report on the monitoring of the election, see www.osce.org/odihr/documents/reports/election_reports/by/bel_sep2001_efr.php3, last retrieved October 2003.

31. See Andrei Ekadumov, "Dynamika reityngu A. Lukashenki i vyniki prezydentskikh vybarau 2001 gody," in *Belaruskaya palitichnaya systema i prezydentskiya vybary 2001 gody*, ed. Pavel Kazanetsky et al. (Warsaw: CDEE, 2001).

32. Oleg Manaev, "Prezidentskie vybory: chto bylo na samom dele?," *Analiticheskii byulleten'* 1(15) (2002): 2–3.

33. *Sovetskaya Belorussiya*, 11 September 2001, 1.

34. *Sovetskaya Belorussiya*, 11 September 2001, 2.

35. *Weekly Digest of Belarusian News*, 10 July 2001, reporting a survey conducted by the Independent Institute for Social, Economic and Political Studies.

36. *RFE/RL Newsline*, 28 August 2001.

37. *Novosti NISEPI*, 28 February 2002.

38. *Sovetskaya Belorussiya*, 11 September 2001, 1.

39. *Respublika*, 11 September 2001, 1.

40. Hill, "Belarus's Presidential Non-election," 135–36.

41. OSCE Statement of Preliminary Findings and Conclusions, 10 September 2001, www.osce.org/odihr/documents/reports/election_reports/by, last retrieved October 2003, 1–2.

42. Cited in www.belarusembassy.org/elections2001.

43. It is called the Belarus Democracy Act 2001. For an assessment of the proposed legislation, see Jeffrey Donovan, "Belarus: New Bill in U.S. Senate Would Isolate Minsk," *RFE/RL*, 11 December 2001.

6 The Belarus Economy: Suspended Animation between State and Markets

D. Mario Nuti

1. Premise

Since 1992, following the breakup of the Soviet Union, Belarus has been generally considered as a postcommunist country in transition to a democratic, market economy—admittedly a laggard but definitely a member of the group.[1] In truth in 1992–1994 the country did make some progress in that direction, with a measure of price liberalization forced by the Russian stabilization program, the introduction of a domestic currency managed by a formally independent central bank, and the issue of mass privatization vouchers. Since 1994, however, it has become increasingly apparent that Belarus is not, politically or economically, a postcommunist transition country like almost all the others. Rather, like Uzbekistan, Belarus still has an authoritarian regime and a state-managed economy.

Politically, Belarus is still characterized by the virtual monopoly of the Communist Party. President Alexander Lukashenko, as we saw in chapter 4, extended his own powers and prolonged his period of office by two years in 1996, dissolving parliament and replacing it by a coopted assembly. He obtained a second term of office in 2001, and rules by decree. Political parties are subject to reregistration and other hurdles; the press is controlled. Heads of local governments are appointed by the president or other central bodies. Local election committees are largely appointed by the center. Specialists refer to the Belarusian model as a case of "quasi-democracy" or "demagogical democracy."[2]

Economically, under a thin layer of markets Belarus is a command economy without central planning, similar to pretransition Poland in the second half of the 1980s. State enterprises are still predominant; there are widespread administrative controls on the output and employment of large state enterprises, on prices, and on exchange rates, and there are directed subsidized credits. An initial macroeconomic stabilization was followed by the resumption of high inflation, in spite of widespread economic and administrative controls, with the reappearance of external imbalances and even occasional domestic shortages, also due to an overvalued currency. Since 2001 inflation has come down steadily, but it is still the highest in the countries of the former Soviet Union. Without significant progress in privatization, and with little foreign direct investment, capacity restructuring is exceedingly slow; foreign trade is still largely with Russia and on an increasing scale (53 percent of exports and 65 percent of imports of goods and services in 2001).

In some respects the Belarusian economy has performed better than its Russian counterpart. Belarus has not squandered state capital through debt-for-equity swaps or insider privatization; it has little domestic and foreign indebtedness—if only for a lack of lenders; the government collects taxes and pays for most of its purchases and for wages and pensions; inter-enterprise arrears are low, though fluctuating, and barter is limited to trade with Russia. Criminality—economic and in its other forms—has been kept in check, as a by-product of a zero-tolerance approach; corruption—which in 1994 Lukashenko was elected to fight—is much less common than in Russia. Above all, Belarus' GDP has resumed growth since 1996, recovering from a smaller recession and much faster than any other former Soviet republics except Uzbekistan.

In all these respects Belarus is an outlier. This chapter reviews Belarus's failure to reform (section 2) and to stabilize (section 3), and assesses its economic performance and prospects (section 4), including the prospective monetary union with Russia (section 5). Some lessons are drawn in conclusion for the sustainability of the Belarusian alternative model and for the reconsideration of the Soviet-type system's collapse.

2. The Transition That Never Was

2.1 EBRD Scores

Since 1994 the EBRD (European Bank for Reconstruction and Development) has published yearly in its *Transition Report* a "Transition Progress Scoreboard" for all countries in which it operates (twenty-eight transition countries in 2003). In addition to the private sector share of GDP, estimated by EBRD taking into account the "informal" economy and reflecting the private or public nature of enterprise governance, transition scores covering other aspects of the economy range from 1 (little or no change) to 4+ (OECD standards). Those scores are subjective (though "expert") assessments by the EBRD Chief Economist office, scales are arbitrary (for a start, they begin from 1 instead of zero and therefore have an over-optimistic bias) and heterogeneous (unless the private sector share is also converted to a 1–4+ scale), and in any case their aggregation into a single index involves arbitrary weights, whether implicit or explicit. Nevertheless, the scores provide some useful guidance, and are widely used in transition literature.

On the EBRD scores Belarus has a very low rating, subject moreover to reversals and fluctuations (see table 6.1). When EBRD scores deteriorate over time (as for price liberalization, or occasionally for foreign exchange and trade liberalization), partly the deterioration is objective, and partly the scores reflect a changing perception of Belarusian achievements, more distant from transition targets than it was believed earlier in EBRD circles. Soon after the series was started, Belarus took the lowest place among the transition countries in which the EBRD is active, or at best it could be placed—with Tajikistan, Turkmenistan, and Uzbekistan—among the least advanced in transition processes.

Belarus' private sector share in GDP, at 25 percent, is the lowest among transition countries. Converting the (+) or (–) signs attached to EBRD scores to a numerical value of +1/3 and –1/3 respectively, Belarus' average score in 2002 was 1.81 on a scale from 1 to 4.3, equivalent to having completed only one-quarter of the distance between the minimum score of 1 and the maximum 4.3 (that is, a progress of only 0.81 over the minimum score of 1, divided by [4.3–1]). In 2003 Belarus' average index rose only imperceptibly to 1.84, thanks to progress in small-scale privatization, but this was still the lowest score among transition countries, although progress in this area can be, and has in general been, very fast. Large-scale privatization, after a temporary success in 1995 (2–), has been scored at 1 ever since. Equally, governance and enterprise restructuring, after an illusory 2– in 1995–1996, was later reassessed and revised downward to a steady 1. Price liberalization, given by EBRD optimistic high scores in 1995–1997 (4–, 4–, 4), was reversed and also more soberly revised downward; only in 2001–2003 did that score rise slightly to a modest 2–. The same reversal and modest recovery has taken place in trade and foreign exchange liberalization, and in banking reform. Neither competition nor securities markets and nonbank financial institutions have made any progress throughout the period 1995–2003 above the modest score of 2 reached initially. Infrastructure reform rose to 1+ in 1999 and remained stuck there ever since. From the viewpoint of system transformation Belarus displays a flat encephalogram.

The EBRD also publishes some of the raw indicators that form the basis of the synthetic scores reviewed above; some of the most significant ones are listed in table 6.2 (from the *Transition Report 2003*). These confirm a picture of slow change, of modest and often reversible achievements. In many respects EBRD scores are overgenerous to Belarus. For instance, the share of administered prices in the consumer price index is underestimated, as it neglects coal, timber, rents, and intercity bus services for lack of data. Privatization is also overassessed, as the government retains golden shares in many privatized enterprises and—what is much worse—can *retrospectively* claim a golden share involving rights of veto and control in any enterprise that is not 100 percent private. Data on budgetary subsidies do not include quasi-fiscal items such as the burden of

Table 6.1. *Belarus: EBRD Transition Progress Scores, 1995–2003*

Year	1995	1996	1997	1998	1999	2000	2001	2002	2003
Private-sector share of GDP (mid-year EBRD estimate, %)	15	15	20	20	20	20	20	25	n.a.
Large-scale privatization	2–	1	1	1	1	1	1	1	1
Small-scale privatization	2	2	2	2	2	2	2	2	2+
Governance and enterprise restructuring	2–	2–	1	1	1	1	1	1	1
Price liberalization	4+	4+	4	3–	2+	2+	3–	3–	3–
Trade and foreign exchange liberalization	2	2	1	1	1	2–	2	2+	2+
Competition policy	2	2	2	2	2	2	2	2	2
Banking reform and interest-rate liberalization	2	1	1	1	1	1	1	2–	2–
Securities markets and nonbank financial institutions	2	2	2	2	2	2	2	2	2
Infrastructure reform	1	1	1	1	1+	1+	1+	1+	1+

Source: Based on EBRD, *Transition Report 2003.*

Note: Scale 1–4+ unless otherwise stated.

nonperforming loans in state banks (see below). Belarus's international standing in the transition league was probably at its lowest in 1998, when both the IMF and the World Bank withdrew their permanent representatives from Minsk (they both returned the following year, but the IMF still does not have a standby arrangement with Belarus). There are positive signs, such as the fall in tariff revenue and the rise of the foreign trade share of GDP, the rise of privatization revenues, a fall in the share of industry and agriculture in GDP, and a fall in inequality (as measured by the Gini coefficient) after an initial rise. But these positive signs are not impressive.

2.2 The Target Model

The target model officially adopted by Belarus is the "socially oriented market economy." In the policy document "Major trends in the social and economic development of the Republic of Belarus in 1996–2000" this was defined as a competitive market economy with mixed private and state ownership on an equal footing supported by social welfare policies including high and stable employment and a social safety net.

This notion evokes a German-style social market economy, or the third way sought at various times in EU countries by social democratic parties or left-wing coalitions, like Tony Blair's New Labour or Gerhard Schröder's Neue Mitte. But this European third way recognizes the primacy of markets both domestically and globally, favors the privatization of state assets and enterprises, and is committed to affordable and sustainable policies, recognizing the importance of hard budget constraints and fiscal and monetary prudence.[3] Belarus's third way, on the contrary, is an old-style pretransition attempt at reconciling state ownership and markets, but does not really imply the construction of a full market economy or the hardening of soft budgets. Too many market elements, even some that could be quickly implemented, are missing or are overridden by central controls; the weight of the state is still overwhelming and there is no sign of new, substantial, and irreversible progress. One cannot socially orient a market economy that is not there and its construction takes more than six McDonald's restaurants in Minsk.[4]

The Belarusian system is in fact very close to the third way adopted by President Islam Karimov of Uzbekistan for his own country in 1993, which he characterized as a model in which the state would maintain its role as a "collective entrepreneur," "production regulator," and "investor in priority sectors of the economy."[5] This is actually the negation of a market economy, where entrepreneurship is diffused among a large number of private and state enterprises, and where the state sets the rules of the game—that is, regulates markets, rather than production—and where there are no priority sectors and the state invests exclusively or for the most part in public infrastructure. Karimov's characterization, however, fits precisely the model adopted by Belarus today—both presidents invoking a gradual, evolutionary, and constrained process of reform. The difference between the two is that Uzbekistan stated clearly what it intended to achieve and since 1998 has moved closer to the standard transition path, whereas Belarus targeted the same model, paying lip service to the market economy, and has never changed its target to date.

The Belarusian model—like the earlier Uzbek approach—does not have the advantages or drawbacks of central planning and there is no way back in that direction, but it retains some of the advantages of a command economy, such as high employment and a dampened inflation. Of course, the administrative containment of inflation is a form of financial repression, which in the Soviet system mounted over time and ultimately wrecked the system. If persistent, repressed inflation could also ruin the Belarusian economy; but the scale of repressed inflation in Belarus today is small, partial, and intermittent compared with the large-scale, general, and endemic repressed inflation of Soviet days. Of course, high labor employment is obtained at the expense of efficiency; higher physical gross output lowers net value added and therefore national income, as it piles up as unsaleable inventories or is traded internationally on unfavorable terms, through disadvantageous barter or even unpaid transactions.

The trouble with this model, as in the old Soviet days, is not only the inconsistency of planned prices and actual achieved quantities, but more generally the adoption of an impossible set of policies and of conflicting policy instruments: the search for noninflationary growth, extensive subsidies, directed credits swelling the nonfiscal deficit, low nominal interest rates that correspond to large negative real rates, multiple official exchange rates (until 2000) administratively fixed at a stable but increasingly overvalued rate, with various freer transactions registering a much higher price for foreign exchange, and exceedingly low savings. These are not consistent policies, and their reconciliation in practice can only be disappointing, inefficient, and costly.[6]

At the same time, Belarus suffers from the typical problems of the Soviet-type model on a much lower scale than the standard Soviet-type economy. Inefficiency involves a loss of potential output but not necessarily stagnation; an economy like that of Belarus, which has enjoyed—until now—access to energy and raw materials from Russia on privileged price and payment terms, can accommodate and even grow with a certain degree of inefficiency—at least until formerly achieved levels are reached. Earlier attempts at this kind of third way in the Soviet era failed precisely because of the failure to allow prices to reach market-clearing levels, and the inertia and lack of incentives associated with state-owned enterprises—but these adverse phenomena are present in Belarus on a manageable scale. There *can* be "socialism in one country" if the country is sufficiently rich or has sufficiently generous rich friends (as Russia has been to Belarus until now). Ultimately, the sustainability of the Belarusian third way depends solely on the continuity of Russian goodwill and generosity.

2.3 Privatization

The EBRD estimate of private sector size, at 25 percent of GDP and roughly also of employment, is not only the lowest among post-Soviet and other transition economies but is also an overestimate, to the extent of residual state holdings in enterprises whose majority shareholders are private. Belarusian official sources give a higher private share of up to 50 percent of enterprise output, but this is a gross overestimate because they treat corporatization—that is, the transformation of state enterprises into joint-stock companies—as a form of "ownership transformation" regardless of actual ownership transfer, let alone a change of control. Moreover, state enterprise subsidiaries are not officially classed as state enterprises. Corporatization is simply a precondition of privatization or just a facilitating factor. The most glaring anomaly in Belarusian privatization, as we have seen, is the possibility of the government retroactively claiming a "golden share" in privatized enterprises—effectively a clause that allows the renationalization of control if not of ownership.

Mass privatization has proceeded more slowly than planned, partly because of the need for prior approval by the president for transactions that involve assets in excess of 10,000 minimum wages, and by enterprise employees; there were also legislative delays. In 1998 it was reported that there was a voucher overhang: the nominal value of the vouchers was greater than that of the shares on offer; 70 percent of privatization vouchers at the time were still unredeemed and, in theory, could have been cashed in by their holders at their nominal value plus interest. By 2002, still only 50 percent of vouchers had been redeemed (voucher privatization was supposed to close at the end of 2003).

The main privatization method has been that of direct sale, but *cumulative* privatization revenue has been truly insignificant, under 3 percent of 2002 GDP in eight years (see table 6.2). Preference has been given to enterprise employees and managers. Decree 591 of 1997 opened the possibility of maintaining state control over privatized enterprises through retention of a golden share.

Recently the government launched the privatization of petrochemicals, hoping to receive at least $1.15 billion for a 43 percent stake in petrochemical plants Polimir, Azot, and Grodno Khimvolokno, and the Naftan oil refinery. However, stringent conditions were set on minimum offer prices, on investment programs that were supposed to match the purchase price, and on the requirements to maintain employment and retain many of the social facilities of the companies. Under such conditions the privatization failed to attract a single bidder, leaving the government to consider postponement, cancellation, or the relaxation of these conditions.[7]

Land ownership rights are far more restricted than in Russia; neither residents nor foreigners may buy agricultural land, which can only be leased, and leases may not be transferred or used as collateral (and in some cases they are subject to the condition that no additional labor may be hired to work the land).

Table 6.2. Belarus: Transition Assessments, 1995–2003

	1995	1996	1997	1998	1999	2000	2001	2002	2003
Liberalization									
Share of administered prices in CPI	45	30	27	27	27	27	25	24	21
Administered prices in "EBRD-15" basket	6	6	6	6	6	6	6	6	4
Share of trade in GDP	98.9	91.9	108.8	91.6	98.0	111.3	124.3	118.7	n.a.
Tariff revenue (% of imports)	3.2	3.5	4.1	4.2	3.9	1.7	2.0	2.4	n.a.
Privatization									
Private sector share in GDP	15	15	20	20	20	20	20	25	n.a.
Private sector share in employment (%)	6.8	9.3	12.0	16.4	18.6	n.a.	n.a.	n.a.	n.a.
Privatization revenues (cumulative, % of GDP)	0.5	0.7	0.9	1.0	1.1	1.1	1.2	2.9	n.a.
Enterprises									
Budgetary subsidies (% of GDP)	n.a.	16.2	17.1	17.2	18.4	18.8	13.6	n.a.	n.a.
Investment rate (% of GDP)	25	22	24.7	26	24	25.4	22.2	n.a.	n.a.
Share of industry in total employment (%)	27.6	24.8	24.5	24.3	24.4	24.2	23.4	22.7	n.a.

Infrastructure

Main telephone lines per 100 inhabitants	19.2	20.8	22.6	24.3	25.7	26.9	27.9	29.9	n.a.
Railway labor productivity (1989 = 100)	29.9	28.8	32.6	32.2	35.9	37.5	35.1	38.3	n.a.
Electricity tariff, US¢/kWh	n.a.	1.5	1.1	0.8	0.4	1.4	1.3	3.2	n.a.
(collection rate in %)	(n.a.)	(n.a.)	(n.a.)	(n.a.)	(50)	(n.a.)	(98)		

Financial Institutions

Number of banks	42	38	38	37	36	31	29	28	n.a.
(of which foreign owned)	(1)	(2)	(2)	(2)	(4)	(6)	(9)	(12)	
Asset share of state-owned banks	62.3	54.1	55.2	59.5	66.6	66.0	53.2	67.6	n.a.
Nonperforming loans (% of total loans)	11.8	14.1	12.5	16.5	13.1	15.2	11.9	8.3	n.a.
Stock market capitalization (% of GDP)	n.a.	n.a.	4.4	3.5	3.4	4.1	2.9	n.a.	n.a.

Social Sector

Life expectancy at birth, total (years)	68.5	68.6	68.5	68.4	67.9	68.0	68.1	n.a.	n.a.
Expenditure on health and education (% of GDP)	10.4	11.2	12.6	11.4	11.1	11.1	11.6	11.7	n.a.
Earnings inequality (Gini coefficient)	37.3	35.6	35.4	35.1	33.7	33.7	34.3	n.a.	n.a.

Source: As table 6.1.

Foreign direct investment is modest, at a cumulative total of $1.7 billion at the end of 2003; that is, only about 3.4 percent of the $50 billion which in 1996 the government announced was the FDI needed by Belarus.[8] On a foreign direct investment per capita basis Belarus ranks only seventh in the CIS. Foreign capital has taken no significant part in the privatization process, and there is hostility toward foreign direct investment on the alleged ground that it leads to trade imbalances with investors' countries, although experience shows that companies with foreign capital have a much higher share of exports—though also a slightly higher share of imports—than they have in employment and output.[9]

2.4 Administered Prices

In the Belarusian transition, prices have largely been administratively controlled, in both level and structure. Directive 249 of December 15, 1994, established the category of "socially significant goods," whose prices are controlled at republican and regional level. Goods whose prices are centrally fixed are claimed to represent only about 5 percent of the total, but in addition there are prices fixed by local authorities (about thirty "socially significant goods"), price ceilings, statutory criteria for price formation, obligations to report and justify price increases, and controls over natural monopolies (such as housing and public utilities). In 1997–2000 these covered a steady 27 percent of transactions; their share has been falling since, to 25 and 24 percent respectively in 2001–2002, and to 21 percent in 2003. There are also controls over supplies to the military.

Law 255-3 of May 10, 1999, "On price setting" ruled that prices for products of enterprises holding a dominant position, and prices for some socially important goods (set by the president or by the Council of Ministers on presidential instructions), would be subject to state control. Presidential Decree 285 of May 19, 1999, "On measures for stabilization of prices (tariffs) in the Republic of Belarus" prohibited any price rise that was not compensated by measures of social protection; annual limits for price indices are set by the Council of Ministers and the National Bank of Belarus.

In addition there are informal controls. Until 2000 there were also presidential decrees fixing the maximum monthly rate of inflation, and latent controls that were activated in case that rate was exceeded. For instance, Decree 590 of December 1996 targeted inflation at a maximum rate of 2 percent per month in retail trade. In August 1997 penalties including fines and even dismissals were introduced for raising prices above the monthly 2 percent rate. As a result, retail prices increased much more slowly than producer prices, squeezing profit margins in retail trade. On March 23, 1998, seeing that prices were exceeding the statutory maximum 2 percent per month, the president decreed that they should go back to the level prevailing on the previous March 1. Thus latent controls cover in practice up to 100 percent of formal transactions.

There is an official view that the presence of inflation is evidence that prices are not controlled in Belarus. This is plainly a *non sequitur*: inflation may be held down administratively below the market-clearing level, and still run fast. The counterproof that price controls actually bite is the appearance of shortages (see section 2.6, below), as well as the controls' negative impact on enterprise profitability (defined as the ratio between profits from sales and the cost of products sold; see below).

In practice wages are also centrally fixed, rather than being the result of negotiations between employers and trade unions. The stated principle of wage policy is a tendency toward the restoration of Soviet real wage levels; the steady rise in minimum wage and the first grade wage in the budgetary sphere provide indicative parameters for public and private enterprises, and for pensions. After rising by 13 percent in 2000, real wages rose by 31 percent in 2001 and by another 8 percent in 2002, for a total increase of 61 percent in three years, while GDP rose by only 16 percent over the period. In his election campaign of 2001, President Lukashenko promised an average monthly wage level of $100, which was temporarily implemented in December 2001, soon to be eroded by inflation. In late 1996, Decree 344 required the timely payment of wages, pensions, and benefits; all the same, Belarus has wage arrears that fluctuate at a lower level than in Russia but are still not negligible (about 10 percent in 2002).

2.5 Other Administrative Controls

Beside controls on prices, wages, and state enterprise output, there are widespread administrative controls, especially financial controls, exercised by a variety of state agencies such as the State Control Committee, the Tax Committee, and the State Committee on Financial Investigation. A 1999 World Bank study, based on a questionnaire administered to a sample of Belarusian enterprises, estimates the direct and indirect cost of administrative controls to be of the order of 4–8 percent of GDP.

The number of private enterprises was slashed as a result of a reregistration campaign of February 1996–April 1997; enterprises not properly registered were not allowed to operate. Only 30 percent of enterprises had reregistered before the deadline; registration was later reopened without a new date, then again halted and reopened. A draft decree of November 1998 limited registrations to three per person. A new reregistration was required in 2001. Decrees, unlike laws, can be retroactive; draft decrees, even if never approved or later withdrawn, once published are often just as effective as those that are approved, and can be more damaging because of underlying uncertainty.

A recent World Bank report on the Belarusian business environment focuses on the emerging twin problems of decreasing competitiveness and falling profitability, due to the combined effect of price and wages controls and of exchange rate policy.[10] Poor competitiveness is also being linked to the scarcity of small and medium enterprises. Belarus suffers from overregulation, in the form of complex and expensive systems of inspection and control for all firms regardless of ownership; and from unpredictability of regulation, due to frequent changes in the rules of the game (laws, decrees, regulations). The result is a decline in the profitability of industrial enterprises (from 17 percent in 1999 to 15.7 percent in 2000 and 11.9 percent in 2001), with an increase of the share of loss-making enterprises from 8.8 percent of the total in 1999 to 29.7 percent in 2001 and a record 36.7 percent in the first half of 2002. This also had a negative impact on the government's fiscal balance. Inventories rose dramatically (especially in textiles, apparel, leather, shoes, machine building, and metal processing, and the medical industry), to average peaks of 70–75 percent in relation to monthly output in the second half of 2002. Inter-enterprise arrears, which dropped sharply in international transactions following exchange rate unification in 2000, re-emerged and grew in domestic trade, thus remaining fairly stable overall in 1998–2002 at between 26 and 31 percent of industrial transactions. Overdue debt rose in 2002 in 41 percent of industrial enterprises surveyed by the National Bank.

In 2001 officially state subsidies were less than 1 percent of industrial output, but a third of enterprises received preferential credits, 17 percent enjoyed preferential tax rates, and tax arrears were 3 percent of 2001 budget revenues (evidently, there is large-scale cross-subsidization implicit in price and credit patterns). The IMF estimated that in 1998–1999 total subsidies were equivalent to 18 percent of GDP.[11] Industrial structure is dominated by large firms, with an average of 433 employees in 2001. Across industrial sectors there has been no significant change in employment structure since 1996. Belarus has approximately 2.8 small and medium-sized enterprises per thousand population, the smallest among the former Soviet republics and the only falling ratio among transition economies. Their output share represents just 6–10 percent of GDP compared with 40 percent in the Czech Republic and over 50 percent in Poland.

2.6 Shortages

Generalized price controls may be ineffective in stemming inflation but are effective enough to bring about shortages. These became visible in March 1998 and were worsened by the Belarusian ruble crisis associated with the Russian crisis in August 1998. The Council of Ministers meeting of February 16, 1999, recognized that "In some districts . . . there are shortages of foodstuffs, shoes, textiles, etc." On arrival at Minsk international airport visitors were handed a 1999 "Welcome to Minsk" pamphlet that actually informed them that Belarus was an economy without general market-clearing prices:

Minsk is a very "cheap" city. Low prices for most types of food products and public transportation are regulated by the state. This leads to the limitation and shortage of many cheap products. Do not be surprised if you will not be able to buy a greater quantity of a product than the amount fixed in the store.

Belarus thus actually advertised that it was not a market economy. Until 2000 the combination of domestic price controls and a domestic currency that was greatly overvalued at the official rate but greatly undervalued at the black or the free market rate (relative to purchasing power parity) led to large-scale informal exports, including cross-border trade. In 1998 it was reported that, in order to avoid this goods drain, scarce goods supplies were delivered to Minsk shops in the evening, only after the last trains to neighboring capitals had departed. In December 1998, confronted with the depletion of shop supplies ahead of Christmas, the president threatened to punish "those responsible" for shortages. The 2000 unification of the exchange rate and the effective elimination of the foreign exchange premium in the parallel market have now eliminated the more glaring instances of shortages and inefficient border trade.

3. Stabilization

3.1 Fiscal Policy

Unlike Russia, Belarus has been able to continue to collect taxes and to keep the budget deficit under control and falling as a percentage of GDP. This favorable trend, however, has been accompanied by a relatively large and—until recently—rising quasi-fiscal deficit, so that the overall deficit has remained of the order of 3.5–5.5 percent of GDP (according to IMF estimates the quasi-fiscal deficit was 2.5 percent of GDP in 1996, 3 percent in 1997, 4 percent in 1998 and 3.3 percent in 1999). The main quasi-fiscal item has been the cost of a large-scale National Bank program of directed subsidized credits to agriculture (distributed by banks to ultimate borrowers at an interest rate of half the refinance rate) and house construction (at symbolic rates, recently raised but still largely negative in real terms). Among other quasi-fiscal items there is also the cost of loan rescheduling (especially in agriculture), the increase in implicit "pay-as-you-earn" pension debt due to a steep worsening in dependency ratios,[12] and the deficit in other extra-budgetary funds. Many assets accumulated by the local authorities and in a number of special funds cannot be used by the republican budget, so that financing requirements are in excess of the general government deficit. Extensive *ad hoc* tax (and tariff) exemptions are used to stimulate production.

The relative size of the budget increased significantly from 46 percent of GDP in 1992 to 56 percent in 1993, fell to 42 percent in 1996 and then started growing again in the second half of the 1990s, up to 47.3 percent in 1999, but

Table 6.3. Belarus: Economic Performance, 1992–2003

	1992	1993	1994	1995	1996	1997	1998	1999	2000	2001	2002	2003
GDP growth at constant prices %	-9.6	-7.6	-12.6	-10.4	2.8	11.4	8.4	3.4	5.8	4.7	4.7	4.0
Registered unemployment % of labor force[a]	0.5	1.4	2.1	2.7	3.9	2.8	2.3	2.1	2.1	2.3	3.0	n.a.
Consumer prices annual average %	969	1,188	2,200	709	52.7	63.8	73.2	293.8	168.9	61.4	42.6	29.0
Gross average wage growth % p.a.	838	1,107	1,504	668.9	60.5	88.0	102.0	322.4	200.9	108.8	54.0	n.a.
General government expenditure % of GDP[b]	46.0	56.2	50.0	43.0	42.4	46.2	45.4	47.3	45.9	46.8	42.0	n.a.
General government balance % of GDP[c]	0	-1.9	-2.5	-2.7	-1.6	-0.7	-1.0	-2.0	-0.2	-1.9	-1.8	-1.5
Refinancing rate of interest %[d]	30.0	210.0	300.0	66.0	35.0	42.2	48.0	120.0	80.0	48.0	38.0	n.a.
Official exchange rate end–year BR/$	0.015	0.698	10.6	11.5	15.5	30.7	106.0	320.0	1,180	1,580	1,920	n.a.
Current account (% GDP)	n.a.	-30.4	-13.2	-4.4	-3.7	-6.1	-6.7	-1.6	-2.5	-2.3	-2.5	-2.6
Trade balance (mn US$)	377	-569	-556	-666	-1,149	-1,407	-1,501	-570	-884	-807	-915	-900
Merchandise exports (mn US$)	3,580	1,970	2,510	4,803	5,790	6,919	6,172	5,646	6,641	7,256	7,985	8,100
Merchandise imports (mn US$)	3,203	2,539	3,066	5,469	6,939	8,326	7,673	6,216	7,525	8,063	8,900	9,000

Net foreign direct investment (mn US$)	n.a.	18	11	15	105	350	201	443	119	96	434	250
Gross reserves (end year, exc. gold, mn US$)	n.a.	91	101	377	469	394	345	309	357	352	601	n.a.
External debt stock (mn US$)[c]	570	1,014	1,251	1,527	991	976	1,011	886	812	763	813	n.a.
External debt stock (% of GDP)	n.a.	27.7	25.7	14.7	7.2	7.0	6.7	7.3	6.4	6.2	5.7	n.a.
Population (millions, end-year)	10.2	10.2	10.3	10.2	10.1	10.1	10.1	10.0	10.0	10.0	9.9	n.a.
GDP (trillion Belarusian rubles)	0.092	0.986	17.8	119.8	184.2	366.8	702.2	3,0261	9,134	17173	25518	34235
GDP per capita (US$)	524	358	472	1,021	1,367	1,388	1,504	1,208	1,274	1,239	1,437	n.a.
Share of industry in GDP %	40.4	30.9	30.8	31.4	34.6	34.3	33.4	31.9	30.1	29.9	30.1	n.a.
Share of agriculture in GDP %	23.8	18.3	15.0	17.7	16.0	15.4	13.9	14.6	14.2	11.9	10.9	n.a.

Notes: [a] Figures do not include emigrant workers abroad, who accounted for an estimated 27.4 percent of the labor force in 2000: EBRD, *Transition Report 2003.*
[b] General government includes the state, municipalities, and extrabudgetary funds.
[c] On a commitment basis.
[d] From 2001 the figures show the repo rate of the Central Bank.
[e] Medium- and long-term public and publicly guaranteed debt.

Source: As table 6.1.

then fell again to 42 percent in 2002. Since 2000 both fiscal and monetary policy have been tightened somewhat, under the regained influence of the Bretton Woods institutions and the prospect of monetary union with Russia (see below).

3.2 Monetary Policy

In theory Belarusian monetary policy is conducted by an independent central bank, which on the basis of the 1994 law is classed in the literature as the seventh most independent bank in the whole world.[13] In practice the president has the power to appoint and remove the head of the National Bank and suspend and revoke any of the bank's decisions; directed credits are decided by presidential decree or by the Council of Ministers. In 1995–1998 the National Bank had four presidents: one resigned under pressure, one was imprisoned before dismissal, and another was dismissed and replaced by the former Minister of Finance and First Deputy Premier Piotr Prokopovich, who as a minister had been associated with expansionary budgetary policies, subsidized credit, and inflationary policies (he was still governor of the National Bank in early 2004 but his permanence could not be taken as evidence of central bank independence from the government). Central bank independence—formally strengthened in 2000—is still one of the issues continuously under discussion with the IMF.

In practice since early 1996 monetary policy has been subordinated to the broader policy goals of the government, including the provision and subsidization of credits to agriculture and housing construction, direct lending to the government by the National Bank, and directed lending to "state programs" and "socially important programs" by state-owned commercial banks. As a result, inflation has remained higher than the statutory (though relatively high) rate of 2 percent a month decreed in 1996, and flared again after the Russian crisis of August 1998, when monetary policy was loosened still further (the velocity of circulation of broad money doubled and the real money stock halved between September 1998 and March 2000[14]). The Belarusian ruble, inevitably, depreciated rapidly. Since then inflation has been falling steadily (see table 6.3), but in 2003 it was still the highest in the whole of the former Soviet area.

Because of inflation Belarus recorded a low degree of monetization, with a ratio between M2 and GDP that at the end of the 1990s fell below 10 percent, as in Russia. This is not, as in the Russian case, the result of high interest rates, inter-enterprise arrears or budget arrears, for in Belarus interest rates have been highly negative, inter-enterprise arrears peaked at only 12 percent of GDP at the end of 1997, and budgetary arrears are negligible. A considerable proportion of industrial enterprise revenues takes a barter form, but primarily in foreign trade with Russia.[15] Commercial banks are undercapitalized, often experience difficult financial conditions, and do not enjoy public confidence. Low monetization is simply the result of economic agents' rational response to a highly inflationary environment. Dollarization is widespread. At the end of the 1990s the National Bank deliberately sought to raise the degree of monetization through additional monetary expansion—a self-defeating, indeed counterproductive, policy.

The National Bank has used several indirect instruments of monetary policy, including bond sales, repurchases at prefixed terms, and foreign exchange swaps, for the management of short-term liquidity, but could not operate them on the scale that would have been necessary to contain the inflationary implications of credit expansion. Real interest rates have always been negative throughout the post-Soviet period, and only in 2002 did they reach a one-digit negative rate.

3.3 Exchange Rate Policy

Until 1995–1996 there was, effectively, a single legal exchange rate, the official one, which appreciated considerably in real terms, plus a black market rate. Then, at the end of 1996, a parallel 50 percent higher rate in Belarusian rubles for foreign exchange was quoted at the Moscow Interbank Currency Exchange (MICEX); the premium fell as a result of official devaluations, then rose again until March 1998 when, as a result of a currency crisis, MICEX trade in Belarusian rubles was closed down in cooperation with the Russian authorities.

Until 2000 there was a free "over the counter" rate for cash transactions, in exchange bureaus where foreign exchange was bought and sold at a premium (30 percent of their receipts must be surrendered to the National Bank at its average cost); purchases were limited to $200 per day per person per bureau, but very often they were simply not possible. The 1999 "Welcome to Minsk" pamphlet candidly acknowledged that

> "valyutchiki" (those who exchange currency illegally) can offer you a more profitable exchange rate. . . . It is practically impossible to buy foreign currency in the local banks. The only place where you can do it is the "black" market.

The official, overvalued rate was adjusted by the National Bank on the basis of weekly inflation data and unspecified "social guidelines"; at that rate exporters surrendered to the Bank a share of their export earnings, say 40 percent, and authorized importers could obtain foreign exchange for the import of essential goods such as energy (although largely unpaid or offset by barter transactions with Russia) and pharmaceuticals. Clearly the compulsory surrender of 40 percent of export earnings at the official rate when the free rate is, say, 60 percent higher is equivalent to a 15 percent tax on gross export earnings ($0.40 \times 0.60/1.60$), which is an inefficient and distortive disincentive to export.

By 2000 the largest banknote (1,000,000 Belarusian rubles) was worth about three US dollars, wallets had been replaced by briefcases, and the exchange rate had come perilously close to that suggested by the old joke about the appropriate exchange rate between the Soviet ruble, the pound, and the dollar: one dollar equals one pound of rubles. Redenomination of the currency eliminated three zeros, without the redistributive implications of earlier currency conversions in Soviet days (1957), which had confiscated a large proportion of the population's liquid assets.

In September 2000 the exchange rate was unified at a devalued rate, in theory pegged to the Russian ruble within a crawling band, in practice targeted to the US dollar. Thanks to Russian financial support and to a temporarily higher interest rate, the exchange rate was stabilized and the premium in the parallel market was virtually eliminated.

4. Belarus's Economic Performance

4.1 Economic Recovery

Untypically for a country that had neither significantly reformed nor stabilized its economy, in 1996–2003 Belarus boasted a rapid recovery of its GDP, by over 55 percent (see table 6.3). By 2002 Belarus had recovered 93 percent of its 1989 GDP level, the second-highest rate of recovery in the CIS after Uzbekistan's 108 percent, compared with Russia's 71 percent.[16] Registered unemployment peaked in 1996 at 3.9 percent but fell steadily to 2.1 percent in 2000, rising only slightly to 3 percent in 2002—a remarkable performance, the downside of which is the probable lack of significant restructuring of productive capacity. The main source of growth has been exports, particularly to Russia, aided by the implementation of a customs union agreed in 1995, the depreciation of the Belarusian ruble compared with the Russian ruble, and direct central exhortations to export even on unattractive terms, on credit or for barter.

4.2 Reality or Mirage?

Was Belarusian recovery reality or fiction? To some extent growth may have been exaggerated by the value of unwanted production without a market outlet, piled up in inventories much greater than in market economies. The quality of statistics is recognized by Western experts and by independent sample inquiries to be better than in most former Soviet republics, so that Belarus' differential performance with respect to them, rather than its absolute performance, may be exaggerated. A possible source of overestimation is the disposal of current output and inventories through barter or, worse, the build-up of unpaid arrears, mostly in trade with Russia. Also, living standards lagged behind GDP; by February 1999 even the president publicly complained that the economic growth recorded in statistical yearbooks was not matched by rising living standards for the mass of ordinary people.

4.3 Capital Consumption

A factor that may not explain Belarus' GDP recovery but might explain the maintenance of living standards (although recovering at a slower rate than GDP owing to the growth of investment) is capital consumption. Investment—fluctuating at about a quarter of GDP—is said to have fallen below the level required to maintain current production capacity. Belarus is eating away the economic potential built in the past, falling behind its Western neighbors.

4.4 The Easier Task of Restructuring

One of the reasons that might explain the smoother recovery of Belarus relative to more ambitious reformers could be the nature of its division of labor with the former Soviet Union. Belarus was not specialized in the vertically integrated production of goods now obsolete or embodying negative value added; it specialized in assembling finished products out of components provided by the rest of the Union, so much as to be labeled "the Soviet assembly shop." Therefore restructuring tasks were probably easier, for the equipment and labor involved in the assembly of components must be less specific and easier to redeploy, or at any rate quantitatively smaller than those involved in vertically integrated production. Another area where Belarus appears to have been able to maintain export capability is that of armaments; we know, for instance, that substantial barter transactions in this sector have been frequently undertaken with China.

But the real cornerstone of Belarusian growth has been its special relationship with Russia. The dominant position of Russian nationals in Belarus; the strategic position of Belarus, defending Russia's western flank (which is claimed by President Lukashenko to cost $1 billion a year, a good bargaining counter in negotiations with Russia) and allowing a transit route to the west (for the gas pipeline and road transport) that is more secure than through Ukraine; the popularity of Belarus with Russian electors; and the genuine long-standing complementarity of their productive structures: all these factors have placed Belarus in an excellent position to export to Russia—as long as Belarus can supply competitively, or regardless of cost, when Russian producers have no spare capacity. Belarus is totally dependent on energy imports from Russia (apart from producing about 10 percent of its own oil consumption), but Gazprom is financing and jointly supervising the trans-European Yamal gas pipeline through Belarus, and is active also as barter broker and financial investor. Until 2003, Belarus obtained Russian oil and gas at a price roughly half of the price paid by Ukraine and a third of the world price.

4.5 Sustainability

The real test of an integrated economic policy elevated to a system, as in Belarus, is its sustainability in the medium to long term. Even full communism could be implemented, perhaps for seven days or even seven months, but over a period of, say, seven years it would not be sustainable.

Can the Belarusian system and policy model be sustained into the medium or longer run? In general, it can be presumed that recovery to earlier levels within the framework of former structures is relatively easy, but after that higher levels than previously attained, or new structures, or both, require a more flexible, market-oriented mechanism of signals and incentives. For a start, idle capacity margins, first selectively then throughout the economy, will be eroded and absorbed; new net investment will be required by sustained growth, which at the moment cannot be expected, whether by domestic or by external investors. Different policies toward both must be devised and implemented. It is no accident that in 2001 and 2002 only two CIS countries grew less rapidly than Belarus, namely Uzbekistan and Kyrgyzstan; all the other CIS countries grew faster In a system that is so export-driven, the question is whether Belarus can compete internationally in the twenty-first century. This will depend on productivity trends that in turn are tied to privatization, restructuring, and investment, three areas in which the Belarusian record is not at all encouraging; on real wage trends, which at the moment are bent on recovering earlier Soviet levels regardless of underlying and reduced circumstances; and on an exchange rate policy capable of accommodating an otherwise deteriorating level of competitiveness. The outlook on all these grounds must be pessimistic.

The most serious threat to the sustainability of the Belarusian model is the price of Russian energy. On September 15, 2003, Russia's President Putin announced that from the start of 2005 gas supplies to Belarus would move to a "market basis" as demanded by cash-strapped Gazprom.[17] As Belarus has been accumulating unpaid arrears, the prospective price hike is going to have a significant effect on both inflation and output in Belarus. This shock is a severe and potentially lethal challenge to the continued existence of the Belarusian economic model. More generally Belarus—like all less developed economies, regardless of their transition status—faces the twin gap of domestic savings and current account balance. Unlike the more successful among those economies, Belarus cannot rely—under present policies and system—on a sustained capital inflow large enough to bridge both gaps.

5. A Belarus–Russia Monetary Union?

5.1 The Schedule

The process of economic integration between Belarus and Russia, relaunched with the treaties of 1996 and 1997 on their economic union, was taken a stage further on December 25, 1998, when President Lukashenko and President Yeltsin signed in Minsk a declaration of intent to implement a monetary union. On February 12, 1999, the chairmen of the Belarusian National Bank and of the Russian Central Bank signed a schedule of concerted actions including monetary policy unification and coordination of exchange rate policy. The National Bank then published its "Concept for the adoption of a single currency, the formation of a single central bank and a common banking system of the Belarusian–Russian Union." On April 28, 1999, in Moscow the two presidents signed eleven documents including the completion of the Russia–Belarus customs union, the Union's budget, and a draft agreement on the unification of the two countries into a Union of Sovereign Republics.[18]

According to the National Bank document, the introduction of a single currency was planned in three phases.[19] In the first quarter of 1999 the monetary policies of Belarus and Russia were to be partially unified; a common capital market for securities would be created; the mutual convertibility of the two countries' currencies would be achieved; and a legal framework for the unification of the currency regulations would be formed. The second phase (April–June 1999) was to deal with the unification of currency regulations and monetary systems of the two countries, and also as with the adoption of a single currency. In the third phase (in the second half of 1999) a single bank of issue would be created and "the process of adopting a single currency" would be completed.

The option preferred by National Bank was the establishment of a common noncash currency that would be in circulation alongside the two national currencies and pegged to a convertible currency. This hasty schedule was accompanied by a long delay expected for the actual introduction of the new currency and the complete replacement of the national currencies, planned for completion in 2008.[20] All this remains to be implemented. At the beginning of 2004 Belarus is not much closer to monetary union with Russia than it was five years earlier. There are still many discussions and open questions.

5.2 The Form

The first question raised by a possible Russia–Belarus Monetary Union is the actual form that this might take; that is, the nature of the common currency and modalities of its issue and management.

Belarus's monetary authorities suggested at first that the common currency might resemble the old-style Transferable Ruble (TR), which was used as a unit of account within CMEA until its dissolution in 1991. This was out of the question. The TR was neither transferable, as TR bilateral balances could not be used automatically in settlement of trade with third member countries without their agreement, nor was it even a ruble, as it could not be used for purchases of Soviet goods and services without Soviet agreement. It was a purely accounting device to record trade imbalances arising in any period, for clearance in subsequent periods through planned trade transactions enshrined in bilateral trade agreements between centrally planned economies. There was absolutely nothing that a new TR could do that could not be done by Russian and Belarusian rubles.

Then the Belarus monetary authorities suggested something along the lines of the ECU–EURO, namely a basket of currencies of the two member countries (in the hope that other FSU countries might join),[21] gradually locked into a permanently fixed exchange rate between themselves and at that point becoming a kind of super-ruble. This was feasible in theory, but in practice such a currency basket would not give the Belarusian ruble, under any criterion (such as relative size of population, national income, or mutual trade shares), a weight greater than, say, 5 percent (possibly less), and a commensurate weight in the management of the currency and the new joint monetary institutions. It would have been futile, indeed pretentious and inefficient, to undertake such complex transformations in order to set up something virtually indistinguishable from the Russian ruble.

Predictably, the only feasible form of a monetary union turned out to be the introduction of the Russian ruble into Belarus. In June 2003 an agreement between the Russian and Belarusian prime ministers fixed January 2005 as the target date for Belarus's adoption of the Russian ruble. Also agreed was the dominant role of the Central Bank of Russia, with two seats for Belarus on the Bank's board of directors and a negotiated share of the joint seigniorage to compensate for the loss of Belarusian ruble seigniorage. However Belarus, which in mid-2002 had rejected a surprise move by President Putin to accelerate the process of monetary unification with January 1, 2004, as the date for the introduction of the Russian ruble in Belarus, again has been holding out for greater concessions: VAT rebates for Russian value-added exports through Belarus, the rate of conversion between Russian and Belarusian ruble, compensation for loss of seigniorage that the Belarusian National Bank estimates at $1.2 billion, presumably in terms of present value,[22] and the price of Russian energy. The January 2005 deadline is unlikely to be met.

5.3 Premature Unification

Whatever form the prospective Russia–Belarus Monetary Union might take, it would be premature; that is, implemented before political unification—which involves much more than the friendship and coordination currently prevailing between the two countries—and before the convergence of their real economic variables (such as labor productivity in real terms, real wages, and unemployment).

Similar considerations apply to the Euro, but the Russia–Belarus Monetary Union would also be premature in a much stronger sense than it might have been the case for the Euro, for several reasons:

- the two countries are subject to likely asymmetric external shocks at least with respect to energy prices, with Russia as a net exporter and Belarus as a net importer of energy respectively suffering and benefiting from an oil and gas price fall (although much oil-refining capacity is located in Belarus);
- the two countries are nowhere near fiscal and monetary convergence, and are not driven to convergence by obligatory parameters such as those fixed for the European Union and the Economic and Monetary Union members by the Maastricht Treaty or by the Growth and Stability Pact;
- Russia, although recovered from the financial crisis of 1998, is still greatly indebted externally but its foreign reserves exceed total public debt and the country has ample access to international financial markets, whereas Belarus enjoys exceptionally low levels of domestic and international debt, but also hardly any foreign reserves and no access to international financial markets or even IMF lending;
- neither country is a fully monetized economy by the standards of advanced market economies;
- there are fragile but highly developed financial markets in Russia, which are missing in Belarus; Belarusian financial vulnerability might increase with the monetary union with Russia because the National Bank of Belarus would lose or reduce its ability to act as a lender of last resort in a liquidity crisis;
- there are different degrees of "marketization" in the two countries, with Russia—for all its faults—approaching a largely private market economy and Belarus having hardly started its own journey toward that objective;
- the Russian ruble is more subject to real revaluation—not only because of oil price trends but also for stronger productivity trends and FDI—than the Belarusian ruble, so that the irreversible introduction of the Russian ruble into Belarus might aggravate competitive pressure in Belarusian industry.[23]

It would therefore be wrong to believe that the pre-1992 experience of joint membership of the ruble area might make it possible for Russia and Belarus simply to reestablish a monetary union: the pre-1992 division of labor is no longer suited to a different economic system (indeed different systems), to a group of two countries instead of the former fifteen, and to different levels and structures of domestic income and production output.

The premature nature of a monetary union between Russia and Belarus, of course, does not mean that it is not feasible. German monetary unification in 1991 was also premature, for instance, with real wages tending to a single level while productivity in the east was just a third of the west German level (although political unification also took place at the same time). It simply was costly in the short and medium run, and it absorbed large-scale resources provided by the German federal budget and international financial market of a kind that would not be available to Belarus and Russia. The political advantages from the operation would also be less substantial for Russia and Belarus than in the case of German reunification. On the positive side, the prospect of monetary union has actually been an incentive for Belarus to implement overdue changes in the direction of transition, facilitated by some financial support from Russia; for instance, the unification of exchange rates, the tightening of budgetary and of monetary policy, and the harmonization of tax policy with Russia.

6. Lessons and Conclusions

Were it not for almost thirty countries today undertaking a transition process from a communist-dominated centrally planned economy with state ownership and enterprise toward a mixed market economy, it would not occur to anyone to label Belarus as a transition economy or society, as it is being done by an undue process of assimilation.

Belarus is still largely a command economy, with dominant large state enterprises, central controls on prices and on economic activities in the state and the small private sector, a central bank subordinated to government, large-scale subsidies, monetary overexpansion and associated open and—to a much lower degree than in the Soviet era—repressed inflation, and internal and external imbalances. These policies are completely at odds with the declared purpose of constructing a socially oriented market economy. Economic stabilization has not been fully achieved.

The survival of the Belarusian system is highly dependent on Russian subsidization of its energy and raw material requirements; indeed, Belarus can be regarded as evidence that the Soviet system's collapse might have been avoided—in resource-rich economies—if relatively minor reforms had been implemented, such as a substantial reduction of the monetary overhang, greater foreign trade integration, and some privatization.

Backwardness in both reform and stabilization has protected Belarus from the worst drawbacks of the Russian transition, but those policies and system are not sustainable without further Russian subsidization; and, in any case, once former income levels are achieved, they will not provide any foundation for sustained recovery and growth.

Notes

1. The writer was economic advisor to the presidential administration of Belarus from January–September 1998, under World Bank auspices, and in 1999 was involved in the EU–TACIS project for the publication of Belarus Economic Trends. The views expressed here are however purely personal and should not necessarily be associated with any of these organizations.

2. See Elena A. Korosteleva, "Why Belarus is Unique: Explaining Institutional and Electoral Allegiances" (paper presented to a Foreign and Commonwealth Office conference, October 2003); Elena A. Korosteleva, Rosalind Marsh, and Colin Lawson (eds.), *Contemporary Belarus: Between Democracy and Dictatorship* (London: RoutledgeCurzon, 2003).

3. See D. M. Nuti, "The Belarusian Alternative: Transition or Solely Reform," *Belarus Economic Trends*, Quarterly Report no. 2 (April–June 1999): 14–20.

4. When I said this at a seminar in Minsk in 2000, someone from the audience asked, only half-jokingly, "How many do you need?"

5. See Islam Karimov, *Building the Future: Uzbekistan—Its Own Model for Transition to a Market Economy* (Tashkent: Uzbekistan Publishers, 1993), 37–60.

6. D. M. Nuti, "Making Sense of the Third Way," *Business Strategy Review* 10, no. 3 (Autumn 1999): 57–67; D. M. Nuti, "Belarus: A Command Economy Without Central Planning," *Russian and East European Finance and Trade* 26, no. 4 (July–August 2000); also in *Transition—The First Decade*, ed. Mario I. Blejer and Marko Skreb (London: Kluwer, 2000).

7. *Business Eastern Europe*, 3 May 2003.

8. Ken Charman, "Foreign Direct Investment in Belarus," *Belarusian Economic Trends*, Quarterly Report, 1999, no. 2.

9. Charman, "Foreign Direct Investment."

10. World Bank, *Belarus: Improving the Business Environment* (Washington, D.C.: World Bank, January 2003).

11. International Monetary Fund, *Republic of Belarus: Recent Economic Developments and Selected Issues*, IMF Staff Country Report no. 00/153, November 2000.

12. The number of workers supporting each pensioner, i.e., the inverse of the dependency ratio, fell from 2.2 in 1990 to 1.7 in 2002, while the replacement rate (the ratio of average pension to average wages) rose from 32.5 percent in 1994 to almost 44 percent in the first half of 2002, targeted to rise to 45 percent in 2003; see International Monetary Fund (IMF), *Republic of Belarus, IMF Country Report, No. 03/119* (Washington, D.C.: IMF, 2003).

13. Alex Cukierman, Geoffrey P. Miller, and Bilin Neyapti, "Central Bank Reform, Liberalization and Inflation in Transition Economies—An International Perspective," *Journal of Monetary Economics* 49 (2002): 237–64.

14. IMF, *Republic of Belarus* 2003.

15. See Simon Commander, "Barter in Belarus and Russia: Why Does It Exist and What Does it Mean?" (paper presented at a conference at the London Business School, 1999).

16. European Bank for Reconstruction and Development (EBRD), *The Transition Report 2003* (London: EBRD, 2003).

17. Current disagreements also involve distribution arrangements; talks with Gazprom about setting up a consortium to manage export pipelines delivering Russian gas to western Europe have stalled, as Gazprom values the gas transit firm, Beltransgaz, at US$600 million while Belarus values it at US$5 billion; Economist Intelligence Unit, *Business Eastern Europe*, 22 September 2003. A political crisis between the two countries was precipitated in January 2004 when, in the midst of a period of exceptionally cold weather, Gazprom suddenly cut its supply of gas to Belarus; see Vital Silitski, "Russia's Latest 'Gas Attack' On Belarus", *RFE/RL Newsline* 8, no. 16, part II (27 January 2004).

18. Anastasia Nesvetailova, "Muddling Through Crisis: Economic Underpinnings of the Russia–Belarus Union" (paper presented to a Foreign and Commonwealth Office conference, London, October 2003).

19. See *Belarus Economic Trends*, March 1999.

20. *Belarus Economic Trends*, March 1999.

21. Belarus forms a customs union with Russia, Kazakhstan, Kyrgyzstan, and Tajikistan, although many trade barriers remain still in place. The other countries of this customs union have not indicated an interest in forming a monetary union.

22. *Business Eastern Europe*, 6 October 2003.

23. See John Odling-Smee, *Monetary Union Between Belarus and Russia: An IMF Perspective* (Washington, D.C.: IMF, 2003), available at www.imf.org.

7 Belarus and the East

Clelia Rontoyanni

Belarusian foreign policy is officially described as multidirectional, ostensibly striving for a balance in relations with various partner countries, international organizations, and geographical regions.[1] In reality, particularly since Alexander Lukashenko's election to the presidency in 1994, Belarus has looked almost exclusively to the east and toward Russia in particular. Russia is unambiguously declared the foremost priority of Belarusian foreign policy. Among all the states that have emerged on the territory of the former Soviet Union, Belarus has been the one most firmly and consistently oriented toward Russia. It has not sought to reduce its dependence on its larger eastern neighbor. On the contrary, from 1993 onward, the Belarusian leadership has actively pursued the expansion of existing economic links to Russia through a range of initiatives aimed at bilateral integration. At the same time, Belarus has been perhaps the most enthusiastic supporter of CIS-wide cooperation in all fields, participating in Russia-led groups, notably the Collective Security Treaty and the Eurasian Economic Community.

Outside the CIS, Belarus has expanded its ties with a number of states that have strained relations with the Western community, such as China, Libya, and Cuba. These countries represent promising export destinations for Belarusian manufacturers and the defense industry in particular.[2] Under Lukashenko, particularly since the international condemnation of the November 1996 referendum, relations with the United States, the European Union, and its member states have deteriorated to the point of being effectively frozen. Belarus stands out among East European states in not seeking accession to the European Union or NATO even in the longer term.

This chapter seeks to account for the peculiarity of the Belarusian external orientation. It examines the rationale underlying the Belarusian leadership's decision to focus on relations with CIS countries and Russia in particular. It outlines the development of the bilateral integration process with Russia and looks at its significance within Belarus—including on the economy and on public opinion. The prospects for a revision of the current reliance on Russia are also considered.

Belarus before Lukashenko

In the immediate period following the dissolution of the Soviet Union, Belarus pursued a course of neutrality and approximate equidistance from Russia, western Europe, and the United States. In May 1992, Belarus was not among the original signatories of the CIS Collective Security Treaty (the Tashkent treaty). In line with its commitment to a nonnuclear status, Belarus agreed to give up the nuclear weapons left on its territory by signing the Lisbon Protocol, promptly ratifying the START-I treaty and acceding to the Non-Proliferation Treaty as a nonnuclear state—with hardly any controversy.[3] Diplomatic efforts at establishing Belarus as a neutral central European country proved rather short-lived owing to a combination of changes in the international environment and in the country's political landscape. As Poland and other central European countries oriented themselves toward accession to the European Union and NATO, Belarusian decision makers felt that Belarus could not realistically hope to follow on its own the Swiss example of neutrality backed by prosperity.

Belarus was no exception in experiencing economic decline following the dismemberment of the Soviet Union. However, perhaps more than in any other country in the region, in Belarus the decline was seen as a direct result of the disruption of interrepublican trade and overall disintegration of the Soviet economic space. Despite the Belarusian economy's high level of development by Soviet standards, prospects for reform pursued independently from Russia and other CIS countries appeared bleak in the eyes of most members of the country's ruling elite. In Soviet times, Belarus had been labeled "the assembly shop of the Soviet Union," and had a developed manufacturing industry that depended almost entirely on other Soviet republics (particularly Russia) for fuel, raw materials, and components. Moreover, Belarusian industrial output far exceeded the consumption capacity of the domestic market. The choice facing Belarusian policy makers was between drastically restructuring the country's economy, which—given the limited resources available—appeared a daunting prospect with painful social consequences, and finding some means of preserving access to Russian and CIS supply chains and export markets. The structure of the Belarusian economy, and of its industrial sector in particular, thus seemed to dictate some form of integration with the CIS or at least with Russia.

Belarus introduced its own currency in May 1992 and left the ruble zone a month later. In April 1994, on the initiative of Belarusian Prime Minister Vyacheslav Kebich, Belarus concluded an agreement "On the Unification of Monetary Systems" with Russia. The agreement also envisaged the elimination of tariff barriers to bilateral trade and the harmonization of customs duties in trade with third countries. Although this agreement was not implemented, it represented the first official expression of the Belarusian leadership's pursuit of bilateral integration with Russia, which was to become the cornerstone of Belarusian foreign policy under the presidency of Alexander Lukashenko.

The economic rationale of integration with Russia was perceived as compelling owing to the absence of a motivation pointing to the opposite direction. During the Gorbachev period, the Belarusian ruling elite had shown barely any inclination to increase its autonomy from Moscow. In the referendum of March 1991, the Belarusian electorate expressed the highest level of loyalty to the Soviet Union among all participating Soviet republics.[4] After the emergence of Belarus as an independent state, the country's rulers saw little appeal in the prospect of attempting to distance Belarus from Russia. Neither the elite nor the population of Belarus shared the Baltic states' determination to "return to Europe" and escape the Russian sphere of influence.[5] With the exception of the Supreme Soviet Speaker, Stanislav Shushkevich, who signed the Belovezh agreements dissolving the Soviet Union on behalf of the Belorussian Soviet Socialist Republic, national-minded political forces remained marginal to the formulation of official policy. In spring 1993, the Belarusian Supreme Soviet overwhelmingly voted in favor of accession to the Tashkent treaty, despite the objections of Shushkevich, who argued that a referendum would have been required to override the commitment to neutrality written into the Belarusian Declaration of Sovereignty.[6]

From Community to Union-State: Integration with Russia under Lukashenko

Alexander Lukashenko has closely associated his political reputation with the cause of integration—both within the CIS and bilaterally with Russia. Although Belarusian efforts in this direction predate his coming to office, Lukashenko may credibly claim the credit for bringing them—at least partly—to fruition. In view of the enormous economic and—most importantly—political barriers that have blocked CIS-wide integration,[7] Belarus has embraced more limited initiatives involving Russia and other CIS countries willing to accept Russian leadership. Belarus was one of the founding members of the "Customs Union of the Four" (Belarus, Russia, Kazakhstan, and Kyrgyzstan), which was established in March 1996, and was later enlarged to include Tajikistan. In May 2001, the "Customs Union of the Five" (in fact a rather malfunctioning free trade area) was replaced by the "Eurasian Economic Community," which was given a more solid institutional basis.[8] In September 2003, Belarus, Russia, Kazakhstan, and Ukraine concluded an agreement to cooperate in the creation of a "single economic space" modeled on the EU single market, with freedom of movement for goods, labor, and capital, and a commitment to monetary union in the longer term.

Belarus has also remained in the Collective Security treaty following the withdrawal of Georgia, Uzbekistan, and Azerbaijan in 1999. Russia is by far the country's most important partner, particularly in economic terms, so most Belarusian diplomatic activity has been devoted to bilateral integration. Until recently, the Belarusian leadership considered the successful development of the bilateral integration process as the most promising path to CIS-wide integration, believing that other CIS countries will come to see concrete advantages in joining in.

Under Lukashenko, Belarus has become linked to Russia through a multitude of bilateral treaties and agreements covering practically all areas of interstate interaction. A Customs Union agreement signed in January 1995 gave rise to the most tangible aspects of economic integration so far, eliminating all quantitative and tariff barriers to bilateral trade and providing for the removal of customs controls on the common border and for the unification of customs and foreign trade legislation. The four-month time frame envisaged for the implementation of these objectives proved too ambitious. Although bilateral trade was liberalized and customs control points were triumphantly removed from the border in June 1995, they were to reappear on several occasions, as the two countries' customs regulations and trade policies with regard to third countries have remained far from uniform. Several high-profile disputes regarding the allegedly uneven benefits resulting from the imperfect customs union have marred the public image of the integration process, especially in Russia.[9] Still, experts have estimated that the implementation rate of relevant bilateral agreements has been significantly higher than that of the Eurasian Economic Community.[10] In spring 2001, most import and export tariffs were unified, with the exception of certain categories of goods covered by bilateral agreements between either of the two member states and third parties. The free trade regime has on the whole operated remarkably smoothly (with only one instance of resort to temporary restrictions in the wake of the August 1998 crisis), leading to an impressive upsurge in bilateral trade.

Following the conclusion of the "Treaty on the Formation of a Community" of April 1996, the process of bilateral integration acquired its own institutional structure modeled on the European Community.[11] The Community of Belarus and Russia was endowed with a Supreme Soviet with a rotating presidency, a Parliamentary Assembly, and an Executive Committee, which have differentiated it from other more informal, looser groupings within the CIS.[12] The treaty required the implementation of a single market characterized by the "four freedoms" (freedom of movement of goods, services, capital, and labor) and by the synchronization of economic reforms. It also envisaged the introduction of a single currency at a later stage. Areas of common policy formulation included the control of Community borders; the elaboration of common positions on defense and issues of international concern; and measures aimed at the development of the two countries' industrial and agricultural sectors.[13]

Exactly a year after its conclusion, the Community treaty was superseded by a treaty on the Union of Belarus and Russia. The original draft treaty, which included significant input from pro-integrationist forces in the Parliamentary Assembly, gave rise to very strong objections from the liberal wing of the Russian government and presidential administration. It was feared that the draft treaty committed Russia to a disproportionate share of the costs of economic integration without adequate checks on Belarus meeting its obligation to approximate to Russian legal norms and economic conditions, as provided in the Community treaty and the attached Program of Actions. Concerns also related to the ostensibly excessive strengthening of supranational institutions, which were perceived as paving the way to a new federal structure in which Belarus would have more influence over common decision making than its share of Union resources would warrant. As a result of a last-minute, highly publicized intervention by Boris Nemtsov, Anatolii Chubais, and other prominent liberal members of the Russian executive, the text of the treaty was sharply curtailed.[14] Perhaps the only noteworthy addition of substance to the content of the Community treaty was a provision referring to the primacy of Union legislation, requiring the amendment of contradictory national legislation (Article 19).[15] The Union Charter, which was later signed and attached as integral part of the Union treaty, extended the policy areas covered by the integrationist project to include military policy, the fight against terrorism and organized crime, and protection of the environment.[16]

December 1998 saw the conclusion of a treaty on the Equal Rights of Citizens in line with the concept of a Union citizenship contained in the Union Charter. According to the treaty, which was implemented quite rapidly (in less than two years), each of the two member states of the Union conferred rights of residence, employment, and access to public services (health care, education at all levels, payment of pensions and social security benefits) on the citizens of the other—on the same basis as these rights are available to its own citizens.[17]

A year later, a new, long debated, and much publicized treaty officially upgraded the Union to a "Union State."[18] The treaty established new institutions and reformed existing ones. It set up a Council of Ministers as "the executive body of the Union State," empowered to issue decrees and directives. This body took over many of the functions previously assigned to the Executive Committee, which the Union State treaty reformed under the name "Permanent Committee." The treaty created the office of the Union State secretary. Pavel Borodin, a former member of the Russian presidential administration, became the first secretary of the Union State. The Parliamentary Assembly, hitherto formed by delegates of the two countries' national legislatures, is to be replaced by a bicameral Union State parliament with a directly elected lower chamber.[19] The new parliament will have legislative powers (in place of the merely consultative functions of its predecessor) within the remit of Union State jurisdiction. The Union State treaty designates policy areas of exclusive Union State competence as well as areas of joint competence, where jurisdiction is to be shared between Union State and national authorities. In the former area, which includes measures toward a unified economic and legal space and military procurement, legislation passed by Union State institutions is immediately valid, while in the latter area, enabling national legislation will be required. Finally, the treaty provides for two new supranational institutions, a Court and an Accounts Chamber, which are to become operational following the elections to the lower house of the Union State Parliament. The Court's decisions are to be directly binding and cover all areas of Union State competence.

The Union treaty did not establish a common presidency or any other attribute of statehood, thereby dispelling speculation related to a possible merger of Belarus and Russia in a new federal entity. The treaty explicitly states that Belarus and the Russian Federation remain separate sovereign states with no prejudice to their respective constitutions and representation in international organizations. However, it also refers to a constitutional act to be adopted by the parliament of the Union State and submitted to national referendums for ratification, stating that national constitutions will subsequently be subject to amendment. Debates on these matters have been taking place in the Parliamentary Assembly, and a working group bringing together the two countries' executive branches has been considering several alternative drafts.[20] Elections to the lower house of a Union State parliament and the formation of a Union State Court and Accounts Chamber have however been persistently delayed because of disagreements on the proposed constitutional act and unresolved economic differences.

The Union State treaty strengthens previous terms of reference regarding military cooperation. It refers to a common border policy, the coordination of military policies, and the formation of a regional military force (Article 17), while the attached Program of Actions provides for a common military doctrine. The establishment of a regional army group was announced during President Putin's visit to Belarus in April 2000. The group, which may reach as many as 300,000 troops drawn from the Belarusian armed forces and the Moscow military district, is to remain under national command and will not to be permanently stationed in Belarus, as this would violate the country's obligations under the Conventional Forces in Europe treaty. It will, however, be deployed on the territory of Belarus in the event of an imminent external threat. Its operation is to be fully in compliance with the Belarusian constitution's prohibition on the deployment of Belarusian troops beyond the country's borders and on the presence of nuclear weapons on Belarusian territory.[21] This development builds on a very extensive foundation of military cooperation encompassing joint officer training; joint procurement; joint planning; common doctrine elaboration; intelligence sharing; a program of bilateral exercises; joint guarding of the Belarusian borders; joint air defense (within the framework of the CIS system); and joint use of military installations in border regions.[22]

Another important provision of the Union State treaty envisages the establishment of a single currency emission center (Article 22), which Belarus had strongly resisted, favoring a Union central bank with a coordinating role between two national emission centers. A follow-up agreement of November 2000 specified that the Russian ruble would replace the Belarusian currency in 2005 and that the two countries' gold and foreign currency reserves would be unified. A new single currency could be introduced at a later date (2008 was originally envisaged) with the establishment of a Union State central bank. Russia has provided financial assistance to support the Belarusian currency in preparation for monetary union.[23] Since the second quarter of 2001 the two national currencies have been locked into a fixed exchange rate. Belarus was supposed to introduce the Russian ruble as a nominal currency in parallel circulation with the Belarusian ruble in July 2003. However, the Belarusian leadership has refused to do so unless Russia agrees to a range of economic demands, including supplying gas, oil, and electricity to Belarus at Russian domestic prices and compensating Belarus for its loss of VAT revenue (Russia retains the VAT on goods exported to Belarus). In a further effort to delay the introduction of the Russian ruble, Minsk has also insisted that the signature of a Union State constitutional act should precede monetary union.[24] Belarus has also continued to insist that currency emission should be controlled by both countries and demanded $1.5 billion in compensation from Russia for alleged costs resulting from monetary union. After talks between the two countries' prime ministers failed to reach a compromise in February 2004, it seems that the earliest possible date for monetary union has been pushed back by a year to 2006.[25]

What Has Integration Meant for Belarus?

It has often been argued that integration has made relatively little progress on the ground as opposed to the ever more ambitious goals declared in the treaties, giving rise to the term "virtual integration." President Lukashenko has repeatedly expressed discontent with the Russian executive's obstruction of more far-reaching forms of integration (particularly when it comes to strengthening the role of supranational bodies with equal representation for the two countries) and with their alleged foot-dragging in releasing resources for the implementation of integration targets. Nevertheless, he has praised the integration process as beneficial to the Belarusian economy and to the population's welfare.[26] Trade with Russia and Belarusian exports in particular expanded impressively following the activation of the Customs Union agreement up to the onset of the Russian financial crisis in August 1998 (see table 7.1), and Belarus has surpassed Ukraine as Russia's second largest trading partner after the European Union.[27] President Lukashenko's activism in pursuing direct economic agreements with subjects of the Russian Federation has boosted Belarusian exports and secured supplies of fuel, raw materials, and industrial commodities, primarily by means of barter

Table 7.1. Belarusian Trade with Russia (millions of US dollars)

	Imports	Exports	Turnover	Balance
1994	3,103	2,094	5,197	–1,009
1995	2,965	2,185	5,150	–780
1996	3,522	3,024	6,546	–498
1997	4,673	4,780	9,453	+107
1998	4,670	4,608	9,278	–52
1999	3,767	3,222	6,987	–545
2000	5,605	3,710	9,315	–1,895
2001	5,348	3,960	9,160	–1,308
2002	6,842	4,054	10,896	–2,788
2003	7,559	4,899	12,458	–2,260

Source: Derived from *Rossiya v tsifrakh* (Moscow: Goskomstat, 2002), 367, and (for 2003) from http://www.president.gov.by/Minstat/en/indicators/ftrade.htm.

transactions.[28] This has been particularly the case of agreements with certain Russian regions, with whose governors the Belarusian president has established close political connections.[29] Since Putin's election to the presidency and his drive to strengthen the federal authorities' control over the regions, however, Lukashenko's tactics of bypassing Moscow has suffered from Russian governors' reluctance to antagonize their head of state.

In addition, Russian and Belarusian economists have estimated Russian direct and indirect subsidies in the region of $1–2 billion annually.[30] Subsidies to the Belarusian economy have included the cancellation of debts (primarily at the outset of the integration process, with $1.5 billion of debt being pardoned in February 1996);[31] low-interest credits for the purchase of Russian products; favorable barter deals; added customs revenue from foreign trade diversion due to the uneven customs legislation; and support for the Belarusian currency, which began to be disbursed in 2001. However, reduced prices (below world market prices) charged to Belarus for gas imports have represented by far the most significant form of subsidy. According to the estimates of the Belarusian authorities, the cost of Russian energy imports dropped by over 40 percent since the beginning of the integration process.[32] According to an agreement reached in April 2002, Belarusian imports of Russian gas and electricity would be charged at the same prices as those paid by neighboring Russian regions, which had been a long-standing objective of the Belarusian authorities. Belarus has covered a significant part of the cost of gas imports with barter payments.[33] The relevant contracts are brokered by direct government involvement on both sides, but they could not be said to serve entirely political purposes at the expense of economic considerations. Russian gas exporters have for some time treated these arrangements less as a necessity (as Belarus would not have been able to pay for higher prices in hard currency in any case, unless it began charging higher transit fees[34]) and more as a form of investment. Until recently, Belarus proved less of a headache to Russian gas exporters than the alternative transit country, Ukraine, where the intertwined problems of nonpayment and illicit gas siphoning have been chronic features of bilateral relations. Belarusian political loyalty, manifested in its commitment to the integration process and cemented by substantial material rewards from Russia, has given the Belarusian route the advantage of longer-term reliability (stable and low transit fees; security of deliveries to hard currency–paying customers), which is essential for large-scale investments in infrastructure.

As a result, Belarus emerged as the transit country of choice for Russian energy exports. Gazprom, Russia's giant gas company, invested over $1 billion in the construction of the Yamal pipeline, which has been bringing Russian gas to central Europe since 1999. Gazprom, in cooperation with western European energy companies, intends to proceed with "Yamal-2," a second pipeline to cross Belarusian territory. The unification of Russian and Belarusian energy systems is identified as a priority sector in the integration treaties. The Program of Actions accompanying the Union State treaty requires that the Belarusian gas transport infrastructure come under Gazprom ownership.[35] However, the Belarusian authorities have resisted the implementation of this clause. The agreement of April 2002 (which provided for Gazprom supplies to Belarus at Russian domestic rates) envisaged the creation of a joint company to manage the Belarusian gas pipeline system by July 2003. Even though President Lukashenko issued a decree for the capitalization of "Beltransgaz" (the Belarusian state-owned company controlling the gas pipelines) in January 2003, Russia (to be more precise, Gazprom) and Belarus have not reached agreement on the ownership of the Gazprom–Beltransgaz joint company.[36] Moreover, as Gazprom became increasingly reluctant to expand gas supplies to Belarus at subsidized prices, instances of pilfering from the export pipeline began to be noted (around 15 billion cubic meters in 2002). These difficulties, in conjunction with a marked improvement in Russian (and Gazprom) relations with Ukraine from the end of 2001 (gas transit agreement of December 2001; establishment of gas pipeline consortium in January 2003), threaten to erode the significance of the Belarusian gas export route. After the failure of negotiations on the sale of a controlling stake in Beltransgaz to Gazprom, in February 2004 Gazprom discontinued gas supplies to Belarus. President Lukashenko responded very emotively, describing the disruption of gas supplies as "an act of terrorism." He also complained that Russia used the Belarusian air defense, road, and rail transport systems "for a pittance" and instructed his government to prepare financial claims "for military services" of $21–25 million per year.[37] Beltransgaz, which imports Russian gas for consumption in Belarus, promptly concluded short-term import contracts with two gas trading companies (including the Gazprom subsidiary Sibur) for a price of $46 per 1,000 cubic meters. Gazprom insists that it will resume supplies only at a price of $50, which is the same price currently paid by Ukraine, unless Belarus agrees to sell a majority stake in Beltransgaz.[38]

Experts argue that Belarus could recover the cost of higher gas prices by raising its gas transit tariffs to levels similar to those charged by Ukraine. Still, higher gas prices raise the cost of electricity generation in Belarus, thereby eroding the competitiveness of Belarusian electricity exports to Poland. Belarus, meanwhile, remains by far the most important route for Russian oil exports. Since the liberalization of the Russian domestic oil market, Belarus itself has paid market rates for Russian oil, while continuing to charge low (compared to European levels) oil transit fees.[39]

Market-minded critics of Lukashenko have argued that he has used Russian subsidies to finance ultimately unsustainable economic and social policies. The common program of the united opposition in the presidential election of September 2001 included the continuation of integration with Russia in conjunction with economic reform at home.[40] For the most part, Russian economic support has functioned as a disincentive for reform, insofar as it has assisted the stability and growth of the largely unreformed Belarusian economy. Despite the warnings of Russian economic liberals, Russia's preferential treatment of Belarus long continued irrespective of the Belarusian authorities' reluctance to implement many of the reforms required to bring the country's legal and economic system into line with Russian norms. In addition, the use of political and administrative means of promoting Belarusian exports to Russia has reduced incentives for industrial restructuring and improving the international competitiveness of Belarusian exports.

The Lukashenko administration has claimed credit for positive economic indicators, most notably rates of economic growth, and for the country's ranking in the UN Human Development Index, ahead of other CIS countries.[41] The so-called "Belarusian model" has aimed to preserve what tend still to be perceived as the positive elements of the Soviet system: almost full employment; low prices for consumer and industrial staples; state control over large and strategic enterprises; free health care and education; and a low but state-guaranteed standard of living. Indeed, survey evidence indicates that the Belarusian population considers President Lukashenko's social and economic policies (alongside the defense of Belarusian national interests) as the most successful aspects of his record in office.[42] The "Belarusian model" has been sustained through strong state intervention in the economy, which has included subsidies to unprofitable enterprises, administrative price controls, and—until recently—inflationary currency emission. The economic course of the Belarusian administration could be summarized as avoidance of market reform, intended to minimize the social disruption experienced by countries undergoing transition to a market economy.

The integration treaties, on the other hand, require Belarus to approximate to Russian economic legislation and indicators. Belarus was to have proceeded with the privatization of land, light industry, construction, and agricultural enterprises by the end of 1997.[43] According to the Union State treaty, it is to adopt Russian standards of financial regulation. Despite repeated demands from the Russian authorities, the Belarusian government took hardly any steps to emulate Russian economic reforms—at least until 2000. Instead, President Lukashenko argued that Russia could learn from the Belarusian example, a view heeded by leftist political forces in Russia, which gained influence over government policy under the Primakov government. The Putin administration's firm reiteration of Russia's commitment to the establishment of a functioning market economy made clear that economic convergence was not to occur on the basis of the Belarusian model. Nevertheless, the Belarusian administration remains unconvinced that the Russia's far more liberal economic system, with its adverse consequences for more vulnerable sections of the population and other accompanying phenomena such as organized crime, represents a model for Belarus to emulate.[44]

Anxious to ensure Russia's continued adherence to the objective of monetary union, Belarus found itself compelled to tighten its monetary policy, which led to the elimination of the perverse phenomenon of multiple exchange rates in 2000. The privatization of large enterprises, which has been keenly awaited by influential Russian business groups, was postponed until after the election of September 2001, as were most other economic reforms. Major privatization deals with Russian enterprises (for instance, of the brewer Baltika) have fallen through as a result of the Belarusian authorities' insistence on stringent conditions, which would require the investor to maintain employment levels and social benefits for the workforce in order to gain majority control following a probationary period of up to five years. Although the Belarusian government has formulated a program of economic reform to meet the expectations of Russia and at the same time of international financial institutions,[45] it has continued to resist those measures that most fundamentally challenge the Belarusian model. For example, the Belarusian government has refused to follow Russia's example in applying a flat income tax rate and has confirmed that there will be no unified income tax rate in a Union State.[46]

Russia in the Eyes of the Belarusian Public

Belarusian public opinion has held predominantly positive views of Russia and the integration process, and perceived Russia's influence on Belarus as broadly beneficial.[47] The Belarusian public has tended to associate the advancement of integration with expectations of improved economic prospects and standards of living. When asked what would be the best path to the country's economic recovery, "strengthening ties to Russia" tends to be the most credible option in the

Table 7.2. Voting in a Hypothetical Referendum on the Adoption of the Constitution of a Union State of Belarus and Russia

	2001	2002	2003
I shall vote in favor	44	46	50
I shall vote against	20	20	23
I shall not take part	18	14	10

Source: Derived from *Novosti NISEPI*, no. 3(29), September 2003; the figures refer respectively to October 2001, December 2002, and September 2003.

eyes of the Belarusian population.[48] Not surprisingly, the cause of integration has been popular with the Belarusian mass public. In a poll commissioned by the US State Department, two-thirds of respondents were in favor of the Union with Russia (19 percent were opposed).[49] A survey conducted by the Minsk-based institute "Novak" in May–June 2001 showed that 63 percent of the Belarusian public thought that the integration process should be accelerated (see table 7.2).[50]

Positive perceptions of Russia and the integration process have also been related to a sense of common identity uniting Russians and Belarusians, which appears to be widespread among the Belarusian population. According to a survey by the Moscow-based Center for Sociological Research, 77 percent of Belarusian respondents supported integration on the grounds that "Russians and Belarusians are historically one people, they are spiritually close, and have similar languages, cultures, and traditions."[51] The Novak poll of March 2000 suggested that only 50 percent of the public regarded Belarusians as "a separate independent nation," with 43 percent endorsing the statement that "Belarusians are one of the branches of the triune Russian nation" (ostensibly consisting of Russians, Belarusians, and Ukrainians). A "human dimension" of dense intersocietal links seems to add to the perception that relations with Russia are of a special nature. Survey evidence shows that as many as 61 percent of Belarusians have at least one close relative living in Russia and that as few as 9 percent would wish to see relations with Russia on the same basis as with other foreign countries, involving border, customs, and visa controls.[52]

Lukashenko has understandably had some success in appealing to the Belarusian electorate's strong sense of affinity toward Russia and nostalgia for the Soviet Union.[53] In May 1995, he called a referendum on the restoration of Soviet symbols; on the establishment of Russian as an official state language; and on the question of economic integration with Russia (see chapter 4). These rather low-cost policies found resonance among the electorate's notion of identity, gathering the support of over three-quarters of Belarusian voters.[54] The Belarusian president has become known for his positive references to the Soviet state and his public statements of solidarity with Russia and calls for Slavic–Orthodox unity. His emphasis on the military aspect of integration with Russia as essential to both countries' defense from an ostensibly aggressive West reached its peak during the controversy over NATO enlargement and during the Alliance's Kosovo campaign. In the eyes of the Belarusian population, Russia appears as the most reliable guarantor of Belarusian national security, and a common defense with Russia is the most popular of the various strategies for advancing national security.[55]

Most Belarusians do not seem prepared to see integration lead to the loss of their country's statehood, overwhelmingly rejecting the possibility of Belarus being simply incorporated into the Russian Federation.[56] Among possible integration options, Belarusians strongly favor a union of independent states (of a confederative type, along the lines of the EU) as opposed to a federal "Union State," which is more popular among the Russian public.[57] When offered a choice concerning the type of relations they would prefer with Russia, the option of good-neighborly relations between two separate states has increased in appeal to become the choice of the majority. At the same time, a majority equally express the intention of casting a "yes" vote in the event of a referendum on the "unification of Belarus and Russia in a *single* state" [emphasis added], which suggests that Belarusian electoral preferences are still in flux.[58] As the Belarusian political analyst Valerii Karbalevich argues, many citizens of Belarus, like the president himself, do not see sovereignty as an absolute value. He argues that they seem to have an understanding of the notion of sovereignty that is quite different from the meaning attached to it in the West, measuring sovereignty using indicators such as economic welfare (table 7.3).[59] The withdrawal of Russian economic support in the form of subsidized gas exports in early 2004 appears to have eroded Belarusian people's support for economic integration with Russia. A poll conducted in March 2004 found that only 33 percent supported the introduction of the Russian ruble as the single currency of Russia and Belarus, a drop of 11 percentage points compared to September 2003; 43 percent also

Table 7.3. Preferred Form of Integration of Belarus and Russia (percentages)

	2002	2003	2004
Belarus and Russia should form a union of independent states with close political and economic relations	52	56	50
Belarus and Russia should have the same relations with each other as with other CIS members	20	21	19
Belarus and Russia should become a single state with a single president, government, army, flag, and currency	21	19	14

Source: Derived from *Novosti NISEPI*, no. 3(29), September 2003; figures are for December 2002, September 2003, and March 2004.

agreed with President Lukashenko's description of the disruption of Russian gas supplies as "an act of terrorism."[60] This suggests that Lukashenko was quite successful in convincing the Belarusian public that the economic disputes that led to Russia ending subsidized gas supplies to Belarus were solely the fault of Russia.

Whither Integration?

The integration process has reached a stage at which its further advancement requires bold steps from the Belarusian leadership. Long-delayed economic reforms, including privatization of major enterprises, have been announced, not least in order to meet the expectations of the Russian leadership, but no large-scale privatization has yet occurred.[61] The Putin administration has affirmed its commitment to the integration process, but at the same time strengthened the conditions attached to the continuation of support for the Belarusian economy.[62] The end of gas supplies at Russian domestic prices (in response to Belarusian intransigence regarding the sale of Beltransgaz), may still prove a powerful lever of Russian pressure on Belarus to do away with the state's exclusive control over the strategic asset of gas pipelines. Overall, however, Russian conditionality has been limited to a few policy areas (privatization and monetary policy), which appears insufficient to push the Belarusian administration to strive toward Russian norms at the expense of government control over the economy.

Internationally isolated, the Belarusian authorities find themselves in a rather weak negotiating position *vis-à-vis* Russia. In August 2002, President Putin caused a stir by calling on Lukashenko (in very undiplomatic, almost offensive language) to make a clear choice between two available integration options, either on the EU model or the incorporation of Belarus into the Russian Federation. The Belarusian president indignantly rejected such a choice.[63] The absorption of Belarus into the Russian Federation is unacceptable both to the Belarusian ruling elite and to the population, as is well known to Russian policy makers. Putin's "blackmail" highlighted the EU model of economic integration based on market principles as the only viable path. Having proposed integration according to the EU model himself on earlier occasions, Lukashenko has been loath to accept the loss of state control over the economy that such a path entails. Instead, he has insisted on continuing on the basis of existing agreements, accusing Russia of backtracking on them. Putin subsequently agreed to negotiate on such a basis, but has stressed that Russia's economic interests cannot be compromised.[64]

Belarus depends on Russia, not only economically, but also for diplomatic support. Belarusian dependence on its larger neighbor has been very much reinforced by the international response to the Lukashenko administration's authoritarian behavior toward the press and the opposition. Unlike the United States and the member states of the European Union, Russia fully recognizes the legitimacy of the Belarusian president and parliament, having acknowledged both the October 2000 parliamentary elections and the September 2001 presidential election as "free and fair." Russian diplomats also defend Belarus in international forums, arguing that the EU and the Council of Europe have been applying double standards in simultaneously isolating Belarus and seeking to obtain the country's return to full participation in international affairs.

Belarus, therefore, needs Russia as a "window to Europe," given that Russia has been far more successful in developing political and economic ties with the prosperous European Union. It is not coincidental that Vladimir Goncharik, Lukashenko's main challenger in the September 2001 election, declared the establishment of a balanced foreign policy and cooperative relations with the West as the foremost priority of his program.[65] Along with the aim of restoring good relations with the West, the United Civic Party, one of the main Belarusian opposition parties and a member of the opposition coalition "Five plus," has put forward an alternative strategy of integration with Russia based on the synchronization of economic reforms. This corresponds to the position of the Putin administration and erodes one of the bases of President Lukashenko's support as the "sole guarantor of Belarusian–Russian friendship." The movement "Republic," led by the rebel member of parliament Valery Frolov, also supports integration with Russia. Other opposition forces such as the coalition "Free Belarus" and the politician Andrei Klimov, one of the first opposition leaders to announce his intention to run in the presidential elections of 2006, advocate a course oriented toward accession to the European Union.

Irrespective of the currently unclear prospects for a change of leadership in Belarus, departing from international isolation and embarking on market-oriented economic reform will be essential to develop relations with Russia on a more equal and pragmatic basis.

Notes

1. Research for this chapter was conducted with the support of the UK Economic and Social Research Council under awards R000429834663 and T026271003.

2. The Belarusian Minister of Defense and President Lukashenko have both strongly denied allegations made by the *Washington Post*, 3 January 2002, A17, and US Senator Campbell concerning Belarusian arms exports to Iraq and Sudan, which the US suspects of sponsoring international terrorism. They have stressed that all Belarusian arms exports are carried out "in strict compliance with all international norms and agreements." Statements by Defense Minister Mal'tsev in *Nezavisimaya gazeta*, 21 February 2002, 5, and by Alexander Lukashenko on Belarusian State Television, 19 February 2002.

3. The Belarusian declaration of sovereignty of July 1990 affirms that Belarus is to be a neutral, nonnuclear state. In signing the Lisbon Protocol of May 1992, the Russian Federation, Ukraine, Belarus, and Kazakhstan (Soviet successor states with nuclear

weapons) became parties to the START-I treaty. Belarus ratified START-I in February 1993 and signed the Non-Proliferation Treaty in July of that year. The issue of handing all nuclear weapons to Russia (in accordance with the Lisbon Protocol) was a lot more controversial in Ukraine, which ratified START-I in February 1994 (the Ukrainian Parliament had rejected it in November 1993) and acceded to the NPT in December 1994.

4. 82.7 percent of votes in Belarus were in favor of preserving the Soviet Union. In Russia and in Ukraine, the rates were 71.3 and 70.2 percent, respectively; Georgia and the Baltic republics did not participate in the referendum; *Izvestiya*, 27 March 1991, 1, 3.

5. Author's interview with Yuri Khodyko, one of the leaders of the Belarusian Popular Front, Minsk, November 1999.

6. Irina Pimonenko, "Belorussko-rossiiskie voennye otnosheniya: ot neitraliteta do kollektivnoi bezopasnosti," *Belorusskii zhurnal mezhdunarodnogo prava i mezhdunarodnykh otnoshenii*, no. 3, 2001: 68.

7. The vast majority of agreements concluded at CIS summits were not signed by all member states and very few of them were actually implemented, with Georgia, Ukraine, and Turkmenistan having the highest rates of abstention; Richard Sakwa and Mark Webber, "The Commonwealth of Independent States, 1991–1998: Stagnation and Survival," *Europe–Asia Studies* 51, no. 3 (May 1999): 396.

8. The Eurasian Economic Community has the following institutions: the Interstate Council, which consists of heads of state and government and meets once or twice a year; the Integration Committee, a standing secretariat based in Moscow; and a Parliamentary Assembly made up of deputies appointed by national parliaments. Weighed voting applies in decision-making procedures, with Russia having 40 percent of the votes, Belarus and Kazakhstan 20 percent each, and Kyrgyzstan and Tajikistan 10 percent each.

9. The most serious disputes related to the export of third-country goods to the Russian market using false Belarusian documentation; to Belarusian customs' authorities retention of levies on goods destined for the Russian market; the influx of smuggled third-country goods through the porous Belarus–Ukraine border into the Russian market; and the illegal reexport of Belarusian goods through Russia.

10. Anatolii Sirotsky, "Tamozhennyi soyuz: plany i realii," *Belorusskii zhurnal mezhdunarodnogo prava i mezhdunarodnykh otnoshenii*, no. 1, 2000: 68–70.

11. Treaty on the Formation of a Community of Russia and Belarus, *Diplomaticheskii vestnik*, May 1996: 39–41.

12. The most noteworthy of these are GUUAM (Georgia, Ukraine, Uzbekistan, Azerbaijan, and Moldova), originally formed in October 1997 as GUAM (Uzbekistan joined later), and the Eurasian Economic Community (Russia, Belarus, Kazakhstan, Kyrgyzstan, and Tajikistan).

13. Treaty on the Formation of a Community (note 11).

14. For details of the liberals' intervention see *Kommersant-Daily*, 1 April 1997, 1. The intervention also led to the dismissal of deputy premier Serov and presidential aide Ryurikov, who had been responsible for negotiating the treaty on Russia's behalf.

15. Treaty on the Union of Belarus and Russia, *Diplomaticheskii vestnik*, April 1997: 41–43.

16. Charter of the Union of Russia and Belarus, *Byulleten' mezhdunarodnykh dogovorov*, September 1997: 68–79.

17. Treaty on Equal Rights of Citizens, *Diplomaticheskii vestnik*, January 1999: 45–46.

18. Treaty on the Formation of a Union State, *Byulleten' mezhdunarodnykh dogovorov*, March 2000: 54–73.

19. The upper house or Chamber of the Union is to consist of an equal number of deputies appointed by the national parliaments of the two member states, as was the case in the Parliamentary Assembly. The Chamber of Representatives is to be composed of seventy-five deputies from Russia and twenty-eight from Belarus, elected by universal suffrage for a four-year term (Article 39). The first elections to the Chamber of Representatives were scheduled for late 2002.

20. *Soyuz Belarus–Rossiya* (weekly publication of the Union State Council of Ministers), 21 February 2002, 1–2.

21. *Nezavisimaya gazeta*, 18 April 2000, 1.

22. In January 1995, Russia acquired the right to use the Baranovichi missile early warning station (where the central CIS air defense administration is located) and the Vileika radio control facility in Belarus free of charge for a minimum of twenty-five years. The agreement of October 1998 "On the Joint Use of Military Infrastructure Objects" covers all types of military installations in both countries' border regions, whose modernization is to be jointly financed.

23. Agreement "On the introduction of a single currency and on the formation of a single emission center of the union-state," *Byulleten' mezhdunarodnykh dogovorov*, October 2001: 60–63.

24. *Nezavisimaya gazeta*, 8 September 2003, 3. For more on the monetary aspects of integration, see Maksim Tumilovich, "Monetary Integration of Belarus and Russia," in *Belarus–Russia Integration: Analytical Articles*, ed. Valer Bulhakaw (Minsk: Minsk Analytical Group, 2003), 95–134; for political aspects of the process, see Vital Silitsky, "The Political Economy of Russian–Belarusian Integration," in *Belarus–Russia Integration*, 221–90; institutional questions are addressed in Iryna Yekadumava, "Structure of the Governing Bodies of the Belarusian–Russian Union State," in *Belarus–Russia Integration*, 333–51; wider issues are discussed in Alyaksandr Tsikhamirau, "Russia in the Foreign Policy of Belarus," in *Belarus–Russia Integration*, 361–81.

25. *Kommersant*, 10 February 2004, 1.

26. Alexander Lukashenko, *Belarus and the CIS: A Path towards a Common Vision* (Geneva: East European Development Association, 1998), 6.

27. In 2000, Russia's trade with Belarus stood at $9.3 billion, compared with $8.6 billion of trade with Ukraine; Economist Intelligence Unit, *Country Report: Russia*, March 2001, 37.

28. Belarus has concluded such agreements with more than two-thirds of Russian federal units: Parliamentary Assembly of the Union of Belarus and Russia, *Informatsionnyi byulleten'*, January–March 1999: 9.

29. Ten Russian regions have accounted for 73 percent of total trade between the two countries (Moscow, Moscow oblast', St. Petersburg, Ingushetia, and the Tyumen', Smolensk, Yaroslavl', Nizhnii Novogorod, Kaliningrad, and Rostov oblasts); document provided by the Belarusian Foreign Ministry (2000). See also Iryna Yekadumava, "The Russian Regional Policy of Alyaksandr Lukashenka," in *Belarus–Russia Integration*, 320–32.

30. Leonid Zlotnikov, "Vyzhivaniye ili integratsiya?," *Pro et Contra* 3, no. 2 (Spring 1998): 85; Valerii Karbalevich, "Vneshnyaya politika Belarusi: popytki samoopredeleniya," in *Natsional'naya i regional'naya bezopasnost'*, ed. V. Karbalevich and

L. Zaiko (Minsk: Analiticheskii tsentr "Strategiya," 2001), 176.

31. This was in return for Belarusian agreement to the "zero option" for the division of Soviet assets and liabilities, which included renunciation of compensation for the removal of nuclear weapons previously stationed on Belarusian territory; Agreement "On the Resolution of Financial Claims," *Byulleten' mezhdunarodnykh dogovorov*, October 1996: 48–49.

32. Author's interview with Belarusian Foreign Ministry official, Minsk, November 1999. In 1997, the price of 1,000 cubic meters of gas for Belarus was $49, compared with a world market price of about $80; by 2000, the price had dropped to $26: *Nezavisimaya gazeta*, 28 January 2000, 4.

33. In 1999, Belarus paid only 8 percent of its debt to Gazprom in cash; *Interfax-ANI*, 10 April 2000. In 2000, Belarus paid $160 million in cash, with the remainder of the $250 million debt to be covered by barter arrangements and Beltransgaz bonds; EBRD, *Transition Report*, November 2001: 119.

34. Belarus charges a fee of $0.55 for the transit of 1,000 cubic meters of gas per 100 kilometers, compared with Ukraine's $1.09; in turn, Gazprom charges Belarus $30 for the supply of 1,000 cubic meters of gas, compared with a price of $50 for Ukraine; to supplement Gazprom supplies, Belarus also imports gas from the alleged Gazprom subsidiary "Itera" for a price of $46; *Kommersant*, 17 September 2003, 1.

35. This was to have occurred by the end of 2001, but was delayed, particularly as the Belarusian leadership was keen to avoid any privatizations before the September presidential elections.

36. Gazprom insists on a controlling stake and a price of no more than $900 million for "Beltransgaz," whereas Belarus demands at least $2.5 billion for a 49 percent stake: *Kommersant*, 17 September 2003, 1. For more on Belarusian dependency on Russian energy, see Natalya Tahanovich, "The Belarusian Fuel and Energy Industry and Its Dependence on Russian Energy Resources," in *Belarus–Russia Integration*, 135–58.

37. *Russian Financial Control Monitor*, 22 March 2004.

38. *Kommersant*, 23 January 2004, 1 and 14, and 19 February 2004, 1.

39. *Belorusskie novosti*, 28 April 2004.

40. *Nasha svaboda*, 4 May 2001, 1–3; *Den'* (Minsk), 5 May 2001, 1.

41. The index includes a range of indicators such as life expectancy and levels of enrollment at all levels of education; in 2001, Belarus was in fifty-third place, with Russia in fifty-fifth and Ukraine in seventy-fourth; United Nations Development Program, *Human Development Report 2001* (New York: Oxford University Press, 2001), 142.

42. US State Department Office of Research, *Opinion Analysis*, M-175-00, 11 October 2000. The survey, which was commissioned by the US government, was conducted in July 2000 by the Belarusian firm "Social and Ecological Surveys," using a nationwide sample of 1,081. Majorities of between 63 and 73 percent credited the president with ensuring adequate food supplies, paying wages and pensions on time, and providing for education and defense.

43. "Program of Synchronization and Coordination of Economic Reforms," *Diplomaticheskii vestnik*, May 1997: 36–38.

44. Author's interviews with Belarusian officials, Minsk, April 2002.

45. A staff-monitored program was agreed to with the IMF in April 2001. On the role of the requirements of the Union State treaty in promoting economic reforms in Bela-

rus, see European Bank for Reconstruction and Development, *Transition Report* (London: EBRD, 2001), 118.

46. Statement by Belarusian Finance Minister Nikolai Korbut, *Nezavisimaya gazeta*, 4 December 2001, 5.

47. A national survey conducted by the Novak Institute in early 2000 indicated that 57 percent of the public believed that Russia exercised a lot of influence over the president and government of Belarus, while 66 percent thought so with regard to the country's economy; 42 percent described Russia's influence on the Belarusian president and government as positive, 33 percent as neutral, and 9 percent as harmful; the figures concerning Russia's influence on the Belarusian economy were 50, 23 and 12 percent, respectively: Novak, *Belarus and the World* (Minsk, March 2000). For an overview see O. G. Bukhovets, *Soyuz RB–RF: elity i massovoe soznanie Belarusi o nastoyashchem i budushchem integratsii s Rossiei* (Moscow: Institute Evropy, 2003).

48. In the above survey, 68 percent of respondents expected that "unification would enable a significant improvement in the economic performance of both countries, reduced unemployment, and higher standards of living." According to another survey conducted by Novak in late 1999, "strengthening economic ties to Russia" was the most popular choice (25 percent of respondents) for the best strategy for Belarus to overcome the economic crisis ("Market reforms" and "ties with western Europe" each gathered 21 percent of responses); Novak, *Public Opinion Monitoring: Republic of Belarus* (Minsk, December 1999).

49. US State Department Office of Research, *Opinion Analysis*, M-175-00, 11 October 2000, 2.

50. Novak, *Public Opinion Monitoring*, May–June 2001; the survey (May 30– June 10, 2001) used a sample of 2,133.

51. Unpublished survey, carried out in April–May 1999 in both Russia and Belarus. The survey was conducted by the Moscow-based Center for Sociological Research (Foundation for National and International Security) and had a Belarusian sample of 837.

52. This survey, based on a national sample of 1390, was organized within the framework of the project *The Outsiders: Russia, Ukraine, Belarus, Moldova, and the New Europe* by Stephen White, John Löwenhardt, and Margot Light within the ESRC "One Europe or Several?" research program. The results are published in Stephen White and Richard Rose, *Nationality and Public Opinion in Belarus and Ukraine*, Studies in Public Policy No. 346 (Glasgow: Centre for the Study of Public Policy, University of Strathclyde, 2001), 18, 45.

53. As already noted, 82.7 percent of Belarusian voters were in favor of the preservation of the Soviet Union, which was the highest percentage among all the participating republics.

54. Of these voters, 76 percent voted for the restoration of Soviet symbols, 83 percent for granting official status to the Russian language, and 82 percent for economic integration with Russia.

55. A common defense with Russia was supported by 46 percent of respondents and 37 percent favored neutral status; only 8 percent were in favor of joining NATO; Novak, *Public Opinion Monitoring*, December 1999. In a later survey, 38 percent of respondents favored an alliance with CIS countries, with 12 percent endorsing NATO membership; White and Rose, *Nationality and Public Opinion in Belarus and Ukraine*, 18; see also Yan Mikalayew, "Military Cooperation Between Belarus and Russia," in

Belarus–Russia Integration, 408–19.

56. A mere 5 percent of respondents endorsed this suggestion; Novak, *Public Opinion Monitoring*, December 1999, and *Belarus and the World*.

57. Survey commissioned by the Secretariat of the Russia–Belarus Union State and conducted in February 2003 in Belarus and Russia. The Belarusian part was conducted by the Independent Institute for Socio-Economic and Political Studies (NISEPI); it indicated 53 percent support for a union of independent states and 33 percent support for a Union State. The Russian part of the survey was carried out by "Romir"; it showed 58 percent support for a Union State, against 28 percent who favored a Union State; results published in *Izvestiya*, 18 March 2003, 3

58. In the May–June 2001 Novak survey, 61.5 percent of respondents said they would vote in favor of the Union State, while 20 percent would vote against it.

59. Karbalevich, "Vneshnyaya politika Belarusi," 167–68. Karbalevich quotes from an interview given by President Lukashenko to a Polish journalist (and published in *Sovetskaya Belorussiya*, 4 July 1997), in which he argued that Belarus had more sovereignty within the Soviet Union on the grounds that guarantees of the population's welfare were stronger in Soviet times.

60. NISEPI survey of March 2004.

61. The Belarusian government drew up a list of 137 major enterprises to be privatized, which included the state-owned oil concern Belneftkhim and Gorizont, the television manufacturing company; *Belapan News Agency* through *BBC Monitoring*, 18 January 2002.

62. Belarus was the only state mentioned by name in President Putin's annual address to the Duma in April 2001; *Diplomaticheskii vestnik*, May 2001: 10.

63. *Belapan News Agency*, 14 August 2002, via *BBC Monitoring*, www. bbcmonitoring.com.

64. *Profil'*, 19 August 2002, 8–9.

65. At the same time, he referred to the Union with Russia as the most effective guarantee of Belarusian security; interview published in *The Viewer*, Weekly Analytical Bulletin, Belapan News Agency, No. 32, 8–14 August 2001, 6.

8 Belarus and the West

John Löwenhardt

Belarusian relations with the West are highly problematic, and have been so ever since 1994 when Alexander Lukashenko came to power. In this, the country contrasts sharply with its five neighbors, including Russia, which have normalized their relations with west European and transatlantic institutions. This isolation is symbolized on the map of member states of the Council of Europe (CoE), where the outline of Belarus is an embarrassingly gaping hole.[1] Whereas both Russia and Ukraine, in spite of repeated setbacks, have succeeded in satisfying the membership criteria of the Council of Europe, Belarus at the start of the twenty-first century is often characterized as Europe's last surviving dictatorship. The regime's lack of commitment to democratic procedures is the most basic reason for the country's isolated status.

This state of affairs dictates the structure of this chapter. In looking at Belarus and the West, domestic determinants of foreign policy are less relevant than in countries where basic democratic procedures are respected. Many movements and parties in the opposition demand both Western democratic standards and a foreign policy in which good relations with Russia are balanced by intensified cooperation with European and transatlantic institutions. But the opposition is suppressed, and this in itself is one of the main stumbling blocks for improved relations with the West. Foreign policy making is the prerogative of the president and his administration, and it has been exceptionally confrontational *vis-à-vis* the West. Before looking at the marginalized Belarusian society and its elite, therefore, the policies of the recent years will first be set out.

The second and third sections of the chapter will be devoted to popular and elite views and expectations. At the moment, these may not impinge strongly on foreign policy, but in the long term they are the basis for more normal, post-Lukashenko relations with the West. The result of this investigation should then provide us with the beginning of an answer to the question whether Belarusian society provides a solid basis for the normalization of relations with the rest of Europe. These sections are based on three different types of sources, most of them collected in the course of a research project on the impact of EU and NATO enlargement on east European countries.[2] In addition to twenty-three elite interviews conducted in June 2000, these are a national survey and three focus groups. The survey was conducted by the Novak Sociological Labora-tory in April 2000, and the sample of 1,090 respondents was representative of the population aged eighteen and over. The first two of the group discussions, organized by Novak as well, took place in Minsk on June 3, 2000, one consisting of eight citizens aged forty to sixty years, the other of eight members of the military forces, in rank between lieutenant and major. A third focus group was organized by the All-Russian Center for the Study of Public Opinion the next day in Grodno, near the borders with Lithuania and Poland. This group had participants between 20 and 40 years old. All unattributed quotes in this chapter are taken from the transcripts of the focus groups in Minsk and Grodno.[3]

Belarus and the West

After independence, Belarus declared itself a neutral state and gave up its nuclear weapons. Its foreign policy would be based on the principle of "multi-vectoredness," an orientation in all main directions of the compass. The country's integration with European institutions was making steady progress until Alexander Lukashenko put a spoke in the wheel. Since the fateful presidential election of 1994, Belarus has come to stand more and more apart from its neighbors in terms of the normalization of relations with the EU and other European institutions. The new president "ran the country like his former state farm" and within two years political parties accused him of trying to establish a dictatorship.[4] The Partnership and Cooperation Agreement with the EU (PCA) was signed in March 1995, and an Interim Agreement (IA) one year later. But Lukashenko's imposition of constitutional change and the referendum that he forced on the country in November 1996 resulted in an immediate EU reaction. Ratification of the PSA and IA was suspended in February 1997, and the European Council decided to limit assistance programs to humanitarian and regional projects and projects supporting democratization.

It did not help Belarus–EU relations that in June 1998 the Belarusian authorities evicted three of the five EU ambassadors (and the US ambassador) from their residences in Drozdy, the district of Minsk where the presidential residence is located. This eviction violated the Vienna Convention on Diplomatic Relations, and EU member states recalled their ambassadors and imposed a visa ban on more than a hundred Belarusian government officials. The Council of Europe suspended Belarus' membership application in December 1998. By the time an agreement was reached and EU ambassadors had returned in January

1999, Lukashenko had succeeded in poisoning relations and creating a huge embarrassment to his country's foreign policy establishment and diplomatic corps.

Since then the EU has kept Belarus on the back burner while stressing that it does not wish to isolate the country. Its CFSP report for the year 1998, adopted by the European Council in April 1999, stated that Belarus "failed to make progress on the issue of respect for human rights and fundamental freedoms as well as in regard to constitutional principles meeting international standards for a democratic state."[5] Whereas Ukraine had been accepted into the Council of Europe in November 1995 and Russia three months later, at the time of this writing Belarus remains the only European country denied membership.

In response to the increasing frequency of human rights violations, the EU, the CoE, and the Organization for Security and Co-operation in Europe (OSCE) decided to pool their efforts in trying to maintain communications with the Minsk authorities. A "Parliamentary Troika" was created, the first in its kind, composed of representatives of the European Parliament and the OSCE and CoE Assemblies. In 1999 the EU adopted a "step-by-step approach" promising a gradual lifting of sanctions upon fulfillment of four "benchmarks" for democratic progress set by the OSCE: free access to the media for all political groupings; opposition representation in electoral commissions; electoral legislation conforming to international standards; and a review of the role of parliament resulting in a substantial increase in its powers.

In September 1997 the OSCE Permanent Council had established an Advisory and Monitoring Group (AMG) in Belarus, which began its activities in February 1998 and became the coordinating center for west European efforts to "assist the Belarusian authorities in promoting democratic institutions and in complying with other OSCE commitments."[6] But soon after his reelection in September 2001 Lukashenko became more confrontational, and in April 2002 the authorities made it clear they no longer appreciated the AMG's assistance. After the departure of the first AMG head in December 2001, Belarus forced the acting head to leave the country. Over protests from Belarusian authorities, the intended new AMG head, the German diplomat Eberhard Heyken, was subsequently appointed special representative for Belarus for the OSCE chairman in office.[7] Only in 2003 was he allowed to head a new OSCE office in Minsk.

Thus, Belarusian authorities facing the West see a united front of European institutions and an American government demanding that they put their house in order. Western institutions, for their part, see a Belarusian president unyielding in his confrontational attitude. Only NATO presents a partial exception. Belarus joined NATO's Partnership for Peace (PfP) in January 1995, half a year after Russia, and has been a member of the Euro-Atlantic Partnership Council since 1997. Belarusian officials present PfP as an "indispensable" instrument in the formation of a "European security structure."[8] The deep military integration between Belarus and Russia, however, has not been balanced by anything but modest cooperation with NATO in the context of PfP.[9] As a result, Belarus stands far apart from neighbors that are either already members of NATO (Poland), expect to gain such status very soon (Lithuania, Latvia), or have a special relationship with the organization (Russia and Ukraine). Belarus's Ministry of Foreign Affairs has asked NATO for a bilateral agreement of the same status as the 1997 NATO–Russia Founding Act and NATO–Ukrainian Charter, but to no avail. Since the events of September 11, 2001, the Belarusian Ministry has declared that the country "considers itself an inseparable link of the anti-terrorist coalition."[10] But repeated reports of Belarusian arms sales to rogue states and terrorist movements have not contributed to any normalization of relations with the United States, NATO, or European institutions.[11]

Popular Views and Expectations

The first thing to be aware of, when discussing popular views and expectations *vis-à-vis* the West, is how closely Belarusian society is intertwined with other societies of the East. Our survey shows that out of every ten adult citizens of Belarus, six have at least one close relative in Russia. In the Vitebsk region in the northeast of the country and in the city of Minsk, this is even more than two out of every three citizens. There are indeed far more Belarusian citizens who have several close relatives in Russia than just one: 44 versus 16 percent. More than half of those having close relatives in Russia also have at least one close relative in one or more other CIS countries, whereas 41 percent of the total Belarusian population has one (10 percent) or several (31 percent) close relatives in CIS countries other than Russia. One focus group participant in Minsk put it succinctly when asked about the most important events of the 1990s: "Well, Belarus became independent. So now all of my relatives live abroad."

The fact that Belarusian society is closely interwoven with that of Russia is also reflected in the language that people speak at home. Of all Belarusian citizens, 77 percent say their nationality is Belarusian, and 14 percent claim Russian nationality.[12] But nowhere in the region (Belarus, Ukraine, and Moldova) is the

Table 8.1. "In what language do you usually converse at home?" (percentages)

	Belarus	Ukraine	Moldova
Titular language	23	51	72
Russian	70	44	19
Other	6	4	9

Source: National surveys commissioned by the "Outsiders" project in Belarus (Novak, fieldwork 13–27 April 2000, *n* = 1,090), Ukraine (Kiev International Institute of Sociology, fieldwork 18 February–3 March 2000, *n* = 1,592), and Moldova ("Opinia" Independent Sociological Service, fieldwork 13–19 February 2000, *n* = 1000, excluding Pridnestrov'e and Bendery).

number of speakers of the "titular" language as low as in Belarus. Only 23 percent speak Belarusian at home, while 70 percent converse in Russian on a day-to-day basis (table 8.1). Taking only those who say their nationality is Belarusian, the percentage of "Russian speakers" drops only five points to 65 percent, and that of "Belarusian speakers" increases by five points to 28 percent. Fewer than 3 percent of Belarusian citizens with Russian nationality speak Belarusian at home.

The density of family networks across borders and the predominance of the Russian language raise the question to what extent Belarusian society has its own distinct identity. The identity problem has in the past been seen as being particularly acute in this country and as the most fundamental reason for its failed transition. One way of measuring this is to ask citizens how proud they are of being a citizen of their country, as was done in the November 2001 New Democracies Barometer (see table 8.2).

Table 8.2. *"How proud are you to be a citizen of your country?"* (percentages)

	Belarus	Russia	Ukraine	Moldova
Very proud	28 (31)	22	14	16
Quite proud	38 (39)	41	34	47
Proud	*66 (70)*	*62*	*48*	*63*
Rather not proud	8 (7)	12	19	16
Not proud at all	6 (5)	9	15	8
Not proud	*14 (12)*	*20*	*33*	*24*
I do not care	12 (11)	10	10	4

Source: Adapted from Christian Haerpfer, *New Democracies Barometer No. 6,* November 2001, sponsored by the European Commission Directorate General Research within the framework of the INCO-COPERNICUS Research Program. Percentages in parentheses refer to those who identify themselves as being of Belarusian nationality.

Surprisingly, citizens of Belarus are the proudest in the region! Of those who consider themselves to be of Belarusian nationality, seven in every ten are proud to be a citizen of their country. Of those who identify themselves as being Russian, 13 percent are very proud, 35 percent quite proud (48 percent are proud) to be a citizen of Belarus, and 24 percent are not proud, whereas 16 percent do not care. Taken together, these data indicate that, although ties with the neighboring societies may still be strong, in the hearts and minds of the Belarusian citizenry their country has definitely been put on the map. But pride in their country is qualified. One such qualification was expressed by a participant in our military focus group: "Personally, I am very proud to live in the Republic of Belarus. But I am very dissatisfied that we are being ruled by nitwits. It's really a shame. Can I develop myself in such a country?" Pride is also moderated by an awareness that, as another officer said, "practically nobody in the world has heard of Belarus" and that if their country is known at all, it is by virtue of "our sportsmen," the country's opposition to NATO expansion, and the regime's violation of human rights. "They never trained us to be proud of our fatherland," said Svetlana, one of the participants in our other focus group in Minsk. "We don't have the kind of national pride as you'll find in the Baltic countries, in the former republics of the USSR, or in Poland."

Most Belarusians understand perfectly well that their international environment cannot be ignored and that isolation is harmful. But which countries are more important to Belarus, and which less? After all, with limited resources a multivectored foreign policy would demand the setting of priorities. In our survey in April 2000 we asked our respondents how important it was in their view for their country to have good relations with six different named states and the EU member states. Not surprisingly, Russia scored highest, followed at a distance by "EU member states" and, named separately, Germany.

Table 8.3 shows the overall percentage of those who consider good relations with the country in question to be very important, and the percentages among the highly educated and the age cohort eighteen to thirty-five. The EU and United States score high, particularly among these two sections of the population. The fact that the US trails behind the EU will have a lot to do with simple geographic proximity and its many consequences; as participants in our focus groups said, Europe is "all that is beyond the gates of Warsaw."

Table 8.3. *"How important is it in your opinion for Belarus to have good relations with the following countries?" (percentage answering "very important")*

With . . .	Sequence on card	Total	Higher educated	Age 18–35
Russia	1	69	69	63
EU member states	7	37	46	45
Germany	5	36	41	43
USA	4	32	37	38
Japan	6	26	27	29
Great Britain	3	25	30	29
China	2	21	23	21

Source: As table 8.1. Respondents received a card with the names of six countries and "the member states of the EU"; they could reply "very important," "somewhat important," "not very important," or "not at all important." "Higher educated" is defined as those with a higher education, from 3–4 years incomplete to completed doctoral level.

From a Belarusian vantage point, the EU starts at the Polish–German frontier. Before moving to examine views and expectations of Europe and the EU, it is appropriate to underline the high regard of many Belarusians for Germany. The devastation and bloodshed caused by Germans during the Second World War are not forgotten. But by the end of the twentieth century, Germany had effectively rehabilitated itself and enjoyed a reputation unsurpassed by any country in western Europe. Such were the fruits of compensation payments and consistent and sustained German support for the social needs of the Belarusian population, particularly in the aftermath of the Chernobyl disaster. Over and again, in focus groups and interviews, Belarusians spontaneously express their appreciation for Germany's "outstanding help, both in the economy and in ecology." They "provide medical treatment for our children" and in doing so, one said, "our former enemies help us better than our former socialist neighbors"— meaning, of course, Russia.

For many, Europe is still a distant desire, even though, as one focus group participant put it, Europe is "where we can go by car." If they use the word "West," they think of "America in the first place." "The West is where life is best." The West is "Prosperity. Culture. A living standard. If a man works, he receives a salary and lives comfortably"; it is "being well provided for when you get old." Europe is "part of the West," the "European Union." It is "where the streets are very clean" and "where they have clean windows." Are they part of Europe? Geographically, of course, yes. Quite often Belarusians proudly claim (as do many Poles and Lithuanians) that they are at the *heart* of Europe because their country hosts its geographical center. Belarus is *in* Europe, "but of course we *are* not yet Europe." "At opposition demonstrations, the slogan is 'Belarus in Europe'," a military officer added; "That says it all. Belarus is not in Europe, she is isolated. The people want to go there but the president says 'Stop! Where are you going? Stay here!' *We* want to."

The question of a European component to the multiple identities of Belarusians is, as in any country, a complicated one. If asked the direct question whether they feel European at all, the population splits into two: just over 50 percent say they never do (38 percent) or don't know, and just under 50 percent answer that they feel European "often" (16 percent) or "sometimes" (34 percent), with the highest score, 62 percent, reached by young Belarusians in their twenties. More revealing is to inquire about nested identities in the terms that have been employed by the New Democracies Barometer. Respondents were asked "which of the following" they identified "most closely" with, and which of the same list of six options, from European (Eurasian) to village, would come second. "Citizen of country" topped the first choice list, with almost 64 percent of respondents, followed by city/village and "Soviet citizen" (10 percent).[13] Only 5 percent of respondents gave "European (Eurasian)" as their first identity. In the list of secondary identities, "Europe" came only in fifth place (just under 9 percent), after city/village (46 percent), country (22 percent), "Soviet citizen"

(11 percent), and region (9 percent). Obviously, and not unlike other Europeans, quite a few Belarusians are prepared to confess to some sort of European identity, particularly the younger, well-educated, and well-traveled ones. But in general, and in comparison with other identities, this identity is weak and superficial.

It is therefore no surprise that Belarusians have little knowledge of the EU. Similar to many other East Europeans, the older age groups in particular have a fairly good idea of what NATO is about. When asked in focus group meetings, they can typify the organization immediately: a "military organization" with "America as leader." But for many, the EU is a mystery. Even when asked to express a general attitude toward the EU in terms of their impression of the organization's aims and activities, four out of every ten find it difficult or impossible to do so (table 8.4). Again, the most positive are people in their twenties, 62 percent of whom have a fairly or very positive impression of the EU: almost 70 percent would be in favor of their country actually joining the EU (54 percent of the general population).

Table 8.4. *"Are your impressions of the aims and activities of the European Union generally. . ."*

	20–29	30–39	40–49	50–59	60+	Total
Very positive	17.4	11.0	11.8	10.4	5.9	10.6
Fairly positive	44.7	38.6	37.4	38.9	27.5	36.4
Fairly to very negative	8.4	12.9	13.3	12.5	14.2	12.4
Difficult to say, no answer	29.5	37.6	37.5	38.2	52.5	40.6

Source: As table 8.1.

Most Belarusians feel reasonably secure in terms of military security. Fewer than 20 percent of the population consider a military attack by "some other country" in the near future "very likely" (4 percent) or "a real possibility" (15 percent). If they see a source of instability, it is the distant West, the former Cold War adversary, the United States. A large majority sees Russia as a stabilizing power (table 8.5).

But a threat to security in the world does not translate automatically into a threat to Belarus. Quite remarkably, even the officers in our military focus group in Minsk could not identify countries that would present a threat to Belarus or could be considered its enemy—not even NATO. "For that to be the case some state would have to be interested in Belarus. Financially, or because of its geography. There would have to be a motive. If you show me a motive by which Belarus would be important. . . ." No, "our enemies are the opposition. That's what Lukashenko says. . . . But in our terms, in military terms, Belarus has no

Table 8.5. "Do you think [country] could be a substantial threat to security and order in the world?"

	United States	49
	Iran	35
	China	27
	Germany	24
	European Union	21
	Russia	12

Source: As table 8.1; responses show the proportion that answered "a big threat" or "some threat."

enemies and cannot have enemies." Other military officers point to the abundance of police and internal security personnel: "they [the authorities] fear the internal enemy far more. We have so many police, it is clear that they expect some sort of attack from within, by our own people."

So is NATO expansion perceived as a threat to the security of their country? Asked about the 1999 admission of Poland, Hungary, and the Czech Republic, 20 percent of Belarusians surveyed in 2000 find it difficult to say; another 20 percent see a "major" (4 percent) or "some" (16 percent) threat, whereas 60 percent see little or no threat at all. If NATO were to expand further into central Europe, slightly more Belarusians (28 percent) would consider this harmful to their country's security. These survey results, however, were not reflected in the three focus group discussions that we monitored. Nobody was particularly concerned, not even the military officers. NATO expansion was seen to be "normal," "no problem," "absolutely no threat." Poland's NATO membership "doesn't mean that they will threaten us with aggression." The one remark that was made by military and civilians alike was that, if a war did indeed begin, "we'll feel it right away, the warning time would be very short" for the simple reason that "two years ago it would have taken a rocket fifteen minutes to reach Minsk, now it will fly there in three minutes." But no Belarusian will lose a night's sleep over this: "I am in favor and I'd even become a NATO member myself, to deal with the matter once and for all. Let's become a member of NATO and have it over with."

Clearly, Belarusians are not particularly concerned about NATO expansion. How about enlargement of the European Union? As was indicated above, attitudes toward the EU are generally positive and uninformed, with a considerable section of the population even being in favor of the entirely unrealistic option of EU membership.

Table 8.6 illustrates the uncertainty of Belarusians concerning the EU. Roughly one-third find it impossible to estimate what the impact would be in the hypothetical case that their country had been accepted for membership. Among those who venture a guess, positive expectations predominate, particularly for

Table 8.6. *"Please indicate for each of these points what in your view would be the most likely results of our country becoming a member of the EU"* (row percentages)

	Positive results	No effect	Negative results	Hard to say/ NA
Political stability	48	12	7	33
Consumer prices	39	12	13	36
Economic development	57	8	7	29
Personal income	35	18	9	38
Unemployment	28	17	16	39

Source: As table 8.1.

the economic development and political stability of their country. In focus groups, Belarusians testify to being well aware of the extent to which this is simply wishful thinking. "As a European country, yes, of course we should become a member." "With both hands." "We want to . . . but as Belarus is now, with our current economic development, it is simply impossible." And a military man: "it's all about the economic and legal basis. Freedom of speech, press. In general, at the moment it is not realistic." In this respect, many Belarusians are realists. They know that their president is the main obstacle *and* they know that "nobody will buy our products." Their immediate concern is the imposition of travel restrictions as a result of Polish accession.

Elite Views and Expectations

Neither is realism absent in official circles. As early as 1999, the Ministry of Foreign Affairs addressed the question of the possible impact of EU enlargement. In a publication on this issue it wrote that, although in the short term Belarusian exports might benefit from the side-effects of industrial reform in the new central European member states, in the long term "it is difficult to imagine a [Belarusian] presence on the EU market without a reconstruction of production and an improvement of the quality of [Belarusian] products."[14] The ministry's Directorate for European Co-operation saw EU enlargement in the context of a struggle for dominance between the "geostrategic interests" of the United States and Germany and it expected this struggle to widen to Belarus and other east European states. Stressing the multidirectionality of its foreign policy, the directorate suggested that Belarus should develop its partnership relations with Poland and the Baltic states in anticipation of their entrance to the EU, and combine a deepening of Belarusian–Russian relations with a "prioritization" of the country's relations with the European Union. It argued that since 40 percent of Russia's foreign trade was with the EU and since the Union with Russia required Belarus to coordinate its foreign policy with that of Moscow, a further development of EU–Belarusian relations was "inevitable."[15]

Officials in the Foreign Ministry underline that processes occurring in Europe are "directly relevant" to Belarus.[16] The younger Belarusian generation, they say, has a "European cast of mind" and the country's isolation has to be broken through a permanent exchange of opinion with the West. Conversely, they state that good relations with Belarus are in the interest of western Europe by pointing out that "by the year 2020, 50 to 67 percent of west European gas consumption will come from Russia *through* Belarus." In the presidential administration, too, one can hear that it is imperative that the country develop its ties with Europe and the EU and that "we should never isolate ourselves from our neighbors."[17]

These attitudes indicate that beneath the hard surface of the president's anti-European rhetoric and deeds, within the top government bureaucracy there was, at least in 1999–2000, considerable support for a pragmatic approach to European integration. At the top of the presidential administration it was said that "in the power system you will find people with different views; some want to go the European way, the others to the East."[18] Indeed, a senior Western diplomat in 2002 confirmed that this is still the case and that large sections of the administration are extremely dissatisfied with the president's course.[19]

This raises the question of divisions within the Belarusian elite concerning the country's foreign policy. For the purpose of this chapter, that question can perhaps best be addressed by dividing the elite into four groups. The main division of course is between the clientele of President-patron Lukashenko and the rest of the political, economic, and cultural elites, including the sidelined opposition forces. It is difficult to escape the impression that the Lukashenko group is rather small, compensating for its weak numerical position by aggressive rhetoric. Next to this group, and perhaps overlapping, is that of the discontented bureaucrats identified above. Opposition leaders, the third group, are almost without exception in favor of an end to the country's self-isolation from Europe and the United States, although many will admit that this cannot be to the detriment of continued cooperation with Russia. Fourth and finally, a large group of elite members can be identified who see no alternative to working with the regime but who would welcome a more sensible foreign policy than that pursued by the president.

Leaders of opposition parties generally see no problem in either NATO or EU enlargement.[20] They feel that Belarus should aim for the closest possible cooperation with both organizations. They do not consider their country to have enemies: "our only enemy is Lukashenko."[21] Their only fear is that the accession of Poland, in particular, may have serious consequences for Belarus in terms of trade and the movement of people across borders. There is an acute awareness of the country's high economic dependence on Russia. European integration is seen not as an alternative, but as a counterweight to the developing union with the big eastern neighbor. Some, however, wonder, "why can't we do as the Finns have done? Once they also were part of Russia, now they are a normal developed state."[22] The opposition has long been campaigning under the slogan "Belarus into Europe." This position is essential, as European institutions insist that the regime should abide by generally accepted rules of democratic procedure as a condition for the normalization of relations. The conditionality of European policy toward the Belarusian regime has resulted in stalemate, the breaking of which would inevitably result in the loss of power of the president and his entourage.

It should thus not come as a surprise that in the eyes of Lukashenko and his immediate associates there is an unholy alliance between the opposition and European and transatlantic institutions. Reacting to the four "benchmarks" formulated by OSCE, CoE, and EU, at a press conference in 2002 five months after his reelection, Lukashenko fulminated that

> nobody will be allowed to put forward opposition demands as conditions for co-operation. Take these notorious four conditions: destroying our entire existing system of government under the mask of some extra parliamentary powers. Do you really want it—a referendum, changes to the constitution with all ensuing consequences?[23]

Of course, the president and his clients do not want this. They feel deceived by the West and accuse the EU, OSCE, and CoE of applying "double standards."[24] Their policy is one of integration by accusation. The OSCE's AMG office in Minsk was termed the "opposition headquarters" by Lukashenko and was forced to close later in 2002.[25] His accusation is laced with a conditionality that answers that of the European institutions. The presidential position is that Belarus is "part of the European home" because "God has destined us to live in Europe as a sovereign and independent state"—and that "nobody will be allowed to exclude Belarus from Europe":

> If the Europeans have a wish to cooperate with Belarus, we are open to this cooperation. If someone does not have such a wish, we are not able to force them to do so. But to ignore Belarus or to attempt to isolate it from European affairs is, as recent years have shown, a futureless and counterproductive policy . . . because Belarus is the geographical center of Europe, and nobody will be allowed to exclude it from Europe, and nobody can do this.[26]

Lukashenko and his clients have also fulminated against NATO enlargement in an effort to use latent fears to strengthen their position among the population and to further integration with Russia. Since 1999, however, they have had to accept that they border a NATO state. Three years later they had no alternative but to accept the institutionalization of a new NATO–Russia relationship.

In a speech on April 11, 2000, Lukashenko said that "we have to take full account of the new geopolitical factor of being a direct neighbor of NATO; we are interested in normal relations with the North Atlantic Alliance and have made proposals in that direction."[27] But NATO has largely ignored Belarus while improving its relations with Russia and Ukraine.

Whereas leaders of the opposition generally have no problem with NATO and its enlargement, elite members who cannot be said to belong to the Lukashenko clientele have a tendency to overdramatize fear of NATO and its enlargement among the Belarusian population. They claim that the impact on the population of NATO's bombing of Serbia in 1999, amplified to the extreme by Lukashenko, has been profound. As an independent journalist said one year later: "The government said 'we may be next'; the opposition said that NATO should bomb Lukashenko."[28] Pressured by these two demagogic positions, many Belarusians in 1999 may have had difficulty not losing their nerve. But as the survey data and focus group results discussed above show, the damage to NATO and its reputation has been limited.

Concerning the EU and its enlargement, independent elite members are generally rather pessimistic. Owing to a lack of investment and innovation, according to an influential journalist, "nobody needs our products."[29] The TV sets, refrigerators, trucks, and tractors that Belarus exports, a leader of the business community said, "are not yesterday's, but the-day-before-yesterday's products. We have lost our opportunity."[30] This evaluation of the country's export potential is typical for those favoring a European choice and underlies their expectations of the impact of EU enlargement on the Belarusian economy. They fear that the country will be "left more and more behind" and will suffer from EU enlargement to central European states. Textile exports, for example, are under serious threat. Only after real economic reform will the problems of trade with EU countries be manageable. Only then, a young entrepreneur said, Poland's accession to the EU would not be a problem; on the contrary, it would be a challenge and a "good chance" for Belarus in stimulating the country's economic development.[31]

The president's policy of integration by accusation has infected many of those who do not belong to his entourage. There is a rather strong tendency in the country's elite to blame the West and the EU for ignoring and isolating Belarus, for not having enough patience with the country. They also show a tendency to turn the argument on its head: if only Belarus were incorporated into the "European process," then there would be a quick improvement of its economic, social, and political situation. European structures, they argue, have to let go of their "double standards" and should provide concrete help to Belarus as they have done for other central and east European states.[32] One influential analyst claimed that by marginalizing Belarus prior to Lukashenko's election in 1994, "the Western countries gave Belarus away to Russia."

Conclusions

For the development of its union with Russia, Belarus, as the previous chapter illustrated, has opted for the institutional model of the European Union. But the Lukashenko regime rejects EU policies as the main obstacle to integration with the West. It is something of a paradox that the country is now in a classic stalemate that can be broken only with Russian help. The country's president has pursued a retrograde policy for too long and has become the prisoner of his own rhetoric. He has failed to come up with new initiatives that could provide an alternative to his policy of integration by accusation. In a country where the new post-Soviet generation longs for a "European way of life," he and his anti-Western clients are a dying but stubborn breed.

Both in senior parliamentary circles and among independent commentators one can hear the accusation that Western countries "gave up" Belarus to Russia and that thereby Europe was to blame for the union with Russia. But at the same time there is very general agreement in Belarus, even among members of the opposition, that the country cannot and must not choose one single direction of integration. Integration with Western institutions and with Russia are not seen as mutually exclusive. This attitude has been strengthened under the serving Russian president and notably since September 11, 2001, when Russia moved quickly in a Western direction. Within the Commonwealth of Independent States, Belarus has become increasingly isolated.[33] An attempt by Lukashenko in May 2002 to create an anti-NATO Collective Security Treaty Organization (CSTO) with Russia and four other ex-Soviet states ended in an embarrassing failure.[34] Russia and other CIS countries have moved on, improving their relations with the West, whereas President Lukashenko has unsuccessfully tried to apply the brakes. He has had to accept the unpleasant fact that in the name of the fight against international terrorism, Russia and other CIS countries have accepted the presence of Western troops and bases in central Asia and Georgia.

Our surveys and focus groups have documented a considerable potential for the normalization of relations with European institutions, a normalization that would be of great interest to Belarus. With the exception of a narrow circle of Lukashenko clients and perhaps sections of the older, rural population, Belarusians favor democratization and integration with Europe. The central issue is how such normalization can be brought about. As long as Lukashenko is in power, European institutions will find it very difficult to bring about change in Minsk. In dealing with the Belarusian regime, they cannot compromise the values they stand for, whereas that regime will find it impossible to yield to European demands in the area of democratization. But in the years to come the economic situation in Belarus may well deteriorate to such extent that popular dissatisfaction will endanger the continued existence of the regime. There are already indications of growing dissatisfaction with the economic situation, particularly among the young.[35]

Were a crisis to arrive, a crucial role would be reserved for the Russian leadership.[36] By endorsing Lukashenko on the eve of the presidential election of September 2001, Vladimir Putin voluntarily accepted a special responsibility for Belarus. His pushing for Russia's integration with European institutions and close collaboration with NATO is difficult to reconcile with continued support for the regime in Minsk. As the previous chapter has shown, Russia has considerable leverage over the Belarusian regime. The responsibilities accepted by Putin in September 2001 *vis-à-vis* both the West and Belarus require him to use that leverage for the benefit of the people of Belarus, Europe, and Russia.

Notes

1. See the web site www.coe.int/T/E/About_CoE/Member_states/default.asp, retrieved 10 May 2004.

2. "The Outsiders: Russia, Ukraine, Belarus, Moldova and the New Europe" (Project Grant L213252007), part of the ESRC "One Europe or Several?" program. Data were collected jointly with Stephen White (University of Glasgow) and Margot Light (London School of Economics and Political Science). The author is grateful to Margot Light for her comments to an earlier version of this chapter.

3. It should be stressed that, in contrast to the survey results, the focus group transcripts cannot be considered representative of the country's adult population. Since they were organized in two major cities, they exclude the rural population.

4. David R. Marples, *Belarus: A Denationalized Nation* (Amsterdam: Harwood, 1999), 86, 89.

5. Annual CFSP Report, 1998, adopted 16 April 1999.

6. OSCE Permanent Council, decision 185, 18 September 1997, at www.osce.org/belarus/documents/files/pced185.pdf, retrieved 14 March 2002.

7. *RFE-RL Newsline*, 19 April 2002.

8. Colonel Alexander Yatskevich, deputy chief of the Defense Ministry's Department for International Military Cooperation, *BelaPAN Military Review*, 1 April 2002.

9. The NATO–Belarus Individual Partnership Program for 2002–2003 contains 170 activity items versus 52 in 2001 and 35 in 2000; see Yatskevich in *BelaPAN Military Review*, 1 April 2002.

10. Statement delivered by Ambassador Sergei Martynov at the Euro-Atlantic Partnership Council Foreign Ministers meeting of 7 December 2001.

11. The reports were angrily denied by Defense Minister Maltsev and the first deputy chairman of the KGB, General Stepan Sukhorenko; see *BelaPAN Newsline*, 18 February and 13 March 2002. General Sukhorenko, however, added that there was indeed "a problem of re-export."

12. 'Nationality" is used here to denote the belonging to a nation, as distinct from citizenship.

13. Calculated from Belarusian data file in Christian Haerpfer, *New Democracies Barometer No. 6,* November 2001. Permission to use NDB-6 data (see also table 8.2) is gratefully acknowledged.

14. "Vozmozhnye posledstviya dlya Respubliki Belarus' rasshireniya Evropeiskogo Soyuza," *Vestnik ministerstva inostrannykh del* (Respubliki Belarus'), no. 3, 1999: 54–62 (60).
15. "Vozmozhnye posledstviya," 58.
16. Interview with two officials of the Foreign Ministry, Minsk, 31 May 2000.
17. Interview with a senior official in the presidential administration, Minsk, 1 June 2000.
18. Interview with a senior official in the presidential administration, Minsk, 1 June 2000.
19. Interview with a Western ambassador, Minsk, 25 January 2002.
20. Interviews with leaders of the Social-Democratic Party "Narodnaya Hromoda," United Civic Party, Belarusian National Front, and a former prime minister, Minsk, 31 May and 3 June 2000.
21. Interview with the leader of a liberal-conservative opposition party, Minsk, 2 June 2000.
22. Interview with a former prime minister, Minsk, 1 June 2000.
23. Press conference, Minsk, 13 February 2002: BelaPAN Information Company.
24. Interview with the chairman of a permanent commission of the Council of the Republic, National Assembly, Minsk, 5 June 2000.
25. Press conference, Minsk, 13 February 2002: BelaPAN Information Company.
26. Speech at the acceptance of the credentials from the new head of the delegation of the European Commission in Belarus, Minsk, 6 February 2002: BelaPAN Information Company, 7 February 2002; see also his speech while accepting the credentials from the Hungarian and Namibian ambassadors, 6 March 2002: BelaPAN Information Company, 6 March 2002.
27. Annual Message to the Parliament, 11 April 2000, *Sovetskaya Belorussiya*, 12 April 2000, 2. See also Lukashenko's interview of 24 May 2000 on the Russian TV program *Vesti* as transcribed in the *Informatsionnyi byulleten'* of the Belarusian Foreign Ministry, no. 413, 29 May 2000.
28. Interview with a journalist, Minsk, 30 May 2000.
29. Interview with a journalist, Minsk, 30 May 2000.
30. Interview with a senior economist and business leader, Minsk, 31 May 2000.
31. Interview with a young entrepreneur, Minsk, 30 May 2000.
32. See also Oleg Laptyonok, "Plurality of Foreign Policy Vectors in Belarus in New International Setting," *Belarus in the World*, 4, no. 4 (1999), who states that "various technical, ecological, and other *artificial* restrictions have to be dealt with in order to clear the way for Belarus products to the European and international markets" (43–47; emphasis added).
33. Aliaksandr Tsikhamirau, "Belarus' attempts to promote anti-Western integration model for CIS doomed to failure," *BelaPAN Weekly Analytical Bulletin*, no. 16 (383), 17 April 2002.
34. The CSTO was to be based on the Collective Security Treaty of Tashkent (1992); see Mikhail Vanyashkin, "Belarusian Leader Calls for Alliance to Oppose NATO," *Transitions OnLine*, 14–20 May 2002, at www.tol.cz, retrieved 21 May 2002.
35. See "Though Still Banking on Lukashenko, Belarusians More Open to Economic Reform," Office of Research, Opinion Analysis, US Department of State, report

M-32-02, 5 April 2002, based on a survey ($n = 1030$) carried out in January–February 2002.

36. See Michael Staack, "Weiter in die Isolierung? Weißrussland nach der Präsidentschaftswahl," *Internationale Politik*, no. 10 (2001): 53–58; Heinz Timmermann, "Strategische Partnerschaft: Wie kann die EU Rußland stärker einbinden?," *SWP-Aktuell*, April 2002. The same position is taken by Leonid Sinitsyn, former head of Lukashenko's presidential administration and one of the candidates in the presidential elections of 2001. In an interview in July 2001, Sinitsyn said that the West "has to involve Russia" in dealing with Belarus, and "offer it a more active role"; *BelaPAN Weekly Analytical Bulletin*, 4 July 2001.

9 Belarus and Postcommunist Democratization

Christian W. Haerpfer

The main aim of this concluding chapter is to place the process of postcommunist democratization in Belarus between 1992 and 2001 within a comparative perspective that embraces the political transformations during the same period in Russia, Ukraine, and Moldova. The first section will analyze the extent of nostalgia on the part of Belarusian citizens for the old communist system and the level of support for a return to communism as a political regime. The following part considers the extent of support by the electorate in Belarus for the current political regime, including the national government and the president. Complementing earlier chapters, a particular focus is the national parliament and its changing place in popular attitudes.

In the following section we consider various alternatives to democracy and the extent to which they are supported by the Belarusian electorate. The first alternative is support for an authoritarian leader, followed by the wish to replace the current political system by a military regime. We also consider the extent to which there is popular support for the introduction (or arguably, the return) of a monarchical system. Finally, the chapter concludes with a comparative test of the "Churchill hypothesis" in terms of which democracy may have deficiencies, but at the end of the day is still better than any other form of government.

Nostalgia for Communist Rule

One of the crucial obstacles to the full acceptance of the new political regime after the end of communism is the fact that considerable segments of the population in central and eastern Europe prefer the old political system and consider that form of regime to be better than the political structures established after the fall of the Iron Curtain in 1989 and immediately thereafter. This nostalgia for communist rule was very apparent in Belarus.[1]

Nostalgia for the communist *ancien régime* decreased in central Europe as a whole from 46 percent in 1992 to 41 percent in 1998.[2] Mass attitudes toward the political past of communism are quite different in central Europe and in southeastern Europe. In central Europe, positive thinking about the *ancien régime* reached a peak very quickly in 1992, with 46 percent of all central Europeans having to different degrees positive evaluations of the communist political system before 1989. Between 1992 and 1994, the group of people with positive evaluations of the *ancien régime* dropped to 40 percent and remained at that level up to 1998. The trend in southern Europe was the reverse: nostalgia increased from 30 percent in 1992 up to 41 percent in 1998.

The proportion of post-Soviet citizens in the Commonwealth of Independent States with some nostalgia for the communist political system shows an interesting longitudinal pattern. The share of nostalgic persons increased steadily from 55 percent in 1992 to 75 percent in 2000, but fell for the first time between 2000 and 2001, when it dropped to 58 percent. Nevertheless it is important to note that there has always been an absolute majority of the electorates in the CIS region that has given the communist political regime a positive evaluation, which is in stark contrast to the pattern in central and eastern Europe, where we find significant groups, but never an absolute majority, with a clear nostalgia for the communist political system (see table 9.1).

Table 9.1. Nostalgia for Communist Rule

	1992	1994	1996	1998	2000	2001
Central Europe	46	40	39	41	n.a.	n.a.
Southern Europe	30	37	40	41	n.a.	n.a.
CIS	55	57	71	71	75	58
Russia	50	51	60	72	70	55
Belarus	60	64	77	60	78	57
Ukraine	55	55	75	82	78	63
Moldova	–	–	–	–	78	79

The question wording was: "Here is a scale for ranking how the government works. The top, +100, is the best; at the bottom, –100 is the worst. Where on this scale would you put the *former communist regime*?" (persons with positive attitudes, percentages).

Nostalgia for communist rule in the Russian Federation, perhaps surprisingly, is less than in Belarus, Ukraine, or Moldova. The share of nostalgic Russians increased during the volatile process of political transformations from 50 percent in 1992 to 72 percent in 1998. In Russia, this represented the peak of communist nostalgia, two years earlier than in other post-Soviet states. Since 1998, the share of nostalgic Russians with regard to the communist political regime has fallen considerably, to 70 percent in 2000 and 55 percent in 2001.

The Belarusian population also showed a high level of nostalgia for communist rule during the first half of the 1990s. At the beginning of political transition in 1992, 60 percent took a positive view of the political system of the Soviet Union. This share went steadily up to 77 percent in 1996, which was as high as in Ukraine. Surprisingly, the extent of nostalgia shrank from 77 percent in 1996 to 60 percent in 1998. One explanation of the different pattern in Belarus in comparison with Ukraine may be that the authoritarian regime of President Lukashenko had been fulfilling the basic needs of political stability of the Belarusian public. The Lukashenko regime is in many respects similar to the previous Soviet form of government and could be seen by the Belarusian electorate as a successful surrogate for the communist political regime of the past. Communist nostalgia increased again in Belarus from 60 percent in 1998 to a historical peak of 78 percent in 2000. As in Russia, nostalgia for communist rule declined substantially at the beginning of the new decade from 78 percent in 2000 to 57 percent in 2001 and is now at a level very close to that of the Russian Federation.

In 1992, an absolute majority of 55 percent of the Ukrainian electorate showed a positive evaluation of the one-party government of the former USSR. This figure went up further during the process of political transformation and reached its peak in 1998, when 82 percent of all our Ukrainian respondents acknowledged that they had a positive view of the former communist regime. Fortunately for the future prospects of democracy in Ukraine, the share of nostalgic Ukrainians has declined since 1998 to 78 percent in 2000 and finally to 63 percent in 2001. In Moldova, by contrast, nostalgia for communist rule is highest among the post-Soviet republics and even increased fractionally from 78 percent in 2000 to 79 percent in 2001. This nostalgia for communist rule is likely to have contributed to the electoral victory of the Communist Party at the Moldovan parliamentary elections of early 2001, and the subsequent election of a Communist president.

Is There a Future for Communism?

On average 10 percent of all citizens in central, southern, and eastern Europe have the conviction that communism is a good way to run things, a good form of government, and a viable alternative to democracy. Can we say that communism is historically dead or that there are tendencies to restore it, in Belarus and elsewhere in the region, as a form of political and economic regime? In order to find out the extent of support for a restoration of the communist *ancien régime* we asked approximately 50,000 postcommunist citizens across twelve countries in 1994, 1996, 1998, 2000, and 2001 whether they favored a restoration of the former communist system (see table 9.2).

Table 9.2. Support for Communist Restoration

	1994	1996	1998	2000	2001
Central Europe	14	14	19	n.a.	n.a.
Southern Europe	15	16	19	n.a.	n.a.
CIS	27	42	42	33	38
Belarus	**34**	**49**	**33**	**27**	**30**
Ukraine	25	43	51	32	42
Russia	23	35	41	39	42
Moldova	n.a.	n.a.	n.a.	39	51

The question wording was: "Do you agree or disagree that it would be better to restore the former communist regime?" (percentage who definitely or somewhat agree).

The first and most striking result is that a considerable section of the postcommunist public still believe that the communist regime is a serious alternative to their emerging new democracies. The idea of a restoration of communism, certainly, is not totally extinguished from the minds of people who lived between forty and seventy years under communist rule. In 1994, 18 percent of all postcommunist citizens supported the idea of a communist restoration, which increased to 21 percent in 1996 and to 24 percent in 1998. This longitudinal analysis shows that the wish for a communist restoration is not vanishing, but has been growing, throughout the process of political transformation, and had reached about a quarter of all citizens in twelve postcommunist countries in 1998. By that year, 19 percent of all citizens in central as well as in southern Europe were in favor of some form of communist restoration. This was is in stark contrast to the former Soviet republics, where 42 percent were favorable regarding the return of communist rule. This high proportion had declined, however, to 38 percent by 2001.

In Belarus, support for a communist restoration is by far the lowest among the former republics of the USSR. The wish for a return to communist rule within the Belarusian electorate peaked at 49 percent in 1996, and has since declined to 33 percent in 1998 and 23 percent in 2004. Currently, in other words, less than a quarter of the electorate in Belarus is still in favor of a communist restoration. In Ukraine, the situation is quite different. We found a peak of support for a communist restoration within the Ukrainian electorate in 1998, when an absolute majority of 51 percent were in favor of a return to communist rule.

This overwhelming support for a communist restoration fell to 42 percent in 2001, but can still be regarded as considerable and politically influential.

In Russia, support for a return to communist rule was never as great as in Ukraine during the period of political transformation, and its development over time displayed a different pattern. The wish for a communist regime in Russia was at its lowest with 23 percent in 1994, but increased steadily up to 42 percent in 2001. Hence, we might speak of a convergence in the levels of support for communist restoration from an initially high level in Ukraine and a lower level in the Russian Federation. The wish for a return to communism has been by far the highest in Moldova, where the share of supporters of a communist restoration went up from 39 percent in 2000 to 51 percent in 2001.

Support for the New Political Regime after 1992

When we measure support for the new political regime, we do not measure an abstract concept of democracy but rather make an assessment of the current political regime in a given postcommunist society. The concept of support for the current regime was operationalized by the following question:

> Here is a scale for ranking how the government works. The top, +100, is the best; at the bottom, –100, is the worst. Where on this scale would you put the *current regime*?

For the purposes of the analysis in this section we selected only respondents who gave the current political system an evaluation in the range between +10 and +100. As we see, support for the current government is quite different in central and southeastern Europe from that in the CIS region (see table 9.3).

Table 9.3 Support for the Current Government

	1992	1994	1996	1998	2000	2001
Central Europe	59	61	66	55	n.a.	n.a.
Southern Europe	56	57	57	46	n.a.	n.a.
CIS	25	29	35	35	38	32
Russia	14	35	38	36	37	47
Belarus	**35**	**29**	**35**	**48**	**47**	**24**
Ukraine	25	24	33	22	31	24
Moldova	n.a.	n.a.	n.a.	n.a.	23	5

The question wording was: "Here is a scale for ranking how the government works. The top, +100, is the best; at the bottom, –100 is the worst. Where on this scale would you put the *current regime*?" (persons with positive attitudes, percentages).

In the countries of central Europe, an absolute majority of the general public has supported the new democracies of Poland, Hungary, Slovenia, and other countries throughout the whole period between 1992 and 1998. These countries were also among those that became members of the European Union in 2004 after the successful consolidation of democracy throughout the region. In southern Europe support for the new regime is not so clear-cut, and we found only 46 percent of postcommunist citizens in Croatia or Bulgaria with a positive assessment of their current political regimes.

Within the Commonwealth of Independent States, there was a clear growth in support for the present regime from 25 percent in 1992 up to 38 percent in 2000, indicating a slow but steady stabilization of political regimes in the region. This comparatively high level of support shrank from 38 percent in 2000 to 32 percent in 2001. This longitudinal development is due to divergent paths of political transformation in Russia, on the one hand, and in Belarus and Ukraine, on the other. The most successful political transformation and establishment of a political regime—within the CIS at least—took place in the Russian Federation. In 1992, only 14 percent of all Russians supported the current regime. The share of supporters of the new Russian regime grew to 35 percent in 1994 and 37 percent in 2000 and rose to 47 percent in late 2001 during the regime of President Vladimir Putin. By this date, a relative if not quite an absolute majority of Russians had given the Putin administration a positive assessment.

The evaluation of the political regime in Belarus by the electorate is quite different from the pattern in the Russian Federation. Popular support for the first Belarusian regime after the end of the Soviet Union was quite high, with a level of 35 percent in 1992. During the mid-1990s more than a third of Belarusian electorate supported the new political regime, and a relative majority of 48 percent gave the regime under President Lukashenko a positive evaluation between 1998 and 2000. This support fell sharply thereafter, however, to a level of just 24 percent by the winter of 2001. By that time, only a quarter of the Belarusian electorate was prepared to give the Lukashenko regime a positive mark between +10 and +100.

The political situation in Ukraine is to some extent similar to that in Belarus with regard to popular support for the existing political regime. In 1992, at the beginning of political transformation, 25 percent of the general public in Ukraine supported the new Ukrainian government. This popular support went up slowly to 31 percent in 2000 but never came close to a majority of the electorate, which was a clear indicator of the chronic dissatisfaction of the Ukrainians with their various administrations. As in Belarus, support for the current regime had fallen to 24 percent by 2001, albeit from a much lower starting point. These figures are evidence of an implicit political crisis in the form of the very low legitimacy of the governments dominated by Presidents Lukashenko and Kuchma. In Moldova, however, support for the existing political regime is even lower than in Belarus or Ukraine, following a similar collapse in political support for the incumbent regime from 23 percent in 2000 to a mere 5 percent in 2001.

The Future of National Parliaments

An important factor in the stability of parliamentary democracy is support for the national parliament. In the postcommunist countries, is there already a readiness to support and protect parliament, if attacked by nondemocratic forces, or is the national parliament as a crucial element of pluralist democracy not yet embedded within the national consciousness? An important indicator of the future chances of survival of a new democracy is the expectation that the national parliament could be suspended in the next few years. If a growing number of people do not expect that their parliament will be dissolved and replaced by some nondemocratic institution, we can hypothesize that the chances of democracy surviving are growing too (see table 9.4).

Table 9.4. *The Future of National Parliaments*

	1992	1994	1996	1998	2000	2001
Central Europe	66	64	68	83	n.a.	n.a.
Southern Europe	69	67	75	77	n.a.	n.a.
CIS	59	55	69	73	59	75
Belarus	**57**	**51**	**64**	**73**	**60**	**77**
Russia	n.a.	62	84	70	68	76
Moldova	n.a.	n.a.	n.a.	n.a.	52	76
Ukraine	60	51	58	75	49	72

The question wording was: "Some people think this country would be better governed if parliament were suspended and we did not have lots of political parties. How likely do you think it is that this could happen here in the next few years?" (persons saying suspension of parliament is unlikely, percentages).

The most important conclusion that can be reached from our survey data is that during the process of democratic transition, more and more postcommunist citizens are convinced that the national parliament will not be suspended in the near future—that is, parliament in particular and democracy in general will survive in the foreseeable future. At the beginning of the process of transition in 1991, only 62 percent of all postcommunist citizens said it was unlikely that their national parliament would be suspended, which means that almost 40 percent were anxious about the possibility of an attack on parliamentary institutions two years after the end of communist rule. Optimism about the prospects of national parliaments grew to 65 percent in 1992, but fell again to the initial level in 1994. Since then, however, the number of postcommunist citizens who believe in the survival of their national parliaments has been steadily increasing to a record level of 78 percent in 1998. This phenomenon shows the enlarging basis of support for parliamentary democracy in postcommunist Europe.

In central Europe, optimism about the survival of parliament is particularly marked, increasing from 66 percent in 1992 to 68 percent in 1996 and 83 percent in 1998. This shows the strengthening of the parliamentary roots of the new democracies in the central European buffer zone in the dawn before integration in the European Union. Expectations about a possible suspension of the national parliament were quite stable in southern Europe in the early 1990s, with figures of between 67 and 69 percent being optimistic about its future survival. In 1998, an average of 83 percent were parliamentary optimists in central Europe and 77 percent in southern Europe, which indicates a convergent pattern between these two regions of postcommunist change. As in central and southern Europe, we find also in eastern Europe the lowest level of expectations for the survival of a democratic parliament in 1994, when only 55 percent thought that their parliament was not under threat of being dissolved in the near future.

The results for central Europe provide strong empirical and comparative evidence that, with regard to parliamentary democracy, we can define the years between 1989 and 1996 as the first period of "transition toward democracy" from the communist political system to parliamentary democracy, whereas 1998 appears to be the starting point of the second period of political transformation, which could be characterized as the period of "consolidation of democracy" in this part of postcommunist Europe.

In Belarus specifically, optimism about the future and stability of the national parliament grew steadily over time from 57 percent in 1992 at the beginning of independent statehood to 77 percent in 2001. In 1992, an absolute majority of the Belarusian electorate was optimistic about the future prospects of the national parliament in Minsk. The share of optimists fell to 51 percent in 1994, showing that 1994 was once again a critical year regarding this dimension of general support for the new political system. Since 1994, the proportion of the electorate that take an optimistic view of the survival of the Belarusian parliament has grown again to 64 percent in 1996 and 73 percent in 1998. In 2000, a crisis of confidence in the future prospects of the Belarusian parliament was reflected in a fall to 60 percent in the proportion of the electorate that are optimistic about the long-term prospects of the highest institution of legislation in their country. In 2001, however, the highest proportion of all were optimistic about the survival of the national parliament (a diminished institution, certainly, as compared with the early postcommunist years)—an overwhelming majority of 77 percent of the electorate thought their parliament would not be suspended or closed down in the coming years. This level of parliamentary optimism was the highest in the entire CIS region among the countries covered by our surveys.

After the suspension of the Russian parliament by President Yeltsin in 1993 and the subsequent political violence the optimism of the Russian electorate in the long-term survival of the new Duma was rather subdued; only 62 percent of the Russian electorate believed that the Duma would not be suspended in the near future, when asked in 1994. But already by 1996 belief in the long-term survival of the Duma had become quite strong, with 84 percent confident in its future. Support for the Russian Federal parliament was stable with 70 percent in 1998 and 68 percent in 2000, rising to 76 percent in 2001.

Despite the continuing political crisis in Moldova, meanwhile, a majority of 76 percent were confident that the parliament in Chişinău would not be dissolved in the foreseeable future. Popular support for the Verkhovna Rada in Ukraine increased in parallel from 60 percent of the electorate in 1992, in the aftermath of the dissolution of the Soviet Union, to 75 percent in 1998. After a crisis of Ukrainian parliamentary legitimacy in 2000, when only 49 percent believed in the long-term survival of the Ukrainian parliament, we identified 72 percent of citizens at the end of 2001 who were optimistic about their parliament and its longer-term prospects.

Popular Support for National Parliaments

After considering the expectations of postcommunist mass publics concerning the survival of their elected institutions we turn now to the question of how deeply the newly created national parliaments are already embedded in the political value systems of the different national populations. We measure this by asking whether respondents would approve or disapprove personally of the undemocratic suspension of the national parliament (see table 9.5). From a longitudinal perspective, we find an interesting pattern in all twelve postcommunist countries taken together. The share of postcommunist citizens opposed to the suspension of a democratically elected parliament was very high at the beginning of democratic transition in 1991, when on average 81 percent of all postcommunist citizens disapproved of any action of this kind. This share of people defending the new national parliament fell to 75 percent in 1992 and 68 percent in 1994, which represented the lowest level in the entire transition period. Here again, we see that 1994 is a turning point in political transformation; from this time onward we can speak of growing support for national parliaments all over postcommunist Europe. After touching the bottom in that year, the share of supporters of parliaments went up to 72 percent in 1996 and 74 percent in 1998.

Looking now at the regional breakdown, we find that in central Europe there has been a constant level of support for newly created national parliaments with shares of between 75 and 78 percent. In southern Europe, the level of popular support for parliaments decreased from 82 percent in 1992 to 77 percent in 1994. The legitimacy of parliaments recovered to 83 percent in 1996, but fell

Table 9.5. Popular Support for National Parliaments

	1992	1994	1996	1998	2000	2001
Central Europe	76	75	77	78	n.a.	n.a.
Southern Europe	82	77	83	76	n.a.	n.a.
CIS	63	51	53	63	53	42
Belarus	**68**	**57**	**60**	**72**	**56**	**54**
Russia	n.a.	40	61	62	61	42
Moldova	n.a.	n.a.	n.a.	n.a.	41	39
Ukraine	58	56	39	55	43	29

The question wording was: "If parliament were suspended and parties abolished, would you approve or disapprove?" (percentage disapproving of the suspension of parliament).

again in 1998 because of the low level of parliamentary legitimacy in the then–Federal Republic of Yugoslavia, now Serbia-Montenegro. The legitimacy of the new national parliaments is lowest in eastern Europe; it fell from 63 percent in 1992 to 51 percent in 1994, which was in that region also a year of political crisis. But even at a very low level, support for democratic parliaments has been increasing slowly in eastern Europe to 53 percent in 1996 and 63 percent in 1998, which shows the slow development of the roots of parliamentary legitimacy even in the least developed part of postcommunist Europe. The proportion of East Europeans that were prepared to defend their national parliaments, however, fell subsequently to 53 percent in 2000 and to just 42 percent in 2001.

Within eastern Europe, the highest level of legitimacy of the new national parliament can be found in Belarus. In 1992, an absolute majority of the mass public was against an undemocratic suspension of the national parliament. This figure reduced to 57 percent in 1994, which is in Belarus as elsewhere the year of lowest legitimacy. Since 1994, however, support for the Belarusian parliament in the face of its possible suspension grew to 60 percent in 1996 and 72 percent in 1998, which is a similar level to that in Romania in the late 1990s. Support for the Supreme Soviet decreased to 53 percent in 2000 and 54 percent in 2001, but this is still the highest level of support of all the CIS countries included in our surveys. Throughout the whole period of political transformation in Belarus between 1992 and 2001, an absolute majority of the Belarusian electorate has always been prepared to support the existence of the national parliament.

In Russia, by contrast, popular support for the Duma against nondemocratic attacks was very low in 1994, when only 40 percent of Russians disapproved of a potential coup, but it subsequently increased. In 1996, 61 percent of the mass public supported the Duma as a political institution and 62 percent gave the Russian parliament its general support in 1998 despite the continuing political crisis, which culminated in the financial collapse of August 1998. Between 1996 and 2000, an absolute majority of the Russian electorate of around 60 percent supported the existence of the national parliament. The legitimacy of the Duma had slipped by 2001, however, with just 42 percent of our respondents actively prepared to support it.

In Moldova, we found only a constant share of around 40 percent of the electorate supporting the national parliament, which is much lower than in Belarus and Russia. The lowest extent of popular support for the national parliament across all twelve postcommunist countries was once again in Ukraine. Support for the Ukrainian national parliament had in addition a downward tendency between 1992 and 1996. In 1992, an absolute majority of 58 percent of all Ukrainians were prepared to defend the national parliament against an undemocratic coup. This figure sank to 56 percent in 1994 and to 39 percent in 1996. The dangerously low level of popular support for the Ukrainian parliament recovered slightly to 55 percent in 1998. But after 1998 popular support for the Verkhovna Rada declined further, to 43 percent in 2000 and finally to a record low of 29 percent in 2001. This means that less than a third of the Ukrainian population is opposed to the suspension of the national parliament.

Alternatives to Democracy: Support for an Authoritarian Leader

The birth and consolidation of democracy are closely linked to the availability and acceptance of alternatives to democracy. In this section we consider the extent of popular support for a "strong and authoritarian leader" in postcommunist Europe (see table 9.6). The most important general conclusion is that support for

Table 9.6. Support for a Strong Authoritarian Leader

	1992	1994	1996	1998	2000	2001
Central Europe	27	27	23	19	n.a.	n.a.
Southern Europe	47	28	19	20	n.a.	n.a.
CIS	65	49	57	43	32	43
Belarus	**76**	**57**	**56**	**37**	**23**	**31**
Russia	n.a.	33	47	36	29	43
Moldova	n.a.	n.a.	n.a.	n.a.	59	54
Ukraine	53	56	67	55	45	56

The question wording was: "Do you agree or disagree with the view that it is best to get rid of parliament and elections and have a strong leader who can quickly decide things?" (percentage of respondents in agreement).

a strong leader, replacing pluralist democracy by the rule of a single person, is melting away throughout the region. At an early stage of political transformations—in 1992—an absolute majority of postcommunist citizens, especially in southern and eastern Europe, were in favor of a strong leader replacing the new democracy. In all twelve countries, support for a strong politician fell to a third of the total by 1994 and went further down to 29 percent by 1996. This linear decline in support for a one-man dictatorship replacing democracy carried on until 1998, when only 25 percent of all postcommunist citizens were in favor of this form of authoritarian rule.

Across the postcommunist countries generally, the lowest level of support for the nondemocratic rule of a single leader is in central Europe. Some 27 percent supported this option in 1992 and 1994, falling to 23 percent in 1996 and 19 percent in 1998. Initial support for a strong man was much higher in southern Europe, at 47 percent. However, here too support fell to 28 percent in 1994 and remained at the level of one-fifth of southern Europeans in 1996 (19 percent). After the negative experiences with Presidents Milošević and Tudjman in Serbia and Croatia only 20 percent of all southern European citizens supported authoritarian one-man rule in 1998. Hence, we can hypothesize that a fifth of the citizens of central as well in southern Europe are in favor of one-man rule as an alternative to democracy about a decade after the end of the communist system.

The wish of the mass public for an authoritarian leader instead of pluralist democracy is by far the greatest in the countries of eastern Europe, in Belarus, Ukraine, Moldova, and Russia. In the aftermath of the collapse of the Soviet Union and the subsequent political confusion in 1992, an absolute majority of 65 percent of all Russians, Belarusians, and Ukrainians expressed their wish to have a strong authoritarian leader. This widespread desire for a strong leader, who would supposedly resolve the problems of political and economic turmoil within the region, decreased during the 1990s to 57 percent in 1996 and 43 percent in 1998 and reached a historical low in 2000, when only 32 percent of post-Soviet citizens supported the regime of a strong political leader. In late 2001, we again found widespread popular support for authoritarian leadership with 43 percent of the citizens in eastern Europe with a longing for a strong leader.

Support for an authoritarian leader was greatest at the beginning of the process of transformation in Belarus, where 76 percent of the electorate wanted such an alternative to democracy. The level of support for a one-man system fell thereafter, to 57 percent in 1994 and to 19 percent in 2004. One explanation for the declining support for a strong leader may come from the fact that Belarus had by this time established a strong authoritarian leader in the person of President Lukashenko—one might almost argue that the popular wish had been fulfilled. At present, less than one-third of the electorate in Belarus (31 percent) are supporters of authoritarian rule of this kind, which is the lowest level of support for this particular undemocratic alternative among the CIS countries included in our surveys.

The wish for an authoritarian leader became prominent in Russia somewhat later than in Belarus. The peak of support for a strong Russian leader was in 1996, when 47 percent of our respondents endorsed this alternative to democracy. The desire for a strong leader fell to 36 percent in 1998 and 29 percent in 2000, but went up again in 2001, when 43 percent of the Russian electorate were again in favor of authoritarian rule. The general public in Moldova has also been quite antidemocratic, with an absolute majority of between 54 and 59 percent consistently supporting the leadership of a strong man as an alternative to a full-fledged democracy. Throughout the whole period between 1992 and 1998 we also find an absolute majority of the Ukrainian population with a declared preference for a strong political leader rather than pluralist democracy. This wish for a one-man regime following a one-party regime even increased, from 53 percent in 1992 to 67 percent in 1996. Only since 1996 has the demand for a strong politician decreased somewhat to 55 percent in 1998, which still represents an absolute majority for that alternative to democracy; and in 2001, 56 percent of Ukrainians were once again prepared to endorse this nondemocratic form of political regime.

Alternatives to Democracy: Support for a Military Regime

Another alternative to democracy, which is less popular than a strong authoritarian leader within postcommunist Europe, is the wish to replace democracy by a military regime. That wish was measured by asking our respondents if in their view the national army should govern the country (see table 9.7). The pattern over time shows that support for military rule is at a low level throughout, at 10 percent or less, without an upward or downward tendency. In 1994, only 9 per-

Table 9.7. Alternatives to Democracy: Support for a Military Regime

	1994	1996	1998	2000	2001
Central Europe	5	3	3	n.a.	n.a.
Southern Europe	12	9	12	n.a.	n.a.
CIS	12	13	13	17	9
Belarus	**15**	**13**	**10**	**9**	**5**
Ukraine	10	15	14	32	9
Moldova	n.a.	n.a.	n.a.	11	10
Russia	10	11	15	11	13

The question wording was: "Do you agree or disagree with the view that it is best that the army should govern the country?" (percentage of respondents in agreement).

cent of the population across the region favored a political takeover by the army, a level of support that was almost unchanged in 1996 (8 percent) and in 1998 (9 percent). In central Europe, almost nobody (3 percent) thought that the army should govern the country; in southern and eastern Europe, however, levels of support were rather higher, at about 12 percent.

In eastern Europe, support for a military regime is clearly much lower than for the restoration of communist rule or a one-person dictatorship, but the patterns are divergent in the former member states of the Soviet Union. The core trend in eastern Europe might be described as a steady increase in support for military rule, from 12 percent in 1994 to 17 percent in 2000. After 2000, however, there was a sharp fall in the idea that the national army should take over politics, down to 9 percent in 2001. Currently, the Latin American model of regime change toward military rule seems a very remote option for political transformations in eastern Europe.

Within the Commonwealth of Independent States, the rule of the military in politics is the least popular in Belarus, where support for a military regime fell from 15 percent in 1994 to 10 percent in 1998 and finally to 5 percent in 2004, which is similar to the very low levels of support for this undemocratic alternative in central Europe. The decline in support for military rule in Belarus has been steady and unbroken, suggesting that the primacy of the political over the armed forces in Belarus seems to be undisputed and that a military coup is out of the question as an option for regime change.

The military option gained increasing support in Ukraine from 10 percent in 1994 and 15 percent in 1996 with an absolute peak of 32 percent in 2000, and seems to be reflective of deep disenchantment with the political regime of that country during the 1990s. Nevertheless the share of Ukrainians in favor of the military taking over politics collapsed from 32 percent in 2000 to 9 percent in 2001. In Moldova, we found a constant group of 10 percent of the electorate who were in favor of military rule, which is *de facto* the case in the Transnistrian region of that divided country. In the Russian Federation, the desire for a military regime has been growing over time from 10 percent in 1994 to 15 percent in 1998, but had declined again to 13 percent in 2001.

Alternatives to Democracy: Support for Monarchy

Many postcommunist countries have the historical experience of monarchy as a form of political regime. We were accordingly concerned to establish the extent to which postcommunist citizens regard monarchy as an alternative to parliamentary democracy at the start of a new century. The main conclusion was that approximately a tenth of the mass public in postcommunist Europe favors monarchy as an alternative to democracy (see table 9.8). The share of monarchists

Table 9.8. Alternatives to Democracy: Support for a Monarchy

	1994	1998	2000	2001
Ukraine	7	12	8	6
Central Europe	4	4	n.a.	n.a.
Southern Europe	14	14	n.a.	n.a.
CIS	8	10	10	7
Belarus	8	8	11	5
Ukraine	7	12	8	6
Moldova	n.a.	n.a.	12	6
Russia	9	11	10	9

The question wording was: "Do you agree or disagree with the view that a return to a monarchy would be better?" (percentage of respondents in agreement).

grew, but only very slightly, from 7 percent in 1994 to 9 percent in 1998. The wish for a monarchist restoration is particularly small in central Europe, where consistently only 4 percent support monarchy as a political regime. The most advanced states of central Europe are indeed the most republican and least monarchist across the region. In southern Europe, by contrast, the wish for a restoration of monarchy is the highest across the entire postcommunist region, with a constant level of support of 14 percent.

In eastern Europe, support for a new tsar grew from 8 percent in 1994 to 10 percent in 1998, reflecting a general dissatisfaction with experience of democratic rule. The share of monarchists remained stable at the level of one-tenth of the electorate in 2000, but fell to 7 percent in 2001, which is higher than in central Europe but lower than in southern Europe. In Belarus, as with military rule, support for a monarchical system is the lowest among the CIS countries included in our surveys, although it gained ground slightly from 8 percent in 1994 to 11 percent in 2000. The wish for a monarchy as a form of government, however, declined further by 2004, when only 7 percent of all Belarusians expressed the view that a return to a monarchy as in the Russian Empire would be better than the current political regime in Minsk.

During the first phase of political transformation in Ukraine the monarchy secured an increasing level of support, from 7 percent in 1994 up to 12 percent in 1998. But since 1998, the wish for a return to dynastic rule has been in steady decline to 8 percent in 2000 and 6 percent in 2001, and seems no longer to be a viable alternative form of political regime. We also found diminishing support for a monarchy in Moldova, from 12 percent in 2000 to 6 percent in 2001. In Russia, on the other hand, there was between 1994 and 2001 a constant share of around one-tenth of the Russian electorate that would apparently appreciate a return to the rule of the tsars.

Support for Democracy as a Form of Political Regime

After analyzing the extent of support for alternatives to democracy, we conclude by measuring support for democracy as a form of political regime. This is also labeled in the literature as the "Churchill hypothesis" and is measured empirically by the statement that "democracy may have deficiencies, but it's better than any other form of government" (see table 9.9). The general trend in the CIS region regarding democracy as a principle of a political system is that the group of "democratic citizens" is small but steadily growing over time. In 1995, we identified 17 percent of "democrats" in the four post-Soviet states. The size of this group grew to 23 percent in 1999 and finally to 33 percent in 2001. One might conclude from this finding that one-third of all post-Soviet citizens have successfully managed the personal transformation toward being democratic citizens after the end of the Soviet Union in 1991, which is much less than, for example, in central Europe.[3]

Table 9.9. *Support for Democracy as a Political Regime (the "Churchill Hypothesis")*

	1995	1999	2001
CIS	17	23	33
Belarus	**24**	**34**	**39**
Ukraine	16	24	33
Russia	10	12	33
Moldova	18	n.a.	26

The question wording was: "Democracy may have deficiencies, but it's better than any other form of government" (percentage of respondents in strong agreement).

Sources: The 1995 World Values Survey; the 1999 European Values Survey; the 2001 New Democracies Barometer 6.

Belarus, in particular, is the post-Soviet country with the largest group of democrats throughout the entire period of political transformation. In 1995, a quarter of the Belarusian electorate could be characterized as "democrats," a share of democratic citizens that increased by 1999 to one-third of all citizens. Finally, by 2001, a relative majority of 39 percent of the Belarusian electorate could be regarded as democrats, using in all cases the typology developed in connection with the World Values Survey.

Ukraine comes in second with regard to the number of democrats within the CIS region. We found 16 percent of democratic citizens in Ukraine in 1995. The share of democrats within the Ukrainian electorate went up to one-fourth in

1999 and to one-third in 2001. The emergence of democratic citizens started much more slowly in the Russian Federation, with 10 percent democrats in 1995 and 12 percent of democratic Russians in 1999. We found a big leap forward in democratic change between 1999 and 2001, when already one-third of the Russian voters regarded democracy as the best form of political regime. In Moldova the share of democrats was already 18 percent in 1995 with only a slow growth process up to 26 percent of democratic Moldavian citizens in 2001.

Conclusions

This study of postcommunist democratization in Belarus in comparative perspective yielded the following main results:

- "Democrats" within the Belarusian electorate have a relative majority of 39 percent, outnumbering all other alternatives to democratic rule. Support for democracy in Belarus is higher than in Ukraine, Russia, or Moldova.
- An absolute majority of 54 percent of all Belarusian citizens support their national parliament. Support for the national parliament is higher than in Russia, Moldova, or Ukraine. Citizens in Belarus are also optimistic about the long-term survival of the national parliament as an actor in the political system.
- The most important alternative to democracy in Belarus is the replacement of democracy by an authoritarian leader. One-third of the Belarusian citizenry supports a strong authoritarian leader like the current president, which is much less than in Russian, Moldova, or Ukraine.
- The second most important alternative to democracy in Belarus is the restoration of communism. One-third of the Belarusian electorate fully or partially supports the return of communist political rule, which is much lower than in Ukraine, Russia, or Moldova.
- Other nondemocratic forms of political regime such as absolute monarchy or military rule found no significant support among the Belarusian public.
- Public support of the existing political regime under President Lukashenko eroded dramatically from one-half of the electorate to one-fourth between 1998 and the end of 2001. Three-quarters of the electorate are currently opposed to the incumbent government in Belarus, which is producing a strong latent tension between democratization at the microlevel of Belarusian politics and authoritarian structures at the macrolevel of the present regime. That tension in its turn is likely to be central to the country's future evolution.

Notes

1. See Kathleen J. Mihalisko, "Belarus: Retreat to Authoritarianism," in *Democratic Changes and Authoritarian Reactions in Russia, Ukraine, Belarus, and Moldova*, ed. Karen Dawisha and Bruce Parrott (Cambridge: Cambridge University Press, 1997), 223–81 (259).
2. See Christian W. Haerpfer, *Democracy and Enlargement in Post-Communist Europe. The Democratisation of the General Public in Fifteen Central and Eastern European Countries, 1991–1998* (London: Routledge, 2002), 12.
3. Haerpfer, *Democracy and Enlargement*, 40–45.

Appendix

The New Democracies Barometer (NDB) is an international comparative survey program to monitor political, economic, and social transformations in post-communist Europe between 1990 and 2001, directed by Christian W. Haerpfer.

NDB 2 - New Democracies Barometer 2

Year   1992
Total   10,518 interviews

1. Belarus   1,225 interviews
    Fieldwork by the Center for Social and Political Research, Belarusian State University, Minsk

2. Ukraine   1,000 interviews
    Fieldwork by Ukrainian Academy of Sciences, Kiev

NDB 3 - New Democracies Barometer 3

Year   1994
Total   14,622 interviews

3. Belarus   2,067 interviews
    Fieldwork by the Center for Social and Political Research, Belarusian State University, Minsk

4. Ukraine   1,000 interviews
    Fieldwork by Socis-Gallup, Kiev

5. Russian Federation 3,535 interviews
    Fieldwork by Mnenie, Moscow

NDB 4 - New Democracies Barometer 4

Year 1996
Total 10,441 interviews

6. Belarus 1,000 interviews
   Fieldwork by the Center for Social and Political Research, Belarusian State University, Minsk

7. Ukraine 1,000 interviews
   Fieldwork by Socis-Gallup, Kiev

NDB 5 - New Democracies Barometer 5

Year 1998
Total 11,595 interviews

8. Belarus 1,000 interviews
   Fieldwork by the Center for Social and Political Research, Belarusian State University, Minsk

9. Ukraine 1,161 interviews
   Fieldwork by Socis-Gallup, Kiev

NDB 6 - New Democracies Barometer 6

Year 2001
Total 18,428 interviews

10. Belarus 2,000 interviews
    Fieldwork by the Center for Social and Political Research, Belarusian State University, Minsk

11. Ukraine 2,400 interviews
    Fieldwork by Eastern Ukrainian Research Foundation, Kharkiv

12. Russian Federation 4,006 interviews
    Fieldwork by Moscow State University

13. Moldova 2,000 interviews
    Fieldwork by Opinia, Chişinău.

Appendix

Selected Socioeconomic Data

Population and Territory

As of January 1, 2003, the population of Belarus was 9,898,600, of whom 1,726,300 lived in the capital city, Minsk. Of the total population 46.9 percent were male and 53.1 percent female; 18.5 percent were below working age, 60.3 per cent were of working age, and 21.2 percent were older than working age. The national territory was 207,600 square kilometers, of which 38 percent was forest; density of settlement was 47.7 inhabitants per square kilometer.

Administrative-Territorial Structure

	Districts	Towns	Urban districts	Urban settlements	Rural settlements	Villages
Belarus	118	110	25	101	1,441	24,049
Regions:						
Brest	16	20	2	9	226	2,178
Gomel	21	17	4	18	275	2,608
Grodno	17	14	2	18	191	4,380
Minsk city	–	1	9	–	–	–
Minsk	22	24	–	19	308	5,234
Mogilev	21	15	5	9	194	3,120
Vitebsk	21	19	3	28	247	6,529

Source: Respublika Belarus' v tsifrakh. Kratkii statisticheskii slovar' (Minsk: Ministerstvo statistiki i analiza Respubliki Belarus', 2003), 25.

Demographic Indicators

	1990	1995	2000	2001	2002	2003
Population, beginning of year (thousands)	10,189	10,210	10,020	9,990	9,951	9,899
of which: urban (%)	66.1	67.9	69.7	70.2	70.7	71.1
rural (%)	33.9	32.1	30.3	29.8	29.3	28.9
Life expectancy at birth (years)	71.1	68.6	69.0	68.5	68.0	n.d.
Infant mortality (per 1000 births)	11.9	12.3	8.3	8.0	6.9	n.d.
Marriages (per 1000 population)	9.7	7.6	6.2	6.9	6.7	6.7
Divorces (per 1000 population)	3.4	4.1	4.3	4.1	3.8	3.8

Source: As above, 54–62.

Labor and Employment (Official Data, Percentages)

	1990	1995	2000	2002
Employed	–	97.5	97.9	97.3
Unemployed	–	2.5	2.1	2.7
Of the total:				
In state sector	73.9	59.8	57.2	55.8
Private	26.1	40.1	42.4	43.3
Foreign	–	0.1	0.4	0.9

Source: As above, 74–75.

Nationality (Census Dates, Percentages and Totals)

	1979	1989	1999	(thousands)
Belarusians	79.4	77.9	81.2	8,159
Russians	11.9	13.2	11.4	1,142
Poles	4.2	4.1	3.9	396
Ukrainians	2.4	2.9	2.4	237
Jews	1.4	1.1	0.3	28
Other	0.7	0.8	0.8	83

Source: As above, 57.

Economic Performance (Indices [1990 = 100], Official Data)

	1990	1992	1993	1994	1995	1996	1997	1998	1999	2000	2001	2002
GDP	100	89	83	73	65	67	75	81	84	89	93	97
Previous year	–	90	92	88	90	103	111	108	103	106	105	105
Industrial production	100	90	81	70	61	64	75	85	93	100.7	107	111
Previous year	102	91	91	85	88	104	119	112	110	108	106	104
Agricultural production	100	87	90	77	74	75	72	71	65	71	73	74
Previous year	92	83	96	84	88	101	103	98	87	111	103	100.4
Capital investment	100	74	63	57	39	37	45	56	51	52	50	52
Previous year	109	71	85	89	69	95	120	125	92	102	97	103
Real incomes	100	91	85	59	56	59	67	79	85	95	123	133
Previous year	114	88	94	69	95	105	114	118	107	112	130	108
Consumer price index (times)	–	16.6	21.0	20.6	3.4	1.4	1.6	2.8	3.5	2.1	1.5	1.3

Source: As above, 28–39.

Language Use (1999 Census, Percentages)

	Mother tongue		Language usually spoken at home	
	Belarusian	*Russian*	*Belarusian*	*Russian*
Minsk city	61.9	36.7	12.9	86.9
Urban population	66.9	31.1	19.8	79.8
Rural population	89.2	8.3	74.7	24.5
Belarusians	85.6	14.3	41.3	58.6
Russians	9.1	90.7	4.3	95.7
Poles	67.1	16.2	57.6	37.7
Ukrainians	14.3	42.8	10.2	83.5
Jews	17.1	77.0	3.8	95.7
Total	73.7	24.1	36.7	62.8

Source: Itogi perepisi naseleniya Respubliki Belarus' 1999 goda, Vol. 1 (Minsk: Ministerstvo statistiki i analiza, 2000), 214–19.

Index

administrative controls, 97–98, 106–8
Agrarian Party, 38, 42, 47–50; and communism, 164–65; and communist system, the present and the future, 21–24; and democracy, 171–75; and electoral mechanism, 26–27; and new political regime, 165–67; and parliament, 167–71; and presidential candidates, 88–89. *See also* elections
authoritarian leader, 171–73. *See also* Lukashenko and authoritarianism

Baltic States, 3–4, 17, 42, 125
Belarus, and Act of Union with Russia, 6, 8; Christian nation, 17; and Commonwealth of Independent States (CIS), 5, 8, 36, 91, 106, 114, 116, 123–26, 128, 132, 138, 156, 162, 166, 168, 172, 175–76; declaration of independence, 36; declaration on state sovereignty, 5, 35, 125, 137–38; and defense of the Soviet Union, 2; economic performance, 98, 114–16, 183; economic recovery, 114–15; foreign policy, 62, 123, 143, 155; history of, 1–2, 5, 57; independence, 2–4, 13–14, 36, 79; and Kingdom of Poland and Lithuania, 17; martyrology, 4; and national identity, 2–5, 12–13, 15, 36; and nationhood, 2, 4, 12; and relations with Russia, 1–3, 5, 7–8, 10, 21–22, 25–26, 28, 31–32, 65–66, 69, 79, 83, 93, 115, 123, 134–35, 137, 152, 166; relations with the West, 2, 7–8, 10, 12, 15, 54–55, 69, 79, 93, 143–60; and Slavic choice, 17, 21, 27, 33; and state emblem of Lithuania, 5; and statehood, 2, 12–13
Belarus Communist Party (KPB), 36, 39, 41–42, 50
Belarusian economy, 8
Belarusian model, 102, 116, 120–21, 132
Belarusian Patriotic Union, 42
Belarusian Popular Front *Adradzhenne*, 3, 4, 36, 55
Belarusian Popular Front political organization, 4-6, 9, 37, 39, 41, 42–43, 47
Belarusian Social-Democratic Gromada (BSDG), 37, 38, 41, 44
Belarusian Soviet Socialist Republic (BSSR), 2–3, 35–36, 51, 125
Belarusian trade, 129–30
Belarus–Russia monetary union, 117–20

Belarus–Russia Union, 14, 127, 143. *See also* Belarus and relations with Russia
Belavezh Treaty, 36, 125
Bogdankevich, Stanislav, 37, 45, 47
Bykov, Vasil, 10

Central Election Commission, 46, 48, 53, 56, 62, 82, 85, 87, 89–92. *See also* elections
central Europe, 23, 35, 152, 161, 163, 166, 168–69, 172, 174–76
central planning, 97, 120. *See also* Belarusian model
Chernobyl', 3, 4
Chigir, Mikhail, 81–82, 87, 91
"Churchill hypothesis," 176
citizen and the state, 24–28
citizens, democratic, 176–77
Civic Party, 37, 45
Cold War, 10
Collective Security Treaty, 6, 123–24, 126, 156
command economy, 97, 120. S*ee also* Belarusian model
Communist Party of Belarus (PKB), 35–38, 40, 41–42, 47–49, 52, 87
communist rule, 17–20, 31, 161–63. *See also* Soviet Union
Community treaty, 126–27
constitution, 18, 57, 59, 61–62, 74–75, 80, 93
Constitutional Court, 43, 47–48, 62–63, 79
Coordinating Council of Democratic Forces (KRDS), 43–44, 49, 81
corruption, 18–19, 27, 34, 69, 98
Council of Europe, 6, 9, 137, 143–45, 154
Council of the Republic, 62–63. *See also* National Assembly
currency, 98, 113–14, 130
customs union, 125–26, 129

"Democratic Club," 35
democratization, 161
demagogical democracy, 97
"disappearances," 64–65, 72, 85–86
Dobrovol'sky, Alexander, 36, 45

eastern Europe, 12–13, 35, 161, 163, 170, 172, 174–75
EBRD, 98–99, 103
economic stagnation, 19
elections, and electoral code, 53–54, 80; parliamentary (1990), 35; (1995), 35, 45–49, 61; (2000), 35, 49–51, 137; presidential (1994), 6; (2001), 79–95, 137
Eurasian Economic Community, 123, 125–26, 138
Europe, 1, 10, 17, 125, 143, 157
"European choice," 17, 33
European democracies, 25
European Union, 1, 8–9, 10–12, 17–25, 45, 54–55, 84, 93, 119, 123, 129, 135–37, 144, 148–49, 151, 153–54, 168; and level of trust in civic institutions, 24–25

fiscal policy, 109
foreign direct investment, 98, 105–6, 119
foreign trade, 98, 101, 109
freedoms, various, 19–20

Gaidukevich, Sergei, 43, 82, 84, 90–92
Gazprom, 115–16, 130–31, 140
glasnost', 3–4
Gonchar, Viktor, 48, 64, 85
Goncharik, Vladimir, 76, 81–86, 88–89, 91–92
Gorbachev, Mikhail (Soviet president), 5, 11, 15, 27, 36, 125

House of Representatives, 7, 41–42, 48, 50, 52, 54, 62–63, 81
human rights, 8, 18–19, 69

IMF, 101, 108, 112, 119, 121, 140
inflation, 9, 98, 102, 106, 120
integration, 136–37

Karpenko, Gennadii, 37, 45, 48
Kebich, Vyacheslav (Prime Minister), 5, 6, 25–26, 40, 59, 74, 124

language, 36, 61, 184
Lebed'ko, Anatolii, 45, 81
liberal democracy, 20, 26–27
Liberal-Democratic Party of Belarus 38, 40, 41, 43, 50, 52, 82, 84, 94
liberalization, 97, 99–100, 104
Lithuania, 3–5, 7–8, 17, 144
Lukashenko, Alexander, President, 1–3, 6–8, 10, 24, 40, 59–60, 63–64, 70, 73–75, 133, 137, 172; anti-Western policies of, 1, 10; and authoritarianism, 2, 8, 9, 10, 12–13, 15, 51, 73, 97; decrees of, 40, 52, 62–63, 106; and dictatorship, 12, 15, 54–55, 93, 143; election (1994), 6, 59, 123, 143; and his electorate, 65, 68–74, 88; and lukashenkism, 9–10; and presidential election 2001, 60, 70, 79–80, 83, 90–92; and referendum (1995), 7, 45–46, 48, 61; and referendum (1996), 48, 54, 61, 79, 123; and regime, 7, 10–11, 32, 51, 54, 59, 63, 93, 163, 166; rise to power, 60–65

Marinich, Mikhail, 82
market economy, 97, 101, 109
Masherov, Piotr, 2, 3, 13, 72
Masherova, Natalia, 82, 90
Mazurov, Kirill, 2

media censorship 7–8, 21, 84–85, 94, 97
military regime, 173–74
Moldova, 1, 161–77, 171–73
monetary policy, 112, 117–20, 124
mornachy, 174–75

National Assembly, 52, 54, 62–64
National Bank, 62, 106, 108, 112–13, 117
NATO military alliance, 1, 7, 17, 80, 92, 123, 135, 144–46, 148–51, 153–55, 157
nomenklatura, 32, 40, 59–60. *See also* old-guard elite

old-guard elite, 36, 51
opposition, 6–8, 10, 61
Orthodox, 17, 34, 86, 135
OSCE Advisory and Monitoring Group, 43, 44, 49–50, 52–53, 57, 79, 86–87, 91, 145, 154

parties, political, 5, 14, 25–6, 30, 35, 45–6, 49, 51–2, 54–6, 97; elite, 44–45; mass, 41–43. *See also under individual parties*
Party of Popular Consent, 37, 39, 47
"party of power," 40
party system, 31, 35, 40–41, 46, 51, 77
perception of change and individual liberties, 19–20; and new democracies, 21
perestroika, 3, 23, 27
Poland, immediate Western neighbor, 1, 5, 17, 19, 45, 108, 144, 148–49, 151, 166
political culture, 17, 32, 67; and perception of communist rule, 18–19; and perception of change, 19–20
political orientations, 28–32
population, 181–82

Poznyak, Zenon, archeologist, 4; and the Conservative-Christian Party, 43, 51; and Kuropaty, 4, 36; leader of the BNF, 4, 6, 10, 42–44, 74, 77, 82, 86–87. *See also* Belarusian Popular Front
presidential administration, 10, 45, 69, 82, 132–33, 153
presidential vertical, 45, 53, 56, 62, 75
privatization, 98–100, 103–4, 133
Putin, Vladimir, 8, 14, 21–22, 80, 84, 85, 116, 128, 130, 136, 157, 166

real wages, 107
regime, superpresidential, 64, 75. *See also* Lukashenko
representative democracy, 35
Russia, 1, 27–28, 59, 80, 136, 171–73
Russia–Belarus Union, 8–9, 11, 42, 55, 65–66, 80, 86, 117–20, 123–29. *See also* Belarus and relations with Russia
Russian stabilization program, 97
Russification, 4

samizdat, 3
Second World War, 1–2, 9, 13, 83
Sharetsky, Semion, 37, 47–48
shortage, 108–9
Shushkevich, Stanislav, and election (1994), 6, 36, 59, 74; and START-1 and nuclear non-proliferation treaties, 6, 124, 138; and the Supreme Soviet, 5, 13, 45, 125. *See also* Belavezh Treaty
social contract, 32
socially oriented market economy, 101, 120. *See also* Belarusian model

Sokolov, Efrem, 36
Soros Foundation, 8, 9
Soviet economic model, 102
Soviet era, Soviet period, 1, 3, 4, 9, 12, 13, 23–24, 27, 30, 46, 61
Soviet propaganda, 3
Soviet regime, 36
Soviet Union, 1–6, 11–12, 15, 17–18, 20, 23–24, 30, 35–36, 51, 59–60, 97–98, 115, 118, 123–25, 134–35, 141, 163, 166, 169; collapse of, 1, 3, 5, 11–12, 97–98, 169, 176. *See also* communist rule, USSR
Soviet-style economic model, 10
state-controlled economy, 69, 97
strong presidency, 7, 18, 60, 65, 76
Supreme Soviet, 5, 7, 46–47, 62–63, 79, 82–83, 85, 125–26. *See also* House of Representatives
survey data, 18, 21, 32–33, 65, 68–69, 76, 90–91, 134, 147–48, 179–80

Transparency International, 27, 34. *See also* corruption
triple transformation, 18
trust in institutions 21, 24–25, 29, 34, 67

Ukraine, neighbor, 3–4, 9–10, 13, 19, 21–23, 25–28, 31–32, 59, 132, 162–77, 171–73; and Gongadze's case, 85, 94; and levels of support of civic institutions, 24–25
unified candidate (2001 presidential election), 82–83
Union Charter, 127
Union State, 127–28, 133–34, 138–40, 142
United Civic Party (OGP), 37, 39, 41, 45, 52, 81, 137

United Democratic Party of Belarus (UDP), 36, 39, 41–42, 45, 47
UN's Human Development Index, 60, 75, 132, 140
United States, 10, 13, 63, 80–82, 92, 94, 123–24, 127–28, 131, 136, 144, 146, 148–49
USSR, 17–18, 60, 148, 163. *See also* Soviet Union

Vecherka, Vintsuk, 42–43, 81. *See also* Belarusian Popular Front

western Europe, 1, 11. *See also* Belarus and relations with the West
Wieck, Hans-Georg, 86–87
Women's Party "Nadzeya," 38, 40, 44–45, 52
World Bank, 101, 107, 121
World Value Survey, 21, 176

Yeltsin, Boris, 5, 59, 117, 169
Yugoslavia, 23, 92, 170

About the Contributors

Christian W. Haerpfer is professor of politics in the Department of Politics at the University of Vienna and residential fellow at the Woodrow Wilson International Center for Scholars in Washington, D.C., during the academic year 2004–2005. He is also visiting fellow at the School of Slavonic, Central and Eastern European Studies at the University of Glasgow. His *Democracy and Enlargement in Post-Communist Europe* was published by Routledge in 2002.

Ronald J. Hill is professor of comparative government and a fellow of Trinity College, Dublin. He has published widely on communist and postcommunist affairs, including books on the Soviet Communist Party and on political change and reform in communist systems, and is style and managing editor of the *Journal of Communist Studies and Transition Politics*. He was involved in developing a program of European studies at the European Humanities University, Minsk.

Elena Korosteleva, formerly British Academy research fellow at Glasgow University, is now lecturer in European politics, Department of International Politics, University of Wales, Aberystwyth. Her recent publications include *Contemporary Belarus: Between Democracy and Dictatorship* (RoutledgeCurzon, 2003, coedited with Rosalind Marsh and Colin Lawson), and *The Quality of Democracy in Post-Communist Europe* (Cass, 2004, coedited with Derek Hutcheson).

John Löwenhardt is senior research fellow at the Netherlands Institute of International Relations "Clingendael." Previously he was at the universities of Amsterdam, Leiden, and Glasgow. His published work includes *The Reincarnation of Russia* (Longman, 1995) and *Army and State in Postcommunist Europe* (coedited with David Betz, Cass, 2001).

David R. Marples is professor of history at the University of Alberta. His published works include two books on Belarus and two on the Chernobyl disaster. His most recent book is *The Collapse of the Soviet Union, 1985–1991* (Pearson

Education–Longman, 2004). In 2003 he was awarded the J. Gordin Kaplan Prize for excellence in research at the University of Alberta.

Ian McAllister is director of the Research School of Social Sciences at the Australian National University, Canberra, and adjunct professor of politics at Queen's University, Belfast. His published work includes *How Russia Votes* (with Stephen White and Richard Rose, Chatham House, 1997) and *The Cambridge Handbook of Social Sciences in Australia* (coedited with Steve Dowrick and Riaz Hassan, Cambridge, 2003).

D. Mario Nuti is professor of comparative economic systems in the Faculty of Economics of the University of Rome "La Sapienza." He is also visiting professor at the Center for New and Emerging Markets at the London Business School. With Milica Uvalic, he is coeditor of *Post-Communist Transition to a Market Economy: Lessons and Challenges* (Longo, 2003).

Uladzimir Padhol holds a Ph.D. in political psychology from the Belarusian State University. He has served as a consultant to the Belarusian Popular Front and the OSCE Advisory and Monitoring Group in Minsk and is director of the public association "Information and Social Innovation." He is author of numerous articles for the Belarusian independent media, most frequently in *Narodnaya volya* and for the Belapan Agency.

Clelia Rontoyanni is attached to the delegation of the European Commission to Russia, but writes in a personal capacity. Her contribution to this volume was prepared while she held a postdoctoral fellowship at the Royal Institute of International Affairs, supported by the UK Economic and Social Research Council. Her publications have appeared in *International Affairs* and *International Politics*.

Stephen White is professor of international politics and a senior associate member of the School of Central and East European Studies at the University of Glasgow. He also holds visiting positions at the Institute of Applied Politics in Moscow and the Institute of Advanced Studies in Vienna, and is chief editor of the *Journal of Communist Studies and Transition Politics*. His recent books include *The Soviet Political Elite* (with Evan Mawdsley, Oxford, 2000) and *Russia's New Politics* (Cambridge, 2000).